SENTINEL

RUSH LIMBAUGH

Zev Chafets is the author of eleven books of fiction, media criticism, and social and political commentary. He is a frequent contributor to *The New York Times Magazine* and a former columnist for the *New York Daily News.*

RUSH LIMBAUGH

AN ARMY OF ONE

ZEV CHAFETS

SENTINEL
Published by the Penguin Group
Penguin Group (USA) Inc., 375 Hudson Street,
New York, New York 10014, U.S.A.
Penguin Group (Canada), 90 Eglinton Avenue East, Suite 700, Toronto, Ontario,
Canada M4P 2Y3 (a division of Pearson Penguin Canada Inc.)
Penguin Books Ltd, 80 Strand, London WC2R 0RL, England
Penguin Ireland, 25 St. Stephen's Green, Dublin 2, Ireland (a division of Penguin Books Ltd)
Penguin Books Australia Ltd, 250 Camberwell Road, Camberwell, Victoria 3124, Australia
(a division of Pearson Australia Group Pty Ltd)
Penguin Books India Pvt Ltd, 11 Community Centre, Panchsheel Park,
New Delhi – 110 017, India
Penguin Group (NZ), 67 Apollo Drive, Rosedale, Auckland 0632, New Zealand
(a division of Pearson New Zealand Ltd)
Penguin Books (South Africa) (Pty) Ltd, 24 Sturdee Avenue, Rosebank,
Johannesburg 2196, South Africa

Penguin Books Ltd, Registered Offices:
80 Strand, London WC2R 0RL, England

First published in the United States of America by Sentinel, a member of
Penguin Group (USA) Inc. 2010
This paperback edition published 2011

1 3 5 7 9 10 8 6 4 2

Portions of this book appeared as "Late Period Limbaugh" in *The New York Times Magazine*.

THE LIBRARY OF CONGRESS HAS CATALOGED THE HARDCOVER EDITION AS FOLLOWS:

Chafets, Ze'ev.
Rush Limbaugh : an army of one / Zev Chafets.
p.   cm.
Includes bibliographical references and index.
ISBN 978-1-59523-063-8 (hc.)
ISBN 978-1-59523-081-2 (pbk.)
1. Limbaugh, Rush H.   2. Radio broadcasters—United States—Biography.
3. Conservatives—United States—Biography.   I. Title.
PN1991.4.L48C53   2010
791.44'028'092-dc22
[B]   2009053904

Printed in the United States of America
Set in Adobe Garamond
Designed by Spring Hoteling

To my brother Joe Chafets and
my sister Julie Chafets Grass with love

I know the liberals call you "the most dangerous man in America," but don't worry about it, they used to say the same thing about me. Keep up the good work.

—Ronald Reagan in a letter to Rush Limbaugh, December 11, 1992

CONTENTS

INTRODUCTION   1

1: *"I Hope He Fails"*   3

2: *Life on the Mississippi*   11

3: *From Rusty to Christie to Rush*   32

4: *The City*   46

5: *The Honorary Freshman*   76

6: *Limbaugh in Limbo*   92

7: *"W"*   100

8: *The Southern Command*   111

9: The Rush Limbaugh Show   120

CONTENTS

10: *Intellectual Engine*   135

11: *The Boss*   141

12: *The Magic Negro*   154

13: *The Guns of August*   167

14: *Welcome to the NFL*   178

15: *Forward to the Past*   186

EPILOGUE: THE PARTY OF "HELL NO"   206

ACKNOWLEDGMENTS   211

APPENDIX   215

INDEX   219

INTRODUCTION

People tend to remember the moment they first heard Rush Limbaugh. Mine came in the fall of 1989 in Detroit, driving down Woodward Avenue in a black Le Baron convertible. I was there researching a book about the racial politics of the city where I grew up and which I had left many years before. Out of habit I had the car radio tuned to 1270 AM, the popular rock-and-roll station of my teenage years. Clarence "Frogman" Henry was singing "Ain't Got No Home," a song that had always made me smile, when suddenly he was interrupted by a baritone voice intoning, "*Dadelut! Dadelut! Dadelut!* Homeless update."

In Detroit you get accustomed to bad news. I listened for the latest installment. But this wasn't about Detroit; it was about a think tank in Washington, D.C., that had, according to the baritone, just put out an inflated figure of the number of homeless Americans—a typical liberal trick to deceive the public and allow Democrats in Congress to funnel "emergency" money to their cronies in big cities. This grew into a riff on the evils of profligate government spending, the debasing effect of welfare on its recipients, and the cynical willingness of the "mainstream media" to treat liberal propaganda as news. The baritone didn't seem angry. On the contrary, he seemed delighted and amused to be catching another bunch of bleeding hearts, rapacious pols, and crooked journalists in the act. He called himself "El Rushbo" and "America's Truth Detector," and he announced that his program was on the "Excellence in Broadcasting Network."

I had been living abroad for many years, but I knew perfectly well that broadcast networks in America sounded nothing like this. They wouldn't have dared to strike such an irreverent tone about homelessness or make raucous fun of revered liberal axioms and icons. It is hard to describe how transgressively original Rush Limbaugh sounded in this media environment. Listening to him on the radio reminded me of the first time I saw Elvis on TV with my father sitting in the next room—a feeling that I was witnessing something completely different and possibly even dangerous.

My friends and relatives in Detroit looked at me blankly when I mentioned hearing Limbaugh. Nobody knew a thing about him. When I described how he had gleefully and artfully ripped into a whole herd of liberal sacred cows, the looks became disapproving. These were their cows, after all. What was funny about a man laughing at feminism? How could a white commentator mock Jesse Jackson? And what sort of troglodyte would dare question the settled science of the environmental movement? This man sounded like a conservative. Whose side was I on, anyway?

Listening to Rush became a guilty pleasure. I didn't agree with everything—in fact, I disagreed with a lot—but agreeing wasn't the point. He was doing something really interesting. Ridicule has always been a weapon used by the left against the right. Limbaugh had somehow seized the cannon and turned it around. I relished his bravado, laughed at his outrageous satire, and admired his willingness to go against the intellectual grain. But I didn't expect him to last long. He was too irreverent and subversive, too bold. The keepers of the culture would never let him get away with it. Somehow, they'd find a way to shut him up and make him go away.

Which, looking back on it more than twenty years later, is pretty much what my father had said about Elvis.

CHAPTER ONE

"I HOPE HE FAILS"

Four days before Barack Obama was sworn in as president of the United States, Rush Limbaugh went on the air and told his millions of listeners what his policy toward the new man in the White House was going to be. He had been asked, he said, by a major American publication—the *Wall Street Journal*, it later turned out—to write four hundred words about his hopes for the new administration. Limbaugh told his audience that he didn't need four hundred words. Four would suffice: "I hope he fails."

Limbaugh said that he fervently disagreed with Republican moderates who were calling on the party to cooperate with Obama or even give him a chance. This was a reference to a meeting between Obama and a group of conservative pundits that had taken place a few days earlier at the home of columnist George Will. The guest list had been unpublished but was immediately leaked, and it included some of the brainiest right-of-center commentators in Washington. They had ideological differences with Obama, but they had a lot in common, too, including a common language. They, like the president-elect, were products of elite liberal educational institutions.

Obama's goal was to flatter and charm the guests, and by all accounts he succeeded. "He's making good on his promise to reach out to Republicans and conservatives with this post-partisan stuff, whatever that means," Larry Kudlow, a conservative economic commentator, later told a reporter. "I was very impressed. He's a nice guy, terribly smart, well informed, great smile. He's just really engaged. He said he likes to know the arguments on all sides."

Obama had no illusions about converting anyone that night (although he evidently made some inroads with *New York Times* columnist David Brooks). He simply wanted these critics to recall his smiling face and reasonable demeanor when they wrote about him. He had another purpose as well: to divide his opponents into "good" and "bad" conservatives.

"The Obama message is a crafty one," blogged *Vanity Fair* media columnist Michael Wolff the next day. "He's choosing these fretting, parsing, neurotic, limp-wristed, desperate-to-be-liked print guys, over the crass, spitting, scary, voluble guys on television and radio, the Ailes-Rove-Limbaugh wing of the Republican Party."

By coincidence, Rush Limbaugh was in Washington on the day of Will's gathering; in fact, he was at the White House, where President George W. Bush threw him an intimate fifty-eighth-birthday luncheon. When word of the Obama dinner got out, the media began buzzing with rumors that Limbaugh had been there.

The following day, Limbaugh laughed at the very idea. He wasn't looking to get along with Obama; he wanted to thwart him. That was the meaning of "I hope he fails." The president was a liberal Democrat, and as far as Limbaugh was concerned, the Republican Party was not in business to expedite or assist liberals. "I've been listening to Barack Obama for a year and a half," he said. "I know what his politics are. I know what his plans are, as he has stated them. I don't want them to succeed. He's talking about the absorption of as much of the private sector by the U.S. government as possible, from the banking business to the mortgage industry, the automobile business, to health care. I do not want the government in charge of all of these things. I don't want this to work."

Some of the moderate conservative pundits were dismayed by this hard-edged approach. The leaders of the mainstream media, who were already comparing the new president to Abraham Lincoln, Franklin Roosevelt, and John F. Kennedy, were appalled. Here was Limbaugh, rain-ing acid on the parade. "I don't care what the Drive-By Media story is," Limbaugh said. "I would be honored if the Drive-By Media headlined me all day long: 'Limbaugh: I Hope Obama Fails.' Somebody's gotta say it."

To reinforce the point, Limbaugh appeared on Sean Hannity's TV show on the FOX News Channel. Hannity got his national start as a substitute host on Rush's radio show. His lawyer is Limbaugh's brother, David, who also represents radio host–author Mark Levin. Hannity tossed Rush a softball and he hit it into deep right field.

"I would hope Obama would succeed if he acts like Reagan," Limbaugh said. "But if he's going to do FDR, if he's going to do the new, New Deal all over, which we will call the raw deal, why would I want him to succeed?" FDR occupies a special place in Limbaugh's personal hall of presidential infamy. Rush's father and mentor, Big Rush, was so vociferously anti-Roosevelt that as a young man he was jumped and beaten by New Dealers after a barroom argument. When Rush began calling Obama "the Black FDR," a lot of left-wing commentators were outraged by the racial modifier. They missed the real insult.

"Look, he's my president," Limbaugh told Hannity. "The fact that he is historic is irrelevant to me now . . . Two trillion in stimulus? The growth of government? I think the intent here is to create as many dependent Americans as possible looking to government for their hope and salvation . . . I shamelessly say, No, I want him to fail, if his agenda is a far-left collectivism."

The new administration saw opportunity in Limbaugh's oppositional stance. The Republican Party had emerged from the 2008 election as a headless horseman. George W. Bush had gone home as an unpopular figure; his near-catatonic handling of the financial crises in his last days of his presidency made it clear that no leadership would be coming out of Crawford. McCain ran one of the worst campaigns in recent memory and alienated much of the party's conservative base in the bargain. Besides, he was too old to run again in 2012, which left a void where the party's titular leader should be.

The GOP's post-2008 congressional leadership was, if possible, even more lackluster. Minority Leader Mitch McConnell, a competent parliamentarian, has the charisma and demeanor of an undertaker. House

Minority Leader John Boehner is equally dreary. President Obama and his advisers saw the Republican leadership vacuum as an opportunity to define their opposition before it could define itself. Obama is a student of the tactics of Saul Alinsky, the legendary Chicago political activist and organizer, who taught that the public pays more attention to personalities than to policy. Obama's strategy started with a scapegoat. George W. Bush had filled that role for eight years but he was gone. So were bogeymen like Dick Cheney, Karl Rove, and Tom DeLay. Who should succeed them? Democratic pollsters came up with a clear candidate. The data made it clear: Rush Limbaugh. Democrats had hated him for years. Independents and moderate Republicans were scandalized and offended by "I hope he fails." Even some conservatives thought Rush had gone too far.

Putting Limbaugh's face on the Republican brand seemed like a brilliant move. Obama himself kicked it off, less than a week after taking office. He invited the Republican congressional leadership to the White House for what was billed as a summit meeting meant to mark the bipartisanship the president had pledged to bring to government. Obama implored the heads of the opposition party to begin by supporting his trillion-dollar economic stimulus bill, and then dropped the Rush Bomb. "You can't just listen to Rush Limbaugh and get things done," he told them.

This raised eyebrows all over Washington. American presidents don't normally single out private individuals, even powerful commentators, and attempt to put them beyond the pale. They certainly don't do this in the first week of a new term. The wildly popular new president was offering the GOP a choice—a place of influence and participation in the gleaming Age of Obama or that symbol of yesterday's harsh partisanship, Rush Limbaugh.

At Limbaugh's studio in Palm Beach, Florida, which he refers to with his trademark grandiosity as "The Southern Command," Obama's words were greeted with incredulity and glee. Limbaugh had been trying to goad him into a fight ever since the Democratic convention in Denver. For a long time it seemed that the young man from Illinois was too cool to engage and that Rush would have to spend the next four or eight years beating up on Harry Reid, Barney Frank, Nancy Pelosi, and other lesser

Democrats. But Obama, for reasons of his own, had called Limbaugh
out. Not since Bill Clinton had Rush had such a worthy adversary.

Limbaugh immediately labeled Obama's stimulus the "porkulus bill"
and demanded that Republicans in Congress oppose it. He also responded
to the idea—being floated all over the capital by White House aides—
that he was now the real head of the Republican Party. His vehicle was an
op-ed article in the *Wall Street Journal* titled "My Bipartisan Stimulus."
The premise was simple: Obama said he wanted a bipartisan administration? Limbaugh would give him one. Let Obama take 54 percent of the
stimulus money—$486 billion, which corresponded to the Democrat's
share of the popular vote—and spend it on infrastructure projects. He,
Limbaugh, as head of the GOP, would take his party's 46 percent—$414
billion—in the form of corporate and capital gains tax cuts. Then they
would compare results and know, once and for all, if John Maynard
Keynes or Milton Friedman got it right.

"The economic crisis is an opportunity to unify people, if we set
aside the politics," Limbaugh wrote. "The leader of the Democrats and
the leader of the Republicans (me, according to Mr. Obama) can get it
done. This will have the overwhelming support of the American people.
Let's stop the acrimony. Let's start solving our problems, together. Why
wait one more day?"

Limbaugh knew perfectly well that Obama didn't really consider him
the Republican leader, and the *Journal* article was his way of saying so; a
signature trick he calls "illustrating the absurd by being absurd." But, at
the same time, the sort of tax cuts Limbaugh was proposing were completely serious and, from a conservative economic perspective, logical.
Over the years, Limbaugh has cultivated a larger-than-life, intentionally
ambiguous persona, which has made him illusive. It is a trick he learned
from Muhammad Ali, whose big mouth, braggadocio, and sheer raw
nerve enabled him to draw and keep a crowd throughout his long career.
The young Ali, still Cassius Clay, invented disparaging nicknames for his
opponents (Sonny Liston was the "Big Ugly Bear") and arrogantly predicted the round of his victories, which led boxing "experts" to denounce
him as merely an entertainer. The first Liston fight dispelled that notion,
but it took the boxing establishment a longer time to finally admit that

Ali was not just a champ at the box office but, truly, the Greatest, a revolutionary talent who transformed the way professional boxers worked.

Ali was also controversial and dead serious about his political beliefs. He became a Black Muslim when it was dangerously unpopular to do so, and he paid for it. He was willing to face prison time rather than serve in a war he didn't support. And yet, despite it all, white reporters couldn't quite take him seriously. When he said alarmingly incorrect things, like calling Joe Louis an Uncle Tom, dubbing his fight with George Foreman in Zaire "the rumble in the jungle," or mocking Joe Frazier as a gorilla, they thought it might be just part of the act. He couldn't really mean those things, could he?

Limbaugh is the Ali of the air, the all-knowing, all-seeing Maha Rishi who defeats his enemies in intellectual combat with half his brain tied behind his back, "just to make it fair." He also happens to be the most important and influential conservative in the country, the one indispensable Republican voice. This can be confusing, which is the way Limbaugh wants it.

After the *Wall Street Journal* article, Rush continued to insist that no true conservative could vote for the president's porkulus bill; Republicans who did would be considered "moderates," one of Limbaugh's supreme insults, and dealt with accordingly. GOP congressmen took this threat seriously, especially after Limbaugh's listeners began bombarding them with e-mail and phone calls. Rush, who is a realist, didn't think he could block the bill, and that wasn't his intention. The Democrats had a clear majority, and he wanted them to pass the stimulus alone, to completely own the spending, which he was sure would prove to be unpopular and ineffective. He got his way, too. Not a single Republican member of the House voted with Obama, who Limbaugh was now calling "The Messiah." Bipartisanship, which Rush considered political and ideological surrender, was off the table. The Republicans were an opposition that would oppose. "I have hijacked Obama's honeymoon," he happily announced.

Not every congressman enjoyed being strong-armed. Phil Gingrey, who represents Georgia's 11th Congressional District, had been a GOP fence-sitter who resented Limbaugh's intervention.

In a moment of candor he complained about the way Rush had been razzing the party's congressional leadership for their alleged softness on spending. Gingrey said it was easy for talk-show hosts "to stand back and throw bricks." In American politics, "talk-show host" is a euphemism for "Rush Limbaugh."

Gingrey was deluged by outraged telephone calls and e-mails. The following day he crawled onto Limbaugh's show and begged El Rushbo to forgive him. He called Limbaugh "a conservative giant" and praised him as a voice of conscience in their movement.

He didn't say *the* voice, but Rush was in a gracious mood and let it pass.

For the moment, both Limbaugh and the Democrats were happy. Rush's ratings were rising by the day, and his party was doing his bidding. This enabled the Democrats to keep using him as the face of the GOP. Paul Begala, a senior Democratic political consultant and informal adviser to the White House, declared that "the real leader of the Republican Party in America today is a corpulent drug addict with an AM radio talk show, Rush Limbaugh." Begala was looking for a twofer; disparaging Limbaugh and, at the same time, starting a fight between him and Michael Steele, the newly elected head of the Republican National Committee. "Steele is going to need to stand up to Limbaugh if he wants to actually lead the party of Lincoln," Begala said.

Attacking Limbaugh for his drug use was a bold Democratic gambit; President Obama, after all, had confessed to serious recreational drugging as an angry young man. But the gloves were off. Hendrik Hertzberg, a former speechwriter for Jimmy Carter who now writes for the *New Yorker*, said that while he wasn't comparing Obama to Martin Luther King or Limbaugh to Bull Connor, he *was* reminded by El Rushbo of the fire hoses and clubs that had been deployed against King by the infamously racist and brutal police chief of Selma, Alabama. Former Air America Radio talk-show host Janeane Garofalo offered a woman's perspective. "The type of female that does like Rush is the same type of female that falls in love with prisoners," she said. "Squeaky Fromme [one of Charles Manson's groupies] is a good example. Eva Braun, Hitler's girlfriend. That is exactly the type of woman that responds really well to Rush."

Tina Brown, the former editor of the *New Yorker* and *Vanity Fair*, was alarmed by all the attention Limbaugh was getting. She warned that the Democrats were turning him into an iconic figure.

Rush couldn't have been happier. After twenty years in the ring, he knew that when you start getting compared to Bull Connor, Charles Manson, and Adolf Hitler, you're landing punches. Dishing out and absorbing punishment was all in a day's work for the self-described harmless little fuzzball who had assigned himself the task of destroying the presidency of Barack Obama. There were risks—you don't take on the most powerful man in the world lightly—but Limbaugh was prepared to take those risks. "This is my destiny," he told his audience. "This is what I was born to do."

CHAPTER TWO

LIFE ON THE MISSISSIPPI

I n 1883 Mark Twain came down the Mississippi River and caught a glimpse of Cape Girardeau, the town of Rush Limbaugh's nativity. "[It] is situated on a hillside, and makes a handsome appearance," he wrote. "There is a great Jesuit school for boys at the foot of the town by the river. Uncle Mumford said it had as high a reputation for thoroughness as any similar institution in Missouri. There was another college higher up on an airy summit—a bright new edifice, picturesquely and peculiarly towered and pinnacled—a sort of gigantic casters, with the cruets all complete. Uncle Mumford said that Cape Girardeau was the Athens of Missouri, and contained several colleges besides those already mentioned; and all of them on a religious basis of one kind or another. He directed my attention to what he called the 'strong and pervasive religious look of the town,' but I could not see that it looked more religious than the other hill towns with the same slope and built of the same kind of bricks. Partialities often make people see more than really exists."

My first encounter with Cape, as the town is affectionately abbreviated by its citizens, came by land. I drove down from St. Louis on I-55, a two-hour stretch of highway through farmland that offers no temptation to stop or sightsee, and entered the town onto a commercial street of faded prosperity. It was a Sunday in mid-December, freezing cold and already dark at five thirty in the afternoon. The downtown district was festively lit for Christmas, but there was absolutely nobody on the street and only one or two places to eat. I chose an Italian ristorante with red-checkered tablecloths, ate a very good steak for the price of a mediocre Manhattan hamburger, and then checked in to the Bellevue Bed and Breakfast, a nineteenth-century Queen Anne Victorian only a couple blocks from the river.

The town gets a fair number of tourists in season, but in the middle of December I was the only guest at the inn. The permanent population is thirty-eight thousand, about the same size as it had been when Rush was growing up there. Most of the Limbaughs are still there: Rush's first cousin, Stephen Jr., a former justice of the Missouri Supreme Court who had recently been appointed to the federal bench by George W. Bush; another cousin, Jimmy, who is a local hospital executive; and David, Rush's only sibling, a commentator and author in his own right who also runs the family law firm. The federal courthouse in town is named for Rush Limbaugh's grandfather Rush Senior. When the courthouse was dedicated, the mayor referred to the family as "Cape Girardeau royalty." The local Limbaughs played it down—"Mayor Knudtson is an immi-grant from Minnesota," David Limbaugh told me—but people who imagine Rush Hudson Limbaugh III is a disembodied voice or a rootless vagabond disc jockey are very much mistaken.

The first American Limbaugh, Rush's great-great-great-great-great-grandfather Johannes Michael Limbaugh (or "Limbach"), was born in Baden, Germany, in 1737 and immigrated to the colony of Pennsylvania before the Revolution. At least four of Rush's ancestors—Peter Clubb, Thomas Coppedge, Conrad Hise, and Johannes Mull—are listed in the Patriotic Index of the National Society, Daughters of the American Revo-lution, making Limbaugh himself eligible for membership in the Sons of the American Revolution. Not all his ancestors were on the same side. His maternal grandmother, Emma Eisenberg, is very possibly descended from Quartermaster Sergeant Henrich Eisenberg, a Hessian mercenary from Waldeck, taken prisoner by the Colonial forces during the war.

At one of our first meetings, Limbaugh introduced me to his girl-friend, Kathryn Rogers, as a lineal descendent of President John Adams.

He seemed vague and not particularly interested in his own genealogy; "somewhere in Germany and then North Carolina I think, before they got to Missouri," he told me. That's ancient history; for Rush, the Limbaugh family saga really begins with his grandfather Rush Hudson Limbaugh Senior.

Rush Senior was born and raised on a farm in nearby Bollinger County. He saw his first electric light at the age of twelve, at the St. Louis World's Fair of 1904. He and his mother traveled to the fair by train on newly laid track.

Before then, St. Louis was three days away by stage coach or twelve hours by boat up the Mississippi. A railroad trip was a novelty in 1904, and the Limbaughs were written up in the local paper.

"I don't think I'd been away from home more than 15 to 20 miles before," Rush Senior recalled in his biography, *Rush Hudson Limbaugh and His Times: Reflections on a Life Well Lived.* "I just discovered the world at that time." Evidently he didn't care that much for what he discovered; at least he never ventured very far. He learned the law, opened his first office in Cape in 1916, and practiced there until 1994. When he finally retired, at the age of 102, he was the oldest attorney working in the United States.

The practice of law in southeast Missouri in those early days was informal—judges sometimes heard cases on their front porch—and not especially lucrative. Rush Senior furnished his "workshop" with a table, three chairs, a set of the latest *Missouri Revised Statutes*, a typewriter, and a spittoon. In his first year he made less than five hundred dollars; it took him six years to save enough money to buy his first car, a second-hand Dodge.

At the age of forty Rush Senior was elected to the Missouri House of Representatives as an anti–New Deal Republican. The job paid five dollars a day plus roundtrip train fare to Jefferson City, the state capital. He served just one term but stayed active in local politics. In 1936 he was a delegate to the Republican National Convention that nominated Alf Landon of Kansas. Landon lost to Franklin D. Roosevelt in a landslide.

Rush Limbaugh Senior was an honest lawyer and a pillar of the community: He helped start the local hospital. He contributed time and money to the Salvation Army. He was a Boy Scout leader. Generations of townsfolk and country people came to him with their legal and personal problems. Young attorneys saw him as a role model. Quietly but inevitably he became well to do, but he lived modestly. "He was a student of Thorstein Veblen's theory of conspicuous consumption," says Frank Nickell, the director of the Center for Regional History at Southeast Missouri State University. "Never ostentatious, but people watched him. He had charisma. He was polished, genteel, and sophisticated, a quiet, wise man who inspired a kind of reverence in Cape Girardeau." Rush III dedicated his second book, *See, I Told You So*, to his grandfather. "You are the Limbaugh America Should Know," he wrote.

In 1949 a tornado hit Cape Girardeau, killing twenty-two people. The Limbaugh home was badly damaged but the family escaped unharmed. Everyone was in Kennett, Missouri, a hundred miles to the south, on the way to Memphis, attending the wedding of Rush Limbaugh Jr. to Millie Armstrong.

"Millie was right out of the cotton fields," says Frank Nickell. "She loved animals. She kept a mynah bird in the kitchen. She sang on the radio in Chicago before she was married, but she was the farthest thing from show biz you could imagine. Everybody in town loved Millie. She was a kind, gracious, gentle lady. To the extent that Rush Limbaugh has any gentility, it comes from his mother."

Frank Kinder, a boyhood friend of Rush and David's, owns an advertising agency in Cape; his brother Peter is the lieutenant governor of Missouri. Kinder's mother was Millie Limbaugh's best friend. "We more or less grew up in each other's houses," Frank told me. "We attended the same church. Rush's father, Big Rush, was my Sunday School teacher. And Millie and my mom sang together in the choir."

When Frank talks about Millie, his eyes tear up. "She was a wonderful woman, not just to her kids but to all of us," he says. "Completely down to earth. She bought her clothes at Kmart. On her sixty-fifth birthday, Rush called my mom and asked her to come with Millie to New York. He sent his plane to bring them and got them a private shopper at Bergdorf Goodman. It was funny, really. Millie didn't have good taste, and she didn't care at all about fashion, but she and my mom had a great time. Five years later, for her seventieth birthday, Rush flew them both down to Florida. He wanted to give them a spa day but Millie put her foot down there. She said she was willing to shop but massages were just plain pampering."

Limbaugh sometimes mentions his mother on the show. By all accounts they were close, but it was his father, Rush Junior, who loomed largest in his son's life. Limbaugh hero-worshipped his father, and he still calls him "the smartest man I ever met."

Certainly he was the most emphatic. Big Rush, who weighed in around three hundred pounds, was a World War II combat pilot who wore his hair in a crew cut and his opinions about politics (and every other subject) on his sleeve. He was not the community leader his father was, nor was he the best lawyer in the family—he was eclipsed by his cousin Stephen, who became a federal judge. As an attorney Big Rush was best known as a passionate advocate. "Clients love my dad," David told me. "He would fight for them to the death. Within the bounds of ethics, of course."

Big Rush Limbaugh was a noted local orator, in demand on patriotic holidays. One of his best-known speeches, on the fathers of the American Revolution, provides an example of the uncompromising attitude and teary-eyed patriotism he bequeathed to his son. Here he is, recounting the story of Abraham Clark, a signer of the Declaration of Independence from New Jersey:

"He gave two sons to the officer corps in the Revolutionary Army. They were captured and sent to that infamous British prison hulk afloat in New York Harbor known as the hell ship *Jersey*, where eleven thousand American captives were to die. The young Clarks were treated with a special brutality because of their father. One was put in solitary and given no food." The British told Clark that they would spare his sons' lives if he recanted his support for the Revolution, but despite the fact that the war was almost won, Clark refused, a decision Big Rush lauded. "The utter despair in this man's heart, the anguish in his very soul, must reach out to each one of us down through two hundred years with his answer: 'No.'"

This is a stirring patriotic sentiment. It thrilled audiences on the

Fourth of July. How it affected young Rusty Limbaugh, as Rush was called in those days, and his brother, David, is another question.

Speechifying wasn't Big Rush's only activity. He had come back from the war an aviation nut, and he remained one long after he could no longer squeeze his bulk into a cockpit. He played a major role in lobbying for an airport in Cape Girardeau. He also dabbled in investments, including a piece of Cape's AM radio station KGMO. And he, like Rush Senior, was a figure in the local Republican Party. In 1956 he proudly played host to Vice President Richard M. Nixon on his visit to southeast Missouri.

Rush's boyhood friends have very vivid memories of Big Rush, who often lectured them on the evils of Communism and liberalism. "We'd go over to his house sometimes just to watch him watch the six o'clock news," recalls Frank Kinder. "He'd sit in front of the television drinking black cherry pop, eating popcorn, and just railing at the anchormen and the reporters. He'd yell at Dan Rather—'They're all typical liberals and Rather's the worst one in the bunch,' he'd say—and we'd try to keep him going, you know, 'Mr. Rush, what do you think about this, Mr. Rush, what do you think about that?' Sometimes he'd say, 'Kinder, you're going to be the first Dutchman on the moon.' I don't exactly know what he meant by that, but he was trying to be friendly. I liked him, but he was a harsh taskmaster with his sons."

Dick Adams was Limbaugh's close friend and high school debate partner. As a teenager he often found himself at the Limbaugh dinner table in the midst of what he calls "spirited political discussions."

"Rush's dad didn't suffer fools lightly," Adams says. "He was always very disapproving of Rush's ambitions to have a career in radio. Rush's mom was a kind, gentle person, but his dad could be pretty rough. He was not above calling down Rush and David in front of their friends, and when he did it, there was a string of expletives attached. I saw that happen many times."

"My dad stood out. Sometimes he provoked people who didn't agree with him to violence," David Limbaugh told me. "Once, for example, he was in a bar slamming FDR, and a couple guys jumped him and beat him up. I never did ask him the details of that one. But it was a couple guys, not a fair fight. I know that much."

Adams remembers Rush as a good debater—"he could argue either side of a proposition without missing a beat"—and generally in agreement with his father's conservative opinions. But I was surprised to learn that Rusty wasn't really very interested in politics. "The only political sentiment I recall him expressing was after the 1960 presidential election," Frank Kinder told me. "Rush wrote on a drywall, 'Kennedy won, darn. Nixon lost, shucks.'" This lack of partisan engagement is a recurring theme in the recollections of Limbaugh's old friends and colleagues in his early radio career. He was in his midthirties before he began giving strong, consistent voice to his conservative beliefs.

On my first morning in Cape Girardeau I took a drive through the town. "It hasn't changed at all," Limbaugh told me later. "Some of the business streets have declined but mostly it looks like it did when I was a kid." It's easy to imagine Rush there, driving down Broadway from the river, the Stars and Stripes flapping over the courthouse on the hill, passing the editorial office of the *Southeast Missourian*, a robust, Republican family–owned newspaper still full of ads and local stories and a daily prayer on the editorial page.

Across the street from the *Missourian* is radio station KZIM-960, which carries Rush's show. An entrepreneur named Oscar Hirsch brought radio to this part of the country in 1924, opening station KFVS. Its inaugural broadcast featured live music by the Pig Meyer Orchestra emanating from the Marquette Hotel, a fine Spanish Revival building that later fell into disuse but has been restored and now houses a fancy continental restaurant.

Cape, like many Midwestern river towns, has maintained an uneasy equilibrium between propriety and pleasure. Sophisticated nightspots like the Marquette Hotel made some local folks uneasy. In the winter of 1926, the Reverend Billy Sunday, the greatest evangelist of Prohibition-era America, came to town for a five-week revival. He raised his own tabernacle and preached against the evils of cards, strong drink, and licentiousness. "It's a damnable insult, some of the rigs a lot of fool women are

wearing up and down our streets," the Reverend Sunday thundered. "No
man with good rich blood in his veins can look at them with prayer-
meeting thoughts." Sunday drew an estimated 250,000 people over the
five weeks, probably more than the total population of southeast Missouri
at the time. At the end of the crusade they totaled up the results: 1,319
sinners converted and 1,482 church members reconsecrated. The town
fathers pronounced themselves satisfied.

The Great Depression hit Cape, but because of the town's economic
diversity, it got off rather lightly. But World War II was devastating. The
sons of southeast Missouri joined up in large numbers. Eighty boys from
Cape Girardeau County were killed and many more were wounded. But
the sacrifice didn't dim the area's patriotism or its fighting spirit. After the
war, Cape was, like the rest of Missouri, a bastion of anti-Communism.
In 1946 at Westminster College in Fulton, Missouri, a three-hour drive
from Cape Girardeau, Winston Churchill delivered his famous warning
about the Soviet Iron Curtain falling across Europe. Democratic President Harry Truman, a son of Missouri, took the country to war in Korea,
declaring that, "the effort of the evil forces of communism to reach out
and dominate the world confronts our Nation and our civilization with
the greatest challenge in our history."

Big Rush shared the president's sentiments, but there was no way he
could support him politically. The Limbaughs had long since become the
town's Republican law firm (just as the rival Oliver family law firm represented the Democrats). For twenty years the Limbaughs led the loyal local
opposition to FDR and Truman. It wasn't until Ike beat Stevenson in
1952 that the balance of power shifted to the Republicans.

The Eisenhower years—the years of Rusty Limbaugh's childhood—
were sweet ones for Cape Girardeau and for the Limbaughs. Rush Sr. was
honored with an appointment as special ambassador to the Indian legal
system. Rush Jr. built a family and prospered. Television arrived in 1954,
courtesy of the enterprising Oscar Hirsch. Southeast Missouri State University, a backwater, was flush with students matriculating thanks to the
G.I. Bill. In 1956, the Army Corps of Engineers began work on what
became a mile-long, sixteen-foot-high floodwall that protects the low-

lying downtown district from the river and provides Cape with a greater sense of security.

Still, some tides couldn't be walled off. It was Harry Truman himself who integrated the U.S. Armed Forces, signaling a new era in race relations. And in 1954, in *Brown v. Board of Education of Topeka*, in neighboring Kansas, the U.S. Supreme Court ruled the racial segregation of public schools unconstitutional.

Race had always been a difficult issue in Cape. During the Civil War, the town and its families had been divided between the Yankees and the Confederates, and its identity—Midwestern or Southern—was never completely settled. Even today there are monuments to both Rebel and Union soldiers on the grounds of the old Common Pleas Courthouse. In the great black northern migration of World War I, hundreds of thousands of African Americans traveled up Highway 61 from Louisiana, Mississippi, Tennessee, and Arkansas bound for St. Louis, but very few stopped in Cape Girardeau. Those who did encountered a pronounced lack of hospitality.

In 1952 Cape built its white students a new school, Central High. Blacks continued to attend Cobb High School. But the Supreme Court—and basketball—changed that.

Cape Girardeau took its high school basketball very seriously and sometimes contended for the state title. The 1953 team was expected to be a powerhouse, but word got around that the kids from Cobb were even better. "An informal game was arranged between Central and Cobb High," says historian Frank Nickell. "Cobb won. Shortly thereafter, Cobb mysteriously burned down." Black students went to school in churches and private homes that year, but a more permanent solution was required. The U.S. Supreme Court had called for desegregation "with all deliberate speed," but even the most deliberate pace couldn't justify building a new black school.

A compromise was reached. Black kids would attend Central High, but virtually all of them would be put in special classes and taught by the former members of the Cobb faculty. It was an inequitable but formally legal scheme, and it succeeded in defusing tension. It was in place by the time Rusty Limbaugh started school.

Rusty had the standard upbringing of a well-born kid of his time and place. He played ball with the neighborhood gang, mowed the family lawn, took piano lessons with no discernible result, dutifully joined the Cub Scouts for one year (during which he received no merit badges), and attended the Methodist Sunday School. From the very beginning he dreaded school, which he considered prison.

The Limbaughs had a large basement rumpus room with a pinball machine and a pool table, and the house became a neighborhood hang-out. "There were always half a dozen kids there, and Rush was the leader," says Frank Kinder. "We shot pool, talked sports, and made a lot of prank calls, which he thought up. One time we convinced the radio station to announce a bogus American history contest. We ordered pizzas and watched as Flo's Taxi delivered them to the neighbors. Pranks. Most of Rush's friends were a year older than him. I'm two years younger, David's friend basically, but Rush was always really nice to me, too."

At thirteen Limbaugh got a job at the Varsity Barber Shop on Broadway, shining shoes. He liked it because it gave him a chance to talk with adults. "I always preferred adults to kids," he told me. "I didn't think kids were interesting."

Rusty loved sports but he wasn't much of an athlete. "We played sandlot baseball," says Kinder, "and one summer he worked on a knuckle-ball, but it didn't amount to much. Basically, he had an aversion to physical exercise." Rusty had a weight problem even then. In high school his beefy physique caught the eye of the football coach, who tried to turn him into a lineman. At first, making the team was a great thrill, but after one season he dropped out. His single moment of glory came when he kicked a game-winning extra point against Illinois's Carbondale High School. But his heart was never in it. "I played to be popular," he told me. "But it didn't work."

Not that Rusty was a social outcast. Limbaughs belonged to the in-crowd by definition. But by the time he reached high school he was awkward around girls. One of the foundational tales of his teenage years, recounted in Paul Colford's very thorough 1993 biography, *The Rush Limbaugh Story*, is how the prettiest girl at a spin-the-bottle party refused to kiss Rusty. "She looked at him and gasped," Colford writes. "Couldn't do it. Not with him, that is. And everyone in the room witnessed his humiliation. It was a wound he would nurse forever."

Jan Seebaugh is fairly sure that she was the girl in the story. Today she is a doctor and the divorced mother of a grown son, but back in high school she had a wild side. "I was the kind of girl who dated the lead guitar player in the rock band," she told me over lunch at the Marquette Hotel. She was also an honor roll student, a cheerleader, and, inevitably, the prom queen, a superstar. Her father was a prominent physician and her family moved in the same social circle as the Limbaughs. In fact, they were distantly related. Maybe that's why she didn't want to kiss Rusty. She doesn't remember. But she does recall liking him, and she merits at least an asterisk in his career as the first to write an article about him—in their high school newspaper. Rush wasn't her type.

Seebaugh also merits an asterisk in Limbaugh's professional biography. As a reporter for the high school newspaper, she wrote the first article about a new young disc jockey on the local radio station:

Fans Find Rusty "Sharpe"

"Here's a song for a sweet little thing named Susie!" comes a deep, masculine voice out of the speaker of the radio. Who would ever guess it belongs to a Central student known to his teachers as Rusty Limbaugh but known to his thousands of admiring fans as RUSTY SHARPE . . .

When asked why "Rusty Sharpe" was chosen for his "radio personality" Rusty stated, "I wanted an adjective that had a double meaning—you know, a pun type thing. I just looked in the phone book and came up with 'Sharpe.'"

Seabaugh asked Rusty whether he was planning a radio career, to which he replied, "Oh, I dunno. Depends on how successful I become. . . . Everything is ad lib and just starting out I sometimes find that hard to do. I've found that if you can't find something to say, keep your mouth shut and run a commercial or something."

Not only was Rusty winningly modest in his Sharpe incarnation, he was also, at least by Cape standards, cutting edge cool. The profile concludes: "Where can I hear this Sharpe guy?" asks one of those poor souls who doesn't know where the action is. All you "unhippies" can "get with it" every weekday afternoon from 3:00 to 6:15, and week-end afternoons from 12 noon to 6:15 on the Rusty Sharpe Show, 1550 on the dial.

"Even when I was a little boy, I dreamed of being on the radio," Limbaugh told me the first time we met. "In the mornings getting ready for school I'd hear the guy on the radio, and he just sounded free and happy, like he was having a wonderful time. That's what I wanted, too." Rusty listened avidly to Harry Caray and Jack Buck, the radio voices of the St. Louis Cardinals (he actually rooted for the L.A. Dodgers, an eccentric choice for that part of the country; his favorite player was Maury Wills). He also played endless hours of Strat-O-Matic, a baseball board game, calling the contests out loud, even when he was all alone.

At first his parents encouraged him. At fourteen they bought him a Remco Caravelle radio set that allowed him to broadcast on any AM channel, within the confines of his house. He played records and did DJ chatter, usually to an audience consisting of his mother. It was such a thrilling experience that Limbaugh never forgot it and sometimes talked with nostalgia about the lost Remco Caravelle of his boyhood. One day a listener sent Rush his own Remco. Limbaugh established his cyber-museum in 2008, and the Remco Caravelle is one of its featured icons.

Rusty's greatest ambition was to expand his audience and become a real top-40 jock—an AM jock, of course; there was no FM to speak of back then. In small towns like Cape Girardeau, radio was the quickest broadcasting route to glamour. Local TV offered only dull opportunities—who wanted to read the news about the Kiwanis Club bake sale or weather predictions? A rock-and-roll disc jockey was in show business, a single dropped needle away from partnership with Elvis and the Beatles. You didn't have to be cool looking or thin to be a radio celebrity. And radio was mysterious. If you lived in the middle of nowhere, you could hear distant voices from the big city and dream about greater vistas. Rusty's favorite was

Larry "Superjock" Lujack, a sardonic, creative radio star who broadcast on Chicago's WLS-AM, a brash, comic radio innovator from whom Rush borrowed some of his early attitude and technique. After Limbaugh became famous, he gave his old mentor public credit for influencing him, but Lujack returned the favor with some nasty remarks about Limbaugh, a slight Rush has neither forgotten nor forgiven.

Rusty Limbaugh was a lazy and indifferent student, much to the chagrin of his father. Limbaughs were expected to be professional men, preferably lawyers, and that meant buckling down, getting good grades, and going to college. But Rusty kept insisting that his future was on the radio, not in an office or a courtroom, and certainly not in a classroom. As it happened, his father owned a small piece of a local station, KGMO-AM. Despite Big Rush's reservations about rock and roll and show biz, he helped his son get an after-school job there spinning records.

In the summer before Rusty's senior year, Big Rush reluctantly gave his son permission (and the tuition) to attend a six-week radio-engineering course at the Elkins Institute of Radio Electronics in Dallas. Rusty lived in a rooming house, started smoking cigarettes, and got a license that permitted him to run the radio without supervision. The management of KGMO was happy enough to leave him there all alone, playing music and wisecracking not just on weekdays after school but weekends, too. A lot of sixteen-year-olds would have been very happy with the way life was going. Rusty had his high school dream job and a degree of celebrity (some of his classmates remember him signing autographs at record hops, although he says that never happened). He was also having fun on the air. The Associated Press used to send out a daily beauty tip, which Limbaugh read with mock solemnity. "I thought it was absurd, getting beauty tips from a wire service," he told me. "A lot of teachers did, too. We used to laugh about it at school."

His father wasn't amused or impressed. He didn't see his son's broadcasting talent, and he didn't get the point of a career dedicated to playing dumb songs for teenagers, anyway. Rusty was going in the wrong direction, and Big Rush let him know it in dinner table harangues that became loud, acrimonious, and painful.

The Cape Girardeau Convention and Visitors Bureau, housed in a small downtown office, is a first stop for the Civil War buffs who come to see the site of a famous battle and the headquarters of General U. S. Grant, and antique hunters in search of local treasures (the PBS series *Antiques Roadshow* was there during my visit). But Cape's biggest attraction is its status as the boyhood home of El Rushbo.

Chuck Martin is the executive director of the Visitors Bureau. "You'd be surprised how many people come in to buy Rush Limbaugh memorabilia and T-shirts here," he told me. "It's amazing how many people come to Cape just because they want to see where Rush grew up." To accommodate them, the bureau offers a drive-it-yourself tour whose itinerary includes the hospital where Rush was born, his childhood home and elementary school, Central High, the Varsity Barber Shop, the KGMO studio, and the campus of Southeast Missouri State University, where he suffered through one utterly unhappy academic year.

Rush often rails against the excesses of liberal academia, but his alma mater was (and still is) a bastion of conservatism. In the spring of 1968, just a few months before he enrolled there, a small group of students and teachers tried to form a chapter of Students for a Democratic Society. The president of the university, Dr. Mark Scully, responded by firing eight members of the faculty, causing the chairman of the department of history to resign in protest. Bobby Kennedy, who was running for the Democratic nomination for president, held a campaign rally in Cape and denounced the firings. The intervention made no difference. Cape wasn't Kennedy country; that year both Republican vice presidential candidate Spiro Agnew and third-party segregationist George Wallace drew bigger audiences.

"The college had a huge contingent of veterans then," says Frank Nickell. "President Scully called in a group of them, handed out T-shirts, and deputized them to defend Academic Hall against the anti-Vietnam protestors." (There are still a lot of military veterans at SEMO, and the place retains its basic outlook. But times change, even in Cape. During my visit, the university hosted a performance of *The Nutcracker* by the Moscow Ballet. Big Rush would not have understood.)

Another event in the spring of 1968 shook the town: on April 4, Martin Luther King was assassinated in Memphis, 160 miles down Highway 61. Cape remained quiet, but Cairo, Illinois, just a half hour across the Mississippi, was a powder keg. Even before the assassination it had been the scene of a long, violent racial confrontation that eventually led the governor to send in units of the Illinois National Guard. The city fathers stationed observers on the bridge to spot and report on cars with Illinois license plates and black occupants. This vigil was maintained for three years.

While all this upheaval was taking place, Limbaugh carried on as usual, living at home, doing *The Rusty Sharpe Show* on KGMO, and stubbornly resisting his father's efforts to make a professional man out of him. He didn't attend any of the political rallies in 1968 and only dimly recalls seeing Bobby Kennedy's motorcade pass by. After King's death he was pressed into service helping NBC-TV and radio reporters upload reports from the station. "I remember talking to them about the broadcast business. I was seventeen, playing records on the radio, not commenting on news. I don't recall feeling any concern," he recounts.

Most of all, he wanted to get out of Cape Girardeau.

"My last three years were miserable," Limbaugh says. In the eleventh grade his heart was broken in a secret romance he still won't discuss. During his senior year his war with his father escalated, and Rusty formally gave in and enrolled at SEMO. He lived at home, continued to spin records, and went to class as rarely as possible. On some days, Millie Limbaugh actually drove him to college to make sure he attended.

The most colorful site on the Limbaugh tour is the flood wall that runs for a mile along the Mississippi. In recent years Cape has, inexplicably, been struck by a passion for historical public art. A mural depicting the town's founding adorns the side of a downtown building. The university's Kent Library features a 38-by-21-foot painting celebrating the pioneers and citizens of southeast Missouri. The grandest project is *Mississippi River Tales*, the 24-panel, 18,000-square-foot graphic narrative on the flood wall. These panels include the Missouri Wall of Fame, forty-six portraits of the greatest sons and daughters, native and adopted, of the Show-Me State, as decided by a panel of Cape's leading citizens. Some are obvious choices: Harry S. Truman, Mark Twain, and Stan "the Man" Musial, for example. Many are Missourians who, like Limbaugh, found fame in distant places—T. S. Eliot, Burt Bacharach, Redd Foxx, General John J. Pershing, Yogi Berra, Walter Cronkite, George Washington Carver, and Ginger Rogers. Dred Scott, America's most famous runaway, was caught and dragged back to Missouri in chains. He is also one of the few members of the Wall of Fame actually buried in the state.

There are also some surprises on the wall. I had no idea Tennessee Williams was from Missouri. I was struck by the absence of Bob Gibson, the greatest pitcher in Cardinals history, and of Chuck Berry, a son of St. Louis whose cultural contribution makes him at least the equal of Marlin Perkins, host of *Mutual of Omaha's Wild Kingdom*, or Rose O'Neill, creator of the Kewpie Doll.

The Cape jury may be guilty of lapses but not of hometown favoritism. There are just three locals on the wall: astronaut Linda Godwin, who grew up in nearby Jackson; Marie Watkins Oliver, who designed the state flag; and Rush Limbaugh. Although he visits his family in Cape regularly, he hasn't seen the Wall of Fame. Perhaps he would be disconcerted to find himself, or even a depiction of himself, stuck in downtown Cape Girardeau in perpetuity.

If David Limbaugh weren't Rush's little brother he might be on the Wall of Fame himself. Certainly he is the most famous current resident of Cape. He has written three best-selling polemical attacks on secular liberalism and produces a nationally syndicated column. Cape has finally got a satellite hook-up, which means that he has recently been able to appear on talk shows without schlepping all the way to St. Louis. And he has a day job as a senior partner in the family law firm.

When Rusty announced that he was quitting college and setting out on a radio career, Big Rush called him in for one last talk. Leaving school, he said, would cost the boy his social standing, force him to settle for intellectually inferior friends, and price him out of the market for a decent bride. It went without saying that it would also deprive him of his birthright, partnership in the Limbaugh law office. But Rusty wasn't swayed by these dire predictions. His mind was made up, and for once he was prepared to stand up to his father.

That left David. He went to SEMO for a year, transferred to the University of Missouri in Columbia, got a B.A. in political science, went to law school, and made law review. Then he came home. His grandfather was still titular head of the firm, and his uncle Steve and cousin Steve Jr.—both future federal judges—were there, too. Big Rush, who suffered from diabetes and obesity, worked intermittently, and having David there gave him a boost. "My dad was really excited to have me back," he says, "and he gave me a lot to do."

David Limbaugh was a devoted brother, but not even a saint could have completely escaped a feeling of resentment. Rusty was out in the world chasing a dream; David was stuck behind a desk. But there were compensations for suddenly becoming Number One Son. "I've never been jealous of Rush," he told me, "probably because I was successful before he was. Does that make sense to you?"

My visit to Cape Girardeau was not the highlight of David Limbaugh's Christmas season. He had received permission from Rush to talk to me, but he couldn't quite shake the idea that I was the enemy, an agent of the hated mainstream media. I was from New York. I had a beard and wire-rim glasses. I wore jeans. "The sixties culture has tried to demonize the unique American culture," he said pointedly at our first meeting.

Yet, despite his suspicions, David proved to be a voluble and gracious guide. His conversational style is a mixture of candor and self-effacing (but sincere) paranoia. Driving around town one afternoon in his Cadillac Escalade he recalled how Rush, even at the age of three or four, knew every make and model of automobile on the road. "He was amazing, like he was reincarnated or something," David said. "The family wanted to get him on *The Ed Sullivan Show*." He shot me a sideways glance. "You're probably going to try to make me sound like an idiot, aren't you?"

When Rush hit it big he turned to his younger brother for legal counsel. It was a display of sibling intimacy and trust—there were far more experienced show business attorneys in California and New York—and David, who calls himself "a country lawyer," did just fine. Over the years he has helped his brother negotiate a series of ever more complex and lucrative deals and, in the process, has attracted some of Rush's acolytes, including FOX News' Sean Hannity and best-selling author and talk-show host Mark Levin.

"Rush is the ideal client," David told me. "He's patient and he knows what he wants. And hey, he knows more about his industry than I do. That makes it easy." David isn't as rich as his brother but he appears to be doing very well. He lives with his wife and five kids in a splendid white-pillared mansion on a hill in horse country.

The Limbaugh brothers don't sound alike—David has kept the reedy Missouri twang that Rush saw as a professional impediment and worked hard to lose—but they think alike when it comes to politics. David described Barack Obama, whose inauguration was a month away, as a "Stalinist liberal," and his supporters in the media and academia as "dictatorial Stalinist aristocrats." The harsh words were softened by an amiable tone; David lacks his brother's emotional velocity, primarily because, unlike Rush, he is not an entertainer. "When Rush gets behind the mike, it's not that he's a different person, he's the same person, but he gets more animated," David explained. "I've heard that Johnny Carson was the same way. A lot of performers are. Do you agree?"

We drove together to pick up one of David's kids at the Christian parochial school he attends. Such schools were not in fashion when the Limbaugh boys were young. They attended public school and confined their religious education to Sunday School instruction at Centenary United Methodist Church. As a young man, David was not what you would describe as pious, but he has lately become a fervent, born-again evangelical. One of his recent books is *Persecution: How Liberals Are Waging War Against Christians.*

I asked David what his brother thought of his religiosity. "I'd say Rush is a Christian," he replied. "But he doesn't go to church and I don't know if I'd say he's born-again. It's something we really don't discuss. I don't try to push religion on people. You're probably going to make me sound like a religious fanatic, aren't you?"

Later, when I mentioned David's observation to his brother, Rush confirmed that he doesn't go to church regularly. "I never enjoyed going when I was a kid. It seemed false to me somehow, just people saying words, going through the motions. On Sundays, some of the local ministers would come into the station to give sermons on the radio, and I'd tell them, 'Hey, I know I should be in church today,' just to see their reaction. You know what? They couldn't have cared less. They were happy I was working." Limbaugh says he does have "a private relationship with Jesus" and speaks to God many times a day. He didn't say who initiates the conversations.

It had been snowing in Cape, and the roads were slick, but David braved the elements to give me a personalized tour of Rush's boyhood. When Big Rush came back from World War II, he, like many veterans, bought a modest cottage—David thinks he paid eleven thousand dollars. As the boys reached their teens, the family upgraded to a brick ranch house with a wraparound porch, big windows, marble floors, and, of course, the downstairs rumpus room. There had been happy times there. David hadn't shared Rush's burning desire to escape, and he pointed out the scenes of their boyhood with what seemed like fondness.

Rush was due home for Christmas in a few days, and David was both happy and sad. He finds it painful that his brother has no children. "He comes every year, flying in with a plane full of presents like Santa Claus. My kids are crazy about him. I don't talk to him very much about how wonderful it is to be a father, because I don't want to cause him any hurt. But I wish he could know the joy of it. I think he'd make a great father."

"David idolized Big Rush and now he idolizes Rush," a high school friend told me. I mentioned this to David and he didn't disagree. "Rush is like a general of a huge army. He's the leader of a movement," he said. "Whatever success I've had with my books and columns, that's not much really when you compare it to him. I guess a lot of people think I ride on his coattails." He gave me one of his sideways looks. "Maybe you think that, too."

"Why would I think that?"

"Everybody does," he said glumly. "I wouldn't be surprised if you did, too."

Unlike a lot of small Midwestern cities, Cape Girardeau hadn't been hurt too badly by the economic dislocations of the past two generations.

In fact, except for some down-at-the-heels stretches of Broadway and a few other commercial streets, things appeared to be booming. The economy is anchored by the university and two large regional hospitals, and it is a commercial center for agricultural products. A Proctor & Gamble factory provides steady work. Retail in Cape ranges from high-end antique galleries and a shining island of national chain stores and restaurants not far from Limbaugh's office to places like Nearly Perfect Shoes ("Actually they are perfect," a saleslady told me, "it's just that they didn't sell, so we get them"). I also spotted The Aggressive Mortgage Company, which soon went under, a victim, presumably, of its own hawkish business philosophy.

I was glad to find the Varsity Barber Shop, Rush's first employer, still open for business. The chair where he once shined shoes is still there; in fact, the entire place looks like it hasn't been so much as painted since the 1960s. I dropped by on a Tuesday morning, about eleven o'clock. The barber, a large man in late middle age dressed in a flannel shirt and droopy jeans, was just finishing up a trim. Otherwise the shop was empty and silent. The barber, whose name was Fred, subjected me to a not-especially-veiled inspection. Clearly the Varsity doesn't get much drop-in business.

"Just came by to get my haircut," I said.

"Sorry," said Fred. "All the slots are taken."

Vacant chairs lined the wall. The unmanned shoe station stood in a corner. Not even a radio was playing. "There's nobody here," I said.

Fred nodded. That was a fact, but not a relevant fact. "Around Christmastime, people come in for a haircut. They make appointments," he said. "You didn't make an appointment."

"I didn't know," I said. "I'm from out of town. Can't you just squeeze me in?"

"Nope."

"When can I make an appointment?"

"After Christmas," he said. "Before Christmas folks come from forty miles to get a haircut."

Christmas was ten days away. "Did Rush Limbaugh really work here?" I asked.

"That's what they say. Never met him."

"Ever hear any good stories about him when he was working here?"

"Nope. Can't say I have."

We looked at one another for a long moment and then I thanked him for his time and left. If there's one thing I have learned in a long career it is that when you can't get a haircut in an empty barbershop at eleven in the morning, you've been in town long enough.

Which is, I think, more or less the way Rusty Limbaugh felt in February 1971 when he left Cape at the wheel of his '69 Pontiac Le Mans.

CHAPTER THREE

FROM RUSTY TO CHRISTIE TO RUSH

In McKeesport, Pennsylvania, twelve miles from Pittsburgh, at the confluence of the Monongahela and Youghiogheny rivers, Rush Limbaugh shed his alter ego, Rusty Sharpe, and was reborn as "Bachelor Jeff" Christie, morning drive-time disc jockey on station WIXZ-AM. McKeesport was smaller than Cape but it was in the Pittsburgh listening area, and for Rush it was a large step up, proof that he could get a serious radio gig outside the orbit of the Limbaugh family influence. Except for the six-week engineering course in Dallas, which had been closely supervised, long-distance, by his mother, this was his first venture into the adult world. He was on his own, earning a living, discovering a new part of the country, and, best of all, permanently paroled from academia.

At WIXZ he hosted the *Solid Rockin' Gold Show*. Here and there on the Internet you can find snippets of these shows. Even at a remove of more than thirty years, the timbre and timing of his voice is instantly recognizable. His job was to play music and deliver traffic reports, but he couldn't repress the urge to make his audience laugh.

"Seven minutes after six in the morning . . . As you know I am a bachelor, I live in a dinky little apartment, and all I have is a lamp and a TV set, but I'm going to play a little joke on the electrical department." Rush dialed the phone and an unsuspecting employee of the electric company answered.

"I just moved here from Florida," said Rush. "I have a thing for palm trees and I have a big backyard, so I thought I might start a palm tree orchard."

"A palm tree orchard?"

"I need heat lamps for that," Rush said. "About fifteen or twenty thousand heat lamps. And I was wondering what it would cost me."

"How many watts?"

Rush said, "About six hundred watts apiece, twenty hours a day. What will that run me?"

The electric company clerk took a minute to calculate. "That would cost you three thousand, six hundred and forty-eight dollars a day," he said.

Rush feigned shock. "*A day!* I could move back to Florida cheaper than that!"

Bits like this were an echo of the crank calls and fake pizza orders from Flo's Taxi, and they signaled that Jeff Christie aspired to something bigger than record spinning. Like all beginning comics, he used the materials he had garnered from his own experience. "The Friar Shuck Radio Ministry of the Air," for example, leaned on his contempt for the radio preachers he had met at the studio on Sunday mornings in Cape, as well as showcased Limbaugh's gift for mimicry.

"Before the show I had the divine joy of talking with the Almighty," Shuck intoned in a fruity Southern accent. "It was in my garage and I got right straight through to Him and I got talking about some real heavy subjects. He told me that there are those of you out there with afflictions and terrible troubles. He said there's a lady out there who believes her daughter is in terrible trouble. I don't know if it's you. Do you believe that your daughter's in trouble? Don't despair, the Almighty told me it could be taken care of. Simply send a hundred dollars. Now if you don't have a hundred dollars, hawk something or borrow it and send it. Get it and send it to Friar Shuck!"

Sometimes Bachelor Jeff gave out faux advice. "Bunch of requests for the Christie quickie DJ course," he said one morning. "Had a letter from a girl who desired to become a radio pronouncer, and she thought it would be a drawback because she's a girl. Not so. You really just have to master two techniques, and I'm going to explain them right now. Number one, the use of the microphone. To use it, simply turn the microphone to the on position and talk into it. The second, which is the biggie, is cuing up the record. Get the record you want to play, take it out of the appropriate shuck, slap it onto the turntable, take the arm and the needle, place it on the outside edge of the record, then turn the record until you hear the beginning of the record, back it up a quarter of a turn, and when you get through talking the record will start." He paused, gave it two beats. "After you have mastered those two techniques, girls, change your sex."

Limbaugh's bosses saw that he was talented and popular, but they worried that his humor was stretching the top-40 drive-time format. "They used to send him memos, telling him 'Shut up and play the records,'" says Bill Figenshu, who worked at the station as "Bill Steele" and shared a two-hundred-dollar-a-month flat with Rush in nearby Irwin, Pennsylvania. "It was supposedly a garden apartment but it was in the basement, so there was no garden. We were both very young, ambitious, hard-working guys. He went in at four in the morning. I worked nights, so we didn't see each other that much. We were friendly, we had a decent time, but we weren't best buds or anything like that. Mostly we did the wash together on Saturdays and ate pizza. Rush had a good personality but he wasn't particularly funny. He was a quiet kid, and so was I. When radio is your life, you're a geek. Especially if you were doing AM, which was becoming uncool at that point. We didn't smoke dope, we did air-checks. Vietnam was going on, all sorts of changes, but I can't remember him talking about politics. We talked about radio and the careers we wanted to have."

According to Figenshu, who went on to become the head of Viacom's radio broadcasting division, the flat they shared was a model of bachelor domesticity, with a ratty green shag carpet, furniture pulled together from forgotten sources, and cold pizza crusting on the kitchen counter. Limbaugh, who is an extremely fastidious housekeeper, is offended by the description. He also denies that the apartment was, as has been reported, the scene of his first sexual conquest. "I have no memory of THAT," he wrote me in an e-mail. "I don't remember where [I lost my virginity]. Honestly I don't. All I know is that there was NO ONE else there. That I am certain of."

In Cape, Rusty Sharpe had been a minor celebrity. In McKeesport, Jeff Christie surpassed Rusty: He did Toys for Tots charity gigs with players of the Pittsburgh Condors, an ABA basketball team that averaged less than a thousand fans a game and whose star, John Brisker, was the dirtiest player in the history of pro basketball. Bachelor Jeff made appearances for the Variety Club and other civic organizations, and showed up on request to schmooze with sponsors at station events.

WIXZ was a starter job, and Limbaugh acquitted himself well enough to take the next step. In 1973 he was hired by station KQV, known as 14K, as a nighttime disc jockey. KQV was an ABC affiliate, the second-most-popular AM station in Pittsburgh. Unfortunately for him, ABC quickly sold the station to Taft Broadcasting. There were different bosses, different expectations, and by 1974 Jeff Christie was out of a job and temporarily unable to find a new one.

The economy was against him—the stock market crashed in 1973, and by the end of '74 it had lost more than 45 percent of its value. Rust Belt cities like Pittsburgh were especially bad places to be. The record industry was changing, too. Singles were being replaced by albums. *Billboard* reported that FM had established dominance in "market after market . . . in the younger demographics"—that was Jeff Christie's demographic. But he had no interest in FM, which he considered a radio band for hippies and phony intellectuals.

Limbaugh put out job feelers, but he got only one offer, from Neenah, Wisconsin. After having been in a top-10 national radio market, even Cape sounded better than Neenah. He hitched a U-Haul trailer to his Buick Riviera and drove home. For the next seven months he lived with his parents, umpired Little League for five dollars a game, sunbathed in the backyard, and cruised Broadway in search of action that didn't materialize ("I felt like I was Dustin Hoffman in *The Graduate* except for the mother and the girlfriend he was banging"). He also spent a good part of his time in the family rumpus room playing Strat-O-Matic baseball. Some of his friends thought he was sulking down there, but to Limbaugh it was a time of reflection and relaxation.

"I did not hibernate in the basement," he wrote to me. "The basement in that house was the greatest room in the house!! And mine was the only bedroom on that floor. It was an above-ground basement with a dumbwaiter right up to the kitchen."

Surprisingly, Big Rush didn't give his son a hard time about his misadventure in Pittsburgh. The old man was approaching sixty. The country he loved and had fought for seemed to be falling apart. Richard Nixon, whom he once hosted in Cape, was forced to resign the presidency in disgrace. The Communists were winning in Vietnam. David was away at college, and it was lonely at home. "I think he liked having me around," says Rush. "He and my mom and I went out to dinner a lot. He told me he knew I'd get my ass in gear eventually."

Limbaugh sent tapes of his work to stations around the country. Joey Reynolds, who hosts a late-night show on WOR in New York City, was at KQV then, and he tried to help Rush get his job back. "My dad gave me the money to go to Pittsburgh to try, but it only lasted a few days," Limbaugh recalls. "When I got back to Cape again I was depressed and frustrated. I always had a sense I would succeed but nothing was coming through. I can remember taking a baseball bat out to the backyard and just beating a tree, over and over."

He was especially stung by a rejection from John Rook. "Rook," he told me, "was a legend in the broadcast business. He had been the program director at WLS in Chicago, which is the station that carried Larry Lujack. By 1974 he had gone to Denver. I sent him a tape and he called me. For one hour he basically told me that the only difference between me and a bag of shit was the bag. He just ripped me to shreds. To this day I have no idea why he did that to me."

Big Rush's reaction was characteristic: "Why," he asked his son, "do you want to stay in the radio business? Nobody has a sense of honor." But he refrained from pushing. It was Millie who grew impatient with her son's indolence. One day Jim Carnegie, who had been program director at KQV in Pittsburgh and was now in Kansas City at KUDL, called Rush to sound out about possibly coming to work there. Rush wasn't sure he wanted to live in Kansas City, but his mother was. She said, "You are going, and if they offer you a job you are going to take it."

Which he did.

Kansas City is 350 miles west of Cape Girardeau, and while it wasn't Limbaugh's dream destination, it was, like Pittsburgh, a real city with major league franchises in baseball, football, and (temporarily) basketball to prove it. His new employer, KUDL, had both AM and FM bands. Limbaugh, still "Jeff Christie," started out playing oldies and bantering with callers on the AM dial. That changed when NBC bought the station and turned AM into an all-talk format. Oddly, it didn't occur to anyone that Limbaugh would make a good fit. Instead he was switched to FM, where he was basically required to supervise the automated and computerized music programs the station ran, make public-service announcements, and take calls from listeners. Insult comedy was coming into its own on the radio, and Jeff Christie decided to try it. He describes the result in his book, *See, I Told You So*:

> I found out something about myself . . . something that was quite disturbing. I found out I was really, really good at insulting people. For example, the topic one day was. "When you die, how do you want to go?"
>
> "I want to go the cheapest and most natural way I can," one nice lady caller from Independence, Missouri, said.
>
> My response was: "Easy. Have your husband throw you in a trash bag and then in the Missouri River with the rest of the garbage."
>
> When I went home after a day of this, I didn't like myself.

The lesson stayed with him. To this day, Limbaugh is polite to his callers who are, in any case, prescreened. He is still insulting, but his targets tend to be institutions, causes, and public figures who can defend themselves.

In time, Limbaugh developed a modest fan base. One of his listeners was George Brett, the Hall of Fame third baseman of the Kansas City Royals. "I liked listening to him," Brett says. "He was funny. I had no idea he knew anything about politics."

Limbaugh had another Kansas City Royals connection, Bryan Burns, a young guy who worked in the team's marketing department. The two men met at the intersection of ticket sales and media, and struck up a friendship. Burns was from a small town in southeast Missouri about ninety miles from Cape. Like Rush, he was single. They both had apartment leases that were expiring and decided to pool their resources and rent a place together in Overland Park, a Kansas City suburb.

"We weren't wild and crazy guys," says Burns, who is now a vice president at ESPN. "On Sundays Rush would put on his Pittsburgh Steelers jersey and we'd watch football. Sometimes a few other guys would join us. Or he'd play music—he was into George Benson, what was called back then contemporary jazz. But it was far from a party atmosphere."

Burns, like Bill Figenshu, had no idea his roommate was a political thinker. "He was scary smart about everything, but I can't recall us talking much about current events. He was funny, though. I was an audience of one. Now his audience is millions, but I don't really hear a difference. The Rush I knew in Kansas City is the same guy I hear on the radio. If I had to choose a word to describe him, I'd say 'real.'"

Soon after moving in with Burns, Rush met Roxy Maxine McNeely, a secretary at one of the other radio stations in town. "Roxy didn't move in with us, but she spent a lot of time at our place," says Burns. "She was a very fun-loving girl. She used to write notes to Rush on the bathroom mirror in lipstick. I liked her a lot." Rush did, too, and in short order he moved in with her, although he continued to pay his share of the Overland Park lease. In 1977 he and Roxy were married in Cape at the Centenary United Methodist Church. It was a large wedding, and for once Rush basked in his father's approval. Perhaps Roxy wasn't quite the wife a real professional man could have snagged, but she was lovely and had a good head on her shoulders. Rush, at twenty-six, was now gainfully employed in Kansas City, plausibly successful, and conventionally coupled.

Like a lot of first marriages, this was a youthful experiment that didn't work out. Rush was focused on his career and he was a homebody; when he wasn't at the studio he wanted to stay home, snack, and watch sports on TV, or tinker with electronic equipment. Roxy liked going out and she felt unappreciated. After two years she filed for divorce on grounds of mutual incompatibility, and Rush didn't object. There were no hard feelings, no kids, and not much in the way of mutual property to distribute—a clean break.

Jeff Christie was doing no better professionally than Rush Limbaugh was doing matrimonially. He was fired twice in 1978, first by KUDL and then by KFIX. The radio business was in flux, and disc jockeys rarely lasted long. Besides, Limbaugh had personality conflicts with superiors who found him argumentative.

Luckily for Rush, Bryan Burns had moved up in the Royals front office. He offered his old roommate a part-time job in the marketing department, and Rush took it. Even when the position went to full-time, Limbaugh was still making far less than he had earned in Pittsburgh a decade earlier. Not only was he broke, he was treated like a nobody.

"On a baseball franchise there are some guys with real important jobs, but Rush wasn't one of them. He did group sales and odd jobs, like finding singers for 'The Star-Spangled Banner.' There was no aura about him," says Burns.

As a teenager, Rush had been accepted by the jocks because he hung out with John Rueseler, a star athlete who went on to play college football at Memphis State. George Brett filled a similar role in Limbaugh's life. They formed a highly improbable friendship—baseball stars seldom pal around with front-office flunkies—and suddenly Limbaugh was a part of the Royals in-crowd.

"Rush didn't have a lot of friends," says Brett. "I don't think he felt very good about himself. But I thought he was smart and funny. On Sundays after games we'd go out for fried chicken dinner at Stroud's, or he'd come over to the house and help me hook up electronic equipment. We talked about personal things, sports trivia, whatever, but I can't recall ever talking about politics. When he left Kansas City and went on to his new career, I was surprised to find out he knew anything about it."

In the off-season Brett included Rush in touch football games with professional athletes and other jocks. "Sam Lacey, the NBA player, was in the games, and a lot of Royals employees, too," Brett told me. "When we chose up sides, Rush was always the last one taken—he was overweight and not very athletic, an old guy. But you know what? He always came up with the play that won the game."

Limbaugh worked for the Royals for five years. In addition to working in group sales he "produced" the scoreboard during games. "Back then baseball teams didn't really believe in marketing themselves," says Burns. "It was looked down on. A team might have a bat day or hold some kind of promotion, but actually putting on a show during the game was considered inappropriate." Putting on a show was what Limbaugh loved. "He played Michael Jackson songs between innings. Nobody was doing anything like that back then. He bought a cart-machine and played sound effects over the scoreboard. I think he was the first one in baseball to produce games that way."

Limbaugh was good at his job, but he rubbed a lot of people the wrong way. "For one thing, they didn't like it when I played Michael Jackson," he told me. "They used to say, 'Where do you think we are, Oakland?'" Rush Limbaugh, racial pioneer.

In 1983 Bryan Burns left the team for a senior role in the office of the commissioner of Major League Baseball. That was the beginning of the end for Rush's career in the Majors. "He had an edgy attitude," says Burns. "He tended to be frank and honest, and when he thought people in the organization were wrong he said so. I was more or less his protector, but after I left he lost his job."

Rush left the Royals and eventually went on to stardom, but he never forgot George Brett's friendship. In 1992 at Brett's wedding reception, he sang a sentimental song (he says he can't recall which one) and handed Brett a letter thanking him and offering to treat the newlyweds to a honeymoon anywhere in the world for as long as they cared to go. When Brett reached his three-thousandth career hit, Limbaugh flew to Kansas City and hosted a large celebratory dinner party at Stroud's. And they are still golfing buddies.

"We were sitting around talking one day, and I suggested to Rush that I come down to Palm Beach to play with him," Brett told me. "He seemed surprised by that. 'You'd want to come all the way down there to play with me?' he said. After all his success, he's still a little bit insecure."

Just before Rush was fired by the Royals he got married for the second time. His bride was Michelle Sixta, a student at Central Missouri State University who was working her way through school as a stadium usher. They were married in a small ceremony at the Stadium Club.

Out of work once more, Limbaugh caught on at KMBZ in Kansas City, where, for the first time, he began openly expressing his conservative opinions on the air and engaging in right-wing satire. This was controversial, and the owner of the station, Bonneville International, a company controlled by The Church of Jesus Christ of Latter-day Saints, was uncomfortable with controversy. Limbaugh drew a crowd but he also upset a lot of people.

Shock radio, rude and irreverent, was catching on around the country at the time. Less than a decade earlier, Larry Lujack had been forced to publicly apologize for telling a listener that he would play more Jim Croce songs when Croce (who had been killed a few months earlier in a plane crash) went back into the studio and recorded some. Now, in New York, at WNBC, Don Imus and Howard Stern scored gigantic ratings with tasteless, offensive, often topical humor.

Sacramento's version was Morton Downey Jr., who was drawing big audiences and national attention for his show, broadcast on KFBK. Downey was a ranter with a taste for pushing boundaries. He reached his boundary when he told a joke about "a Chinaman," an ethnic term that offended many, especially City Councilman Tom Chinn, who thought it had been aimed at him personally. Chinn complained to the owner of the station, C. K. McClatchy, who fired Downey. As luck would have it, Limbaugh was fired again right around the same time. He was done in by football. Unbeknownst to him, KMBZ was trying to get the rights to broadcast the Kansas City Chiefs games. Limbaugh, a fanatical football fan, had taken to blasting the team and its executives as price-gouging, incompetent cheapskates. That made him a liability, and he was canned. The pink slip came with a curt note. "Unfortunately," the station manager wrote to him, "I cannot share your enthusiasm for your performance."

Norm Woodruff, who met Limbaugh while working as a consultant to KMBZ, was now the acting program director of Sacramento's KFBK. He knew Limbaugh's show, and he thought Rush would be an ideal replacement for Downey. Limbaugh had too much attitude for Kansas City, but compared with Downey he was a model of easy listening and good humor. Woodruff hired Limbaugh and gave him marching orders that Rush described in a speech in the summer of 2009: "We want controversy, but don't make it up. If you actually think something—if you actually believe it, and you can tell people why—we'll back you up. But if you're going to say stuff just to make people mad—if all you want to do is rabble-rouse, if all you want to do is offend and get noticed—that's not what we're interested in, and we won't back you up."

Limbaugh was a hit in Sacramento. He was using his real name now. The station let him go on the air solo, unencumbered by sidekicks or guests, and encouraged his highly personal, right-wing monologues. For the first time in his career he was marketed heavily and aggressively. There were billboards around town showing a finger hitting a button, captioned: "How Would You Like to Punch Rush Limbaugh?" Rush was so pleased by these that he sent Bryan a snapshot. Morton Downey Jr. had been a big star in Sacramento, with a 5 share of the market—5 percent of people listening to the radio in a given fifteen-minute segment. Limbaugh tripled that. He was sharp edged but good humored. "The new morning host espouses many of the same beliefs of his predecessor, Morton Downey Jr.," reported the *Sacramento Bee*, "but he skates a little farther from the edge of the hole in the ice."

Rush was rewarded for his success with a six-figure salary, an estimable income in the mid-1980s, even by his father's standards. More important, for the first time in his life he really mattered. He was invited to deliver speeches, just like Big Rush. He was an occasional commentator on television and wrote newspaper columns. Politicians and celebrities sought him out. He and Michelle bought a new house and furnished it with products he endorsed on the air.

The audience in Sacramento was more sophisticated than the one he had had in Kansas City, and more liberal. Jerry Brown, known as "Governor Moonbeam," had just finished his years in the statehouse, and California was swinging to the right, but it was still a long way from Kansas. I was in Sacramento in the mid-'80s, and I vividly recall boarding a bus bound for San Francisco on which the driver nonchalantly announced that smoking cigarettes, cigars, pipes, and joints was prohibited.

Marijuana wasn't Rush's thing. (In 1993 he told an interviewer for *Playboy* that he had only tried it twice, inhaled but hadn't liked it.) Hippies smoked marijuana. Rush wanted to belong to the square adult world, and in Sacramento he had that chance. "For the first time in my life I actively appreciated where I lived," he wrote in *The Way Things Ought to Be*. "I was no longer a passing personality but rather a functioning, practicing, and participating member of my community—aspects of life that were new to me. And I loved it."

Michelle loved it less. She had a job at a printing company but quit to become her husband's assistant, and she found the job boring and tedious. She was an outdoors type; he hated nature. When he did venture out he was a klutz. One day fellow disc jockeys Bob Nathan and Dave Williams convinced him to go rafting on the American River, which runs through Sacramento. "It's a very, very mild ride," Williams later wrote. "Bob gave Rush an oar and told him to absorb the blow of the canyon wall to give us a little spring back into the current . . . Rush panicked, stuck the oar out, his arms stiff as a board, and upon impact he fell overboard . . . We got Rush back in the raft and the next day he spent the entire three hours of his show talking about his horrendous whitewater grapple with the grim reaper."

Rush's fun, as always, came in the studio. An evangelist in Ohio claimed that the theme song for the old *Mister Ed* television series (*"A horse is a horse, of course, of course . . ."*) contained a satanic message when played backward. Limbaugh told his audience about it and informed them a Slim Whitman recording played backward also contained a message from the devil. To his delight, a lot of listeners took him seriously, calling the station to report that they were trashing all their Whitman albums to "keep the devil out of the house."

The Limbaugh persona, which had been germinating since the "Jeff Christie School for DJs" in Pittsburgh, flowered in Sacramento. Limbaugh became "El Rushbo, the all-knowing, all-caring, all-sensing Maha

Rushi," "a harmless little fuzzball," and the "Epitome of Morality and Virtue." His show was carried "across the fruited plain" on the (fictitious) Excellence in Broadcasting Network, from behind the golden EIB microphone. He was on "the cutting edge of societal evolution," "serving humanity" with "talent on loan from God," and opinions "documented to be almost always right, 97.9 percent of the time" by the Sullivan Group (another fictitious entity named for local DJ and Limbaugh buddy Tom Sullivan).

The stylized, satirical lingo began then, too. He mocked the multicultural style of California by proposing to keep "Uglo-Americans" off the streets. Militant feminists became "Feminazis." The green movement was full of "environmental whackos," the American left became "Commie pinko liberals," and the residents of Rio Linda, California, were synonymous with stupidity. A ringing *"Dadelut! Dadelut! Dadelut!"* introduced news updates on what he regarded the absurdities of liberal activism. Liberals, of course, hated him, which he found inspiring. When they attacked him as a dimwit, he responded by claiming that he was so much smarter than his critics that he could vanquish them "with half my brain tied behind my back, just to make it fair."

Bruce Marr saw that Limbaugh had the ability to go beyond Sacramento and introduced him to Ed McLaughlin, the former head of ABC Radio. McLaughlin had started his own company, and he was syndicating the *Dr. Dean Edell Show* nationally. He agreed with Marr that Limbaugh had the potential to go national as well. McLaughlin offered a partnership. Rush brought in his brother, David, to work out the details. The arrangement made a fortune for both Limbaugh and McLaughlin, and revolutionized the style and content of American radio.

But first Limbaugh had to get out of Sacramento. His contract with KBFK stipulated that he could leave only to accept an offer by a top-market station. But city stations wanted local programming, not shows aimed at a national audience. McLaughlin came up with an ingenious solution. Limbaugh would go to WABC in New York, where he would do a local program, essentially for free. In return, the ABC Radio Networks would carry a second, national program each day on its affiliates.

The New York City show started in July 1988. A month later, on

August 1, the national program followed on fifty-six stations in second-tier markets with a total of about 250,000 listeners. The EIB Network was on the air. It had been twenty-one years since Rusty Sharpe's first show in Cape Girardeau. He was thirty-seven years old, and he had finally made it to what he hoped would be the big time.

CHAPTER FOUR

THE CITY

Limbaugh came to New York with trepidation. "I decided to leave Sacramento in April but didn't go till July," he told a reporter for the *Sacramento Bee*. "I realized that everything I'd been searching for in seventeen years I'd found in Sacramento in the last year and a half. Friends. Security. Stability. A house." After being fired in Pittsburgh, Limbaugh had retreated to Cape; in Sacramento, with New York looming, he once more holed up. "I got so depressed, I guess you could say I sat around the house in my underwear, sulking," he said.

Bryan Burns had moved to New York. One Saturday morning he got a call from Limbaugh. "You're not going to believe this," Rush said, "but we're moving to New York City. Can you help us find a place to live?"

"Rush and Michelle came to town, and my wife and I took them all over the city looking at places," says Burns. "Finally we found an apartment near Lincoln Center for twenty-seven hundred dollars a month." The flat was still occupied and wouldn't be ready for a few months, so Ed McLaughlin found Limbaugh a suite at the Parker Meridien Hotel.

Professionally Limbaugh was more than ready for the big city. His technique and timing, honed during thousands of hours on the air, were flawless. Studio engineers at ABC were impressed to find that he knew almost as much about the latest broadcasting technology as they did. His voice, shorn of its regional accent through practice, was a fine instrument.

And he had a great selection of bumper music. Like Lee Atwater, George H. W. Bush's hard-driving political consultant, Limbaugh understood that cool music could make a conservative message seem contemporary and energetic.

All these tools were necessary for success but not nearly sufficient. New York was full of disc jockeys with musical taste, good voices, and broadcasting chops, but no one—in Manhattan or anywhere else—was doing unabashed, balls-to-the-wall right-wing satire. That was Limbaugh's niche, and he seized it immediately.

Limbaugh brought with him from Sacramento the same style he uses today—unscripted, free-flow monologues on the topical issues of the moment, full of demeaning nicknames (Ted Kennedy, for example, was "the swimmer"), wicked imitations and parodies, relentless mockery of the mainstream media, unabashed Republican partisanship, and a willingness to transgress almost every kind of political correctness. But, beyond this bag of tricks, there was a bedrock seriousness of belief that came not from his years on the road, but from his home in Cape Girardeau.

In 1988, before coming to New York, Limbaugh published a column in the now-defunct *Sacramento Union* titled "35 Undeniable Truths." It read like an eclectic and sometimes whimsical collection of axioms and pronouncements by Thomas Hobbes (*"War is not obsolete; ours is a world governed by the aggressive use of force"*); Howard Cosell (*"The greatest football team in the history of civilization is the Pittsburgh Steelers of 1975–1980; the L.A. Raiders will never be the team that they were when they called Oakland home"*); Billy Graham (*"There is a God; abortion is wrong; morality is not defined and cannot be defined by individual choice; evolution cannot explain Creation"*); John D. Rockefeller (*"There will always be poor people. This is not the fault of the rich"*); Norman Mailer (*"Feminism was established so as to allow unattractive women access to the mainstream of society"*); General George Patton (*"The US will again to war. There is no such thing as war atrocities. War itself is an atrocity. The only way to get rid of nuclear weapons is to use them"*); a high school history teacher (*"Abraham Lincoln saved this nation"*); Paul McCartney (*"Love is the only human emotion that cannot be controlled"*); and Thomas Jefferson (*"Freedom is God given"*).

By far the greatest number of "undeniable truths" came from the anti-Communist dinner table rants of Big Rush: *"The greatest threat to humanity lies in the nuclear arsenal of the USSR. The greatest threat to humanity lies in the USSR. Peace does not mean the elimination of nuclear weapons. Peace does not mean the absence of war. Peace can't be achieved by developing an 'understanding' with the Russian people. When Americans oppose America, it is not always courageous and sacred; it is sometimes dangerous. Communism kills. In the USSR, peace means the absence of opposition. To free peoples, peace means the absence of threats and the presence of justice. The Peace Movement in the United States—whether by accident or design—is pro-Communist. The only difference between Mikhail Gorbachev and previous Soviet leaders is that Gorbachev is alive. Soviet leaders are just left-wing dictators. To more and more people, a victorious United States is a sinful United States. This is frightening and ominous. You should thank God for making you an American; and instead of feeling guilty about it, help spread our ideas worldwide."*

And, as Big Rush certainly believed, *"The collective knowledge and wisdom of seasoned citizens is the most valuable—yet untapped—resource our young people have."*

Very few of Rush Limbaugh's "truths" were the product of personal observation or experience. His life had been remarkably untouched by many of the affiliations and responsibilities of his generation. He had been a Cub Scout (under pressure) for one year and quit without earning a single merit badge. He was on the high school football team for a season and then dropped out. He spent one year in college, living at home. He never served in the army or the Peace Corps, had not traveled abroad (and, in fact, had only been in New York once, on a three-day business trip, before moving there), and did not belong to any church or clubs. He also had no children. Since his midteens he had spent his life in the circumscribed environment of top-40 AM radio, with a few years in the marketing department of the Royals. While he was in the studio, or at the ballpark, the world and the American culture were in a state of exceptional flux.

Rusty Limbaugh's reaction to the events of 1968—an apolitical shrug, conversations with newsmen about how he could break into big-time broadcasting—became Rush's pattern. He did not participate, one way or the other, in the great causes of his time. The civil rights movement, the Vietnam War, Stonewall, the feminist revolution, political assassinations, Watergate, Jimmy Carter, even the Reagan counterrevolution didn't engage him until he was nearly forty. He had his opinions, of course. Once a station manager in Pittsburgh cautioned him not to talk positively about Richard Nixon on the air. He read newspapers and kept up but didn't talk politics with his roommates or his closest friends, like George Brett. He was so detached and apolitical that he didn't register to vote until he was thirty-five years old.

When he did begin talking about politics, in Kansas City, he reached for the doctrines he had been raised on. That they were not original or less absolutely true than he imagined was secondary; what mattered, what was unusual, was that he was a talking disc jockey with a coherent, conservative credo. They were an honest representation of how Limbaugh saw the world. They also were sufficiently overstated to give him a plausible, Ali-like, just-kidding deniability when it suited him.

Limbaugh came to New York with many ambitions, not all of them complementary. First, he wanted to become the country's leading radio personality, and he accomplished that in short order. Within five years, *Playboy* noted that his show was so widespread on the American air that it ought to come with its own environmental-impact statement. By most standards he was rich and famous, but not by the standards of Manhattan. In interviews he gave in the early 1990s, he often remarked on how disconcerting it was for him, after his celebrity in Sacramento, to go unrecognized on the streets of New York.

He was especially hurt and disappointed by the rejection of his peers. Limbaugh arrived believing that there was an elite club of broadcasters ("not media people, broadcasters," he says) who would recognize his ability and welcome him into their fraternity with fellowship and camaraderie. "These guys had millions of listeners every night. I looked up to them. I wanted to be accepted as one of them. But that's not what happened." In fact, the only mainstream broadcasters who were even remotely welcoming were Tim Russert and Ted Koppel.

Limbaugh was right: there was (and is) a broadcast elite in New York with connections to one another (not always friendly) and other very important people in the arts and entertainment, the news business, politics, publishing, academia, and Wall Street. Outsiders are always welcome—Walter Cronkite himself came from Missouri; Tom Brokaw, from Nebraska; and Peter Jennings, from Canada, of all places—but the price of admission is accepting and, in some small way propagating, the group ethos. Get in and you become eligible for prizes and awards, college commencement gigs, famous neighbors, social respectability (if not popularity), front-row-center seats, and great tables. In that respect, acceptance by the Manhattan media elite is not different from membership in any high school in-crowd. Dobie Gray sang about the experience on a hit record Rusty Sharpe used to spin: *"You ain't been nowhere 'til you've been in . . . with the in crowd, yeah!"*

Internalizing the lyrics of hit songs is an occupational hazard for disc jockeys. Besides, Dobie Gray didn't spell out the Manhattan rules. Members of the club had to be (and still have to be) secular, socially liberal, politically Democratic (or at least not Republican), aspirationally Ivy League, discreetly avaricious, and unwilling to express opinions not sanctioned by the editorial page of the *New York Times*. Of these values, Limbaugh shared only avarice. There was precisely no chance that he could ever be accepted, even if he wasn't simultaneously using his show to mock and satirize them as members of the mainstream (later, "Drive-By," and currently, "State-Run") media.

Limbaugh's "truths" resonated with millions of Americans, which is how he built his audience. But in Manhattan they sounded weird, offensive, or just plain crazy. "What does he mean, evolution can't explain creation? Who is this guy, William Jennings Bryan (and wasn't Spencer Tracy great in the movie)? God created the world? Everyone knows the world was created by a big bang and tiny protozoa. That's settled science." And how about: "Morality isn't a matter of individual choice? What's that supposed to mean, that all lifestyles aren't equally valid?"

The most infamous of Limbaugh's dicta was Number 24: "Feminism was established so as to allow unattractive women access to the mainstream of society." The most politically charged was: "Abortion is wrong." Those were fighting words in Manhattan, atomic invitation killers.

When Limbaugh began his show he got relatively little attention in the New York press. AM radio was considered a second-rate medium. Don Imus and Howard Stern were listened to, but they were on during drive-time, not during the middle of the day. In his early days in New York, Limbaugh continued with his invention of a new form of radio, but the supposedly cutting edge critics of the big city didn't even notice. And those who did pay attention didn't like what they were hearing.

Soon after his national show went on the air, Limbaugh got a message from his partner and mentor, Ed McLaughlin. According to Rush, the management of the Parker Meridien wanted him to leave. "They think you're an anti-Semite," McLaughlin told him.

Limbaugh was dumbstruck by the accusation. In Cape the Limbaughs lived next to a Jewish family, and they all got along just fine. If there had been prejudice, it had worked in the opposite direction. In high school, David Limbaugh had a mad crush on the girl next door. When her disapproving parents found out about it, after graduation they had her shipped off to a college where she could find a suitable—i.e., Jewish—husband.

Rush hadn't socialized with many Jews on his long journey down the AM highway or in the front office of the Kansas City Royals; neither is a particularly Jewish milieu. They simply weren't on his radar, nor was he on theirs. One Sunday night Limbaugh saw a *60 Minutes* segment about the power of the pro-Israel lobby in Washington, done in reporter Mike Wallace's tabloid style. It is doubtful that Limbaugh was even aware that Wallace was Jewish (Wallace himself doesn't advertise it) or that the piece was meant to be negative. Limbaugh knew very little about the nuances of the American–Middle East discourse. He liked Israel for the same reason that most Americans did—it was pro-American, anti-Communist, democratic, and the land of the Bible. What was there not to like?

The following day on his show, Limbaugh riffed on the power of various lobbies in Washington. He wasn't putting it down; in his world lobbying is a constitutional right. But someone at one of New York's Jewish organizations heard about the broadcast and put out the word that the new right-wing broadcaster at WABC was a Jew-hater. To many New York Jewish liberals it was (and remains) an article of faith that conserva-

tive Republicans are anti-Semites by definition. This belief has tran-
scended every possible proof to the contrary, including the obvious fact
that hostility to Israel and its supporters in the United States is almost
entirely located on the "progressive left."

A campaign was quickly mounted. People called the station, sent let-
ters of protest to advertisers, and complained to the management of the
Parker Meriden, which declared Limbaugh persona non grata . . .

Needless to say, he was disconcerted. "This incident did not cause me
to feel any animus," he told me years later. "If anything, it frightened me.
The message for me in this story is my discovery of those very clichés
["conservatives" equal "racists," "sexists," "bigots," "homophobes," "anti-
Semites"] attached to me when they weren't true. Remember, this happened when I had only fifty-six radio stations . . . and in the following
two years I felt the full force, nationwide, of being associated with those
clichés simply because of my politics . . . I had no idea how to deal with
it. And no one to advise me how to deal with it."

Limbaugh informed his listeners that he was the target of a campaign.
But one day, a listener, Nathan Segal, an Orthodox rabbi from Staten
Island, called the station and got Limbaugh on the phone. "I heard what
you said; you haven't done anything wrong," Segal told him. "I will protect you." It was the start of a friendship that has lasted more than twenty
years.

"One of the instigators of the campaign against Rush was the actor
Ron Silver," says Segal. That was ironic. Silver, who had been the president of the progressive Creative Coalition, eventually quit the group, in
part because of its coolness toward Israel and its opposition to the war in
Iraq. In 2004 he delivered a speech at the Republican National Convention endorsing President Bush's Mideast policies, for which Silver was
widely ostracized by the "artistic" community.

An accusation of anti-Semitism, even an unfair one, was nothing to
take lightly in the media world of New York. Limbaugh was right to be
frightened by the damage it could do. The effort to smear him as a Jew-
hater persisted, and eventually he confronted it head on, publicly offering
a million dollars to anyone who could demonstrate that he was, in any
way, an anti-Semite. Not long after that challenge, Abe Hirschfeld, an

eccentric millionaire, bought the *New York Post*. It was a scandal—
Hirschfeld was not only a kook but a lowlife; he eventually went to prison
for trying to have his ex–business partner murdered. Limbaugh, in discussing the sale of the *Post*, mistakenly referred to Hirschfeld as "Irv."
When he was corrected by a member of his staff, he said, "Irv, Abe, what's
the difference?" A listener in California heard this and demanded to collect the million dollars. Limbaugh refused, the listener sued, and the case
was laughed out of court.

By 1990 Limbaugh's national audience had grown to almost twenty
million listeners, and imitators were springing up on local stations around
the country. The national press began to take notice. Lewis Grossberger,
in an early profile in the *New York Times Magazine*, described Limbaugh
as "some odd combination of Teddy Roosevelt, Willard Scott and the old
Jackie Gleason character, Reginald Van Gleason 3rd." *Vanity Fair*'s Peter
Boyle compared him to Garrison Keillor and Paul Harvey, as someone
who used radio as a theater of the mind and said his show was similar to
David Letterman's ironic takedown of the "phony decorum of the studio
setting itself." A profile in *Cigar Aficionado* written by a *New York Times*
reporter presented Limbaugh as a modern-day W. C. Fields. Ted Koppel
hosted him on *Nightline* and declared, "There is absolutely no one and
nothing else out there like him, anywhere on the political spectrum."

In 1993 the *New York Times*' Maureen Dowd went out to a four-hour
dinner with Rush Limbaugh at "21" and came away confused. She had
been expecting a caveman, or at the very least a male chauvinist pig. "But
oddly enough," she reported, "beneath the bombast, there beats the heart
of a romantic."

Limbaugh confessed to Dowd that he was very rarely invited out, a
statement she found hard to believe. "New York loves celebrities, no matter what they are famous for," she wrote, but, of course, that isn't quite
right. Billionaire tax cheats, debauched rock singers, crooked (Democratic) politicians, journalistic plagiarists, society pimps—almost anyone
could (and can) be part of the celebrity social life of New York—at least
the New York that Dowd was talking about. But Limbaugh was a pariah.
"You have no earthly idea how detested and hated I am. I'm not even a
good circus act for the liberals in this town . . . You can look at my calen-

dar for the past two years and see all of the invitations. You'll find two, both by Robert and Georgette Mosbacher."

Dowd reported that despite his anti-feminist rhetoric, Rush liked girls and tear-jerking movies. "I'm an incurable romantic," he told her. Dowd seemed nonplussed by such sentimentality.

She had bearded the lion at New York's posh supper club "21" only to discover that while he was, of course, a provincial doofus and a bigot, he was also, puzzlingly, a big sweetie.

Or maybe not. In November 2004, eleven years after their date, Limbaugh had an opportunity to share his impression of Maureen Dowd with his audience. She had appeared on *Meet the Press* after George W. Bush's reelection and had made it clear she considered it a cataclysm. "Maureen Dowd," Rush remarked, "is literally a shadow of her former self, both physically and intellectually; it's a shame what's happened to MoDo. She was, at one time, she was pretty funny. She had a caustic, rapierlike wit. She's just become embittered, just totally embittered." For "reasons," he added gallantly, "we won't go into."

■ ■ ■ ■

Not everyone shunned Limbaugh in Manhattan. He was taken up by William F. Buckley, the publisher of *National Review*. For Limbaugh, entering the Buckley orbit was like walking through the looking glass and finding himself in a magical kingdom.

Buckley was a hero to Limbaugh, as he was to all American conservatives. His book *God and Man at Yale*, published in 1951, was the beginning of the right-wing counteroffensive to the political and cultural dominance of New Deal liberalism. Before Buckley, conservatives were stodgy budget scolds from the Midwest, like Senator Robert Taft of Ohio; or unattractive anti-Communists like Whittaker Chambers; or Southern segregationists like Senator Strom Thurmond of South Carolina and Senator William Fulbright of Arkansas. The term "conservative thinker" was regarded by the cultural and media establishment as oxymoronic. As Lionel Trilling wrote in 1950, "Liberalism is not only the dominant but even the sole intellectual tradition . . . there are no conservative or reactionary ideas in general circulation."

Buckley's aim was to change this, and in the process, he almost single-handedly debunked every one of the anti-conservative stereotypes. He was a handsome, dashing, and hyperarticulate debater and polemicist, the scion of a large fortune married to the daughter of an even bigger one, a convivial and charming man with a sophisticated tolerance for opposing views and a social circle broad enough to include some of New York's best-known liberals.

On matters of principle Buckley was unyielding. He was a Catholic anti-Communist who spoke and wrote about liberating Eastern Europe and the Baltic states at a time when the very idea seemed absurd. A partisan Republican who once ran for mayor of New York and whose brother James served as a Republican senator from New York, he supported Barry Goldwater's right-wing takeover of the party in 1964 and was invaluable to the political ambitions of his close friend Ronald Reagan. Buckley's magazine was the intellectual boiler room of modern American conservatism, and he—through his books, his syndicated newspaper column, and, most especially, his TV show *Firing Line*, in which Buckley debated the country's most prominent liberals—its most important spokesman.

Limbaugh had once read a book by Buckley that he had found in his father's library, and he sometimes watched *Firing Line*. Rush even did a very funny imitation of Buckley's mellifluous, multisyllabic English. But it wasn't until Limbaugh began doing political satire full-time that he actually began reading *National Review* on a regular basis.

"I thought you had to be invited to read it," he said in an emotional broadcast on the day Buckley died. "I thought there was a select group of people that were entitled to be part of that. I'd never seen it on a newsstand. I had never seen it anywhere at anybody's house."

Limbaugh recounted how he had called the magazine from Sacramento and meekly asked if he could subscribe. "I was as nervous making that phone call as any phone call I can remember making," he said. The magazine was his first introduction into formalized post–Cape Girardeau conservatism. *National Review* was a revelation, a clear enunciation of the modern conservative movement's agenda and policy prescriptions. It was especially influential on his economic thinking: "My first real understanding of the concept of lowering tax rates to generate revenue came from Bill Buckley."

About a month after Limbaugh began doing his national show, he was invited to a reception at the home of Lewis Lehrman, a major conservative benefactor. He met several *National Review* editors and was thrilled to learn that he was being listened to by Buckley himself. Not long afterward he was invited to attend a *National Review* editorial meeting at Buckley's apartment on Park Avenue. Limbaugh was so excited that he began shaking when he got the call, and he prepared for the event like a kid going to his first prom. "I did not want to go in there and make a fool of myself. The time arrived, the day arrived, and I had my driver drive around the block four times while I'm mustering the courage to get out of the car and go in."

The first thing Limbaugh noticed when he entered the salon was a harpsichord. Buckley was an accomplished musician, a world-class sailor, a proficient skier, and a novelist who wrote spy fiction based partly on his own experience as a covert CIA agent in Latin America. Limbaugh, who had an aversion to physical exertion and cultural pursuits (he told Maureen Dowd that he would start visiting museums when they got golf carts to ride around in), was suitably awed.

Buckley himself poured Limbaugh a drink, and Rush sat silently as the editors discussed a burning question: could James Joyce have published *Ulysses* today? Limbaugh had no idea what they were talking about, but, like the harpsichord, it awed him, as did the grand entrance of Buckley's socialite wife, Pat.

At dinner, Limbaugh found himself the center of attention.

Buckley and the others grilled him on his thoughts and opinions, his broadcasting secrets, what his goals were. "They were fans!" Limbaugh said, still amazed after all these years. "It was one of the most memorable nights of my life . . . that night I was made to feel welcome in the conservative movement as started by its leader."

Some of Buckley's friends and associates looked askance at their leader's enthusiasm for Limbaugh, whom they regarded as crude and poorly educated. But the imprimatur of William F. Buckley and his wife, Pat, was more than sufficient. Through them he met and socialized with Henry Kissinger, Norman Podhoretz, Richard Brookhiser, and other prominent conservative intellectuals. He lunched with Buckley from time to time, visited him in Connecticut, even went on a *National Review* cruise. And on one memorable occasion, in the mid-1990s, he hosted Buckley and some other conservative dignitaries, including Newt Gingrich, in his newly acquired New York penthouse. After dinner they smoked cigars and drank brandy, and Limbaugh, who wasn't much of a drinker, found himself on his feet, snifter in hand. He raised the glass to Buckley and said, "You know, my father passed away in 1990, but you make me think my dad's still alive here with me."

In 1990 Limbaugh struck up another strategic friendship. Roger Ailes was a television producer and political media consultant who helped Richard Nixon re-create himself as the "New" Nixon in 1968, coached Ronald Reagan in his crushing debate victory over Walter Mondale in 1984, and helped George H. W. Bush craft his media campaign in 1988. He was a rare bird in the world of TV, a hard-line conservative and partisan Republican who was also a highly respected professional, with two Emmy Awards as executive producer of *The Mike Douglas Show* and another for a 1984 documentary on the presidency.

In the fall of 1990, Ailes met Limbaugh and discussed the possibility of producing and syndicating a TV show starring Limbaugh. They worked on the deal for almost a year, then took it to Multimedia Entertainment, which also syndicated *The Phil Donahue Show*.

At first Limbaugh was ambivalent about his venture into television. EIB had more than four hundred radio stations and was growing, as he often bragged on the air, "by leaps and bounds." He was making perhaps three million dollars a year.

He also had a book deal with Pocket Books, a division of Simon & Schuster, which had netted him a six-figure advance. Besides, he was a radio guy. He'd done some television commentary in Sacramento but never a whole show. And New York was a different world than the mellow media atmosphere of California. He had made a guest appearance on *Live with Regis and Kathie Lee*, where he had been ambushed by the dyspeptic liberal columnist Jimmy Breslin, who disparaged him as a fat blowhard as the hosts looked on innocently. But that was nothing compared with his one-night stint as a sit-in for Pat Sajak.

The Pat Sajak Show was a national late-night talk program on CBS, which was on its last legs when Limbaugh was invited to guest-host in early 1990. He took the opportunity seriously and prepared several topics. One was abortion. The governor of Idaho had just vetoed a bill that would have outlawed abortion in his state, and Limbaugh was critical of the decision. He took his microphone into the studio audience to hear reactions and ran into a group of screaming protestors who called him a Nazi. He changed the topic to AIDS, and activists in the crowd began chanting, "You want people to die!" and "Murderer!" Limbaugh was visibly taken aback but restrained in his response. "I am not responsible for your behavior," he told the activists. Some in the studio audience jeered, while others gave him a standing ovation.

Limbaugh then went to the subject of affirmative action, which he said was an "insult" to African Americans because it implied they couldn't compete fairly. Once more there was a chorus of heckling.

The show was taped in advance, and the producers decided to shoot the last segment in an empty studio. Media critics interpreted this as a surrender by Limbaugh. In fact, it was a gimmick, aimed at stirring controversy ahead of the show. It worked. Limbaugh's enemies thought he had been humiliated, while his fans saw it as an illustration of the intolerance of the far left. Rush himself didn't think he had done badly. But Big Rush, who had seen the program in Cape, called with a bleak assessment. "Son," he said, "these things don't just happen by themselves. They set you up."

Nobody would set up Limbaugh again. He and Ailes were in complete control of the format and the content. They taped every day at 5:00 p.m., making sure that the show was freshly topical. Limbaugh commented on the news, bantered with the crew, and clowned around. But there was a serious purpose to the program, just as there was to the radio show. Limbaugh was seeking conservative converts. "They call me the most dangerous man in America," he boasted. "Know why? Because I am."

The mainstream critics were dismissive. The show exposed Limbaugh as "a blowhard casting about for a TV persona," said the *Boston Globe*. But

Limbaugh and Ailes couldn't have cared less about the voices of the liberal establishment. Their audience was elsewhere.

The show ran at various hours on more than two hundred stations. In cities where he competed in the late-night slot, his ratings often topped both Jay Leno's and David Letterman's. By the end of his first season, he had more than three million viewers a night, a very respectable number, especially considering that some stations put him on at 1:00 a.m.

On the air, Limbaugh did some memorable stunts. Once he sent a reporter out into a snowstorm to interview people about global warming. He showed a clip of Vice President Al Gore at Monticello asking the curator who the plaster busts were (one of them, Gore was told, was George Washington). He ran a video clip of Bill Clinton telling an audience of children how he had learned to count to ten to control his temper, and then showed him cursing and chewing out the mayor of Washington for messing up a photo op.

Some of his bits went in surprising directions. He showed congresswoman and feminist icon Pat Schroeder praising Martha Washington for spending three terrible winters with the Revolutionary Army and boosting the morale of the troops, while Limbaugh, on a split screen, played an imaginary violin. He said that Martha had been in Valley Forge to boost her husband's morale, not the troops'; and that Washington had made up the troop morale story in order to bill the Continental Congress for her expenses, "under the table." He then clarified, for the "males in the audience," that the term "under the table" referred only to money. Not too many comics were doing ribald Colonial humor on television.

As always, a lot of Limbaugh's humor was self-referential. He ran a home movie of himself visiting Israel (a trip on which he was accompanied by Rabbi Segal), meeting dignitaries, and praying at the Wailing Wall. The clip ended with his standing in the turret of an Israeli Merkava wearing, Dukakis-like, a helmet and commanding the tank.

Some of the TV humor misfired. He ran a training film by a homeless-activist group, Project Dignity, that showed how to salvage edible food from restaurant Dumpsters. Limbaugh thought this was hilarious, but it wasn't; it was callous and cringe inducing. Sometimes he got it just right. Katie Couric took the *Today* show to a Boston restaurant and girlishly grimaced as the chef cut up and fried a lobster. Limbaugh added a soundtrack of the lobster's groans and screams of pain to mock Couric's empathy for an essentially brainless (and soon to be devoured) crustacean.

One of Limbaugh's recurring themes was his admiration for Ronald Reagan, whom he called "Ronaldus Maximus" and "the greatest president of the twentieth century."

In mid-October of 1994, Limbaugh received a fan letter from the great man himself. "I am comforted to know that our country is in the capable hands of gifted young individuals like you and your listeners," Reagan wrote. "You are the backbone of our great nation, solely responsible for the success of our worldwide crusade. God bless you and your audience for believing; for having faith in America's future; and for making a difference in this world." It was signed "Ron."

Limbaugh had never quite captured the admiration of his father, but this was the next best thing, Ronald Reagan sitting in his living room in California watching him on television. Despite his "El Rushbo" shtick and his considerable political and cultural power, Limbaugh had never really been certain that he deserved his place in the conservative movement or the national media. He had been put down too often by his father, and fired too many times by dissatisfied station managers, to easily believe that he had truly and finally made it. The validation of Buckley, and especially Reagan, were critically important to him. He could finally say to himself, in the words of Jesse Jackson, a man Rush despises but in some ways resembles, "I am Somebody."

Limbaugh was a television star but he didn't like it. TV was profitable and ego gratifying, but it was also exhausting when coupled with the radio show. In 1996 he pulled the plug. "Rush didn't like being dependent on so many people, which is the nature of television," Roger Ailes, who went on to found FOX News, told me. "There are too many meetings for him. He likes the solo style of radio, the fact that it is all up to him. But his TV show was a success, don't forget that. Believe me, if Rush wanted to go back on television, he could have a program of his own tomorrow. And not just on FOX."

"I've done television and I've done radio—and radio, to me, is incomparable and irreplaceable," Limbaugh said to a convention of broadcasters in 2009. "You own that audience member. It's not Muzak. They're not doing anything else. This is direct, hands-on. This is primary listening . . . Television provides the pictures. Radio doesn't. The host either paints them or the listener paints the image him- or herself. But once that starts happening, you've got them locked."

In the fall of 2009, not long after Limbaugh's speech, the White House launched a campaign against FOX News. Obama himself said that FOX was more like talk radio than a conventional television network. This was, obviously, a political judgment; FOX, at that time, was the only TV network actually engaged in adversarial journalism in the first part of the Obama administration. It had broken scoops about Obama's mentor, the Reverend Jeremiah Wright, and played excepts from his incendiary anti-American sermons; revealed the political and professional connection between Obama and former Weatherman terrorist leader Bill Ayers; raised questions about Van Jones, a presidential adviser who had signed a petition accusing President Bush of collusion in the 9/11 terrorist attacks; and broadcast hidden-camera clips showing employees of ACORN—the Association of Community Organizations for Reform Now, a left-wing group with which Obama had close ties—advising a pimp on how to import underage prostitutes into the United States. These stories were profoundly embarrassing to the Obama administration—the president had been forced to sever his ties with Wright, accept Jones's resignation, and watch as Congress cut off ACORN's federal funding. Naturally, the president wanted to discredit the network.

Still, Obama wasn't entirely wrong when he referred to FOX News as "talk radio." In fact, Limbaugh himself had told me the same thing a year or so before. Later Rush had second thoughts and wrote to clarify that he hadn't meant to put down Roger Ailes.

"I want to ensure that you didn't take my comment that Fox News is Talk Radio on TV as a slam. Roger is one of my closest friends. I was speaking within the context of being proud of the things the success of my radio show spawned."

. . . .

In 1992 Limbaugh published his first book, *The Way Things Ought to Be*. He wasn't a writer and he knew it—"I don't have the iron butt you need for it," he says.

Limbaugh enlisted John Fund, a young editorial writer at the *Wall Street Journal*, to tape conversations with him on the topics he wanted to discuss and shape them into a first draft. His brother, David, worked with him on the final version. "I'm more of a writer, Rush is more of a talker," David told me. "In fact, he does his best thinking when he's talking." Rush dedicated the book, "To my parents, whose love and devotion made me the terrific guy I am."

The Way Things Ought to Be, with a picture of a sweetly smiling Limbaugh on the jacket, became a publishing phenomenon. It hit number one on the *New York Times* best-seller list and stayed there for almost half a year. More than a million copies were sold. When it got to be too big to ignore, the *Times* assigned TV critic Walter Goodman to review it.

"Some passages," Goodman wrote, "alternate between slobberings of sincerity and slaverings of invective, but it is all in the service of the same cause."

That cause, of course, was Limbaugh's promotion of conservatism as he understood it. "This is a work for its time," Goodman wrote. "Despite Bill Clinton's recent victory, right-wing populism, an American perennial, is in bloom, and at the moment Mr. Limbaugh is its gaudiest flower. His appeal is to a part of middle America—call it the silent majority or The American People or the booboisie—that feels it has been on the receiving end of the droppings of the bicoastals as they wing first class from abortion-rights rallies to AIDS galas to save-the-pornographer parties."

When a writer uses "gaudiest flower" and "booboisie" in the same paragraph, you can be pretty sure he is attempting to channel H. L. Mencken, the journalistic patron saint of irreverence, self-promotion, brutal satire, and public combat. Mencken often expressed his contempt for the influential right-thinkers of his time with a theatrical mockery. In 1926, for example, after an issue of his magazine, *The American Mercury*, was banned in Boston for publishing an "obscene" story about a prostitute who conducted her business in a graveyard, Mencken publicly broke the law by selling a copy of the magazine to the famous Massachusetts moralist J. Frank Chase—comically biting Chase's coin to ascertain its authenticity (in an odd coincidence, the offending story, "Hatrack," was set in Farmington, Missouri, just down the road from Cape Girardeau). The *New York Herald Tribune* editorialized against Mencken's "incurable vulgarity" and "business acumen," and derided him as a "professional smart-Aleck."

A less antagonistic reviewer might have noticed that Limbaugh and Mencken had quite a lot in common, from self-educated disdain for schoolteachers to their incendiary satire and the impact it had on the culture.[1]

To Goodman, Limbaugh was merely a demagogue, devoid of ideas worth considering. Like most liberal intellectuals, the reviewer knew next to nothing about American conservatism, and it showed, especially when he tried to put Limbaugh and Pat Robertson into the same bag. Limbaugh did share many of Robertson's political views—the two men were, after all, both conservative Republicans—but Robertson was the sort of televangelist Limbaugh had been mocking since his "Friar Shuck" bits in Pittsburgh. Rush might have a daily chat or two with Jesus, but his on-air banter about adult beverages, sexual innuendo, and at times profane language was anything but pious, and he certainly didn't share Robertson's belief that the Reverend Robertson could perform miracles.

Goodman conceded that dogmatic liberals sometimes invited Rush's mockery and that he was a pretty fair radio comic. "The satire here is not subtle . . . I especially like the commercial for the Bungee condom, which has a daughter bringing Dad up to date on 'the Bungee X27 model himhugger with extra torque capability' which came in a Kennedy Weekend dozen or the Wilt Chamberlain carry-home crate."

---

1. There were also profound differences. Mencken was a transcendent stylist but a terrible public speaker. He was an aggressive enemy of clericalism and gained his greatest lasting fame by ridiculing primitive, Christian anti-evolutionists at the 1927 Scopes "Monkey Trial." But Mencken was far more reactionary that Limbaugh ever dreamed of being. The Sage of Baltimore was an outright racist who believed that blacks were inherently and permanently intellectually inferior. He was also a misogynist, an anti-Semite, a proponent of racial eugenics, a militant anti-Communist, and, during World War II, a sullen "neutral" who found Hitler no worse that Churchill or Roosevelt.

The review ended with a prediction based on a quotation. "'We conservatives are the future,' announces Mr. Limbaugh, and the reader may construe that as a political promise. On the evidence of *The Way Things Ought to Be*, with its deference to religion and patriotism, its relentless self-promotion (which may be a put-on, but then again maybe not), its no-budge line on crime, welfare, and sexual disarray, its massagings of honest, hard-working, clean-living, do-it-on-their-own folks, I'd guess Mr. Limbaugh will be running for office before very long, as America's white hope." Mr. Goodman would have lost that bet. By then Rush Limbaugh was too rich and too influential to run for anything.

Limbaugh was not only rich—his income in 1993, from books, radio, television, and his other ventures, was estimated at between fifteen and twenty million dollars—he was still growing. The EIB now consisted of 636 stations with about twenty-one million listeners a week. The TV show was prospering. He founded *The Limbaugh Letter*, a monthly publication that quickly attracted 430,000 subscribers—five or six times more than the circulation of the leading magazines of opinion on both the left and the right. His stage show, when he bothered going on the road, packed theaters and auditoriums. And, that year, he published his second (and thus far, last) book.[2]

See, I Told You So was dedicated to Rush's 102-year-old grandfather: "For Rush Hudson Limbaugh Senior, You are the Limbaugh America should know." Joseph Farah, Rush's "conservative soul brother" from Sacramento, replaced John Fund as the designated journalist on the project, but, once again, the tone and content were unmistakably Rushian. The book went directly to first place on the *Times* list, and by the end of 1994 there were an estimated 7.5 million copies of Rush's books, in print or on audio, in the hands of his fans.[3]

Rush's first book, *The Way Things Ought to Be*, could have fairly been entitled "The Way Things Used to Be." He had devoted several chapters

---

2. Limbaugh told me that he is planning to write another, tentatively titled *The Back Nine*, which will discuss the lessons he has learned about friendship and success. God only knows how many of those he can sell.

3. According to *New York Times* reporter Mervyn Rothstein, writing in *Cigar Aficionado* magazine.

to defending the expired presidency of Ronald Reagan and attacking the defunct Soviet Union and the hapless Mikhail Gorbachev. Big Rush was dead, but his adamant anti-Communism lived on in his son's geopolitical outlook. But the new book had a more contemporary feel. For one thing, the USSR was now gone. For another, Limbaugh was now clearly influenced by Buckley and his agenda. It is startling to realize, after rereading *The Way Things Ought to Be* today, how much of that agenda is still relevant; very few issues have been resolved in the past twenty years. And nowhere are they better preserved than on Limbaugh's show. Many of the book's targets—the Clintons, Jesse Jackson, Barney Frank, the mainstream media, Paul "the Forehead" Begala, even Jimmy Carter ("an utter disgrace and embarrassment," Limbaugh called him in 2009)—continue to make frequent appearances in Rush's monologues. The issues, too, are strikingly familiar, from global warming ("a hoax") to labor unions ("goons") to big government ("an infringement on the rights of every American").

When Obama came into office, his chief of staff, Rahm Emanuel, was quoted as saying, "You never want a serious crisis to go to waste." The conservative bloggers lit up at the cynicism of the remark, but Limbaugh was fifteen years ahead of them. He observed in his book, and on the air, that crisis creation was standard operating procedure for the left. "They overstate a problem and work society into a frenzied state in order to justify their invariable big-government solution."

Another theme was the failure of the Democrats to appreciate the exceptional nature of America and its role as the natural leader of the world; and Bill Clinton's alleged belief that the country had seen better days. "Don't believe the doomsayers," wrote Limbaugh. "Don't believe the negativity mongers. Don't believe the America bashers—even if one of them is the President of the United States." Sixteen years later, after Barack Obama's first speech to the UN General Assembly, Limbaugh returned to the same complaint about the new Democratic president. "[Obama] is saying, 'no there is nothing exceptional about our country . . . we are tarnished, stained, we have been immoral and unjust and our Constitution is flawed.'"

In *See, I Told You So*, Limbaugh also developed his thesis that environmentalism is a scam, seized upon by former Communists orphaned by the death of the USSR, to redistribute Americans' wealth. He discerned in the movement a quasi religion (much like Communism itself) based not on empirical evidence but on faith.

"Despite the hysterics of a few pseudo scientists, there is no reason to believe in global warming," he wrote. "The Earth's ecosystem is not fragile and humans are not capable of destroying it." He was especially scathing about the apocalyptic scenarios for the destruction of the planet whose purpose was to instill "terror, dread and apprehension about the future."

It took more than a little chutzpah for a college dropout to take on the august scientists and Ivy League progressive activists who were the spokespeople for environmentalism. But Limbaugh was a skeptic, unimpressed by the expertise of the experts, and willing to challenge them.

He had been given his first chance to really take on the environmentalists in 1992, when Ted Koppel invited him to debate Senator Al Gore on ABC's *Nightline*. Like the first Ali-Liston bout, it looked like a ridiculous mismatch: Al Gore, of St. Albans Prep and Harvard, the esteemed author of the critically acclaimed *Earth in the Balance*, up against a dumb, right-wing radio ranter (the epithet "global warming denier" had not yet been invented). Liberals were looking forward to a slaughter.

Gore opened by warning of "a global ecological crisis that is more serious than anything human civilization has ever faced." There were many ecological challenges facing the world, he said, but singled out "the hole in the ozone layer—which now could appear above the United States," climate change, the imminent destruction of the rain forests, and pollution of the oceans and the atmosphere.

Limbaugh was visibly amused by this litany of present and future disaster. "There is no ozone hole above the United States," he stated flatly. "I don't think the ecology is fragilely balanced." He attributed such concerns to a "doomsday industry" typified by Hollywood airheads whose naïveté and need for image-building charities made them useful idiots for the environmentalist movement.

Gore responded by agreeing with Limbaugh that their key disagreement was whether the earth is fragile. He mentioned the growing number of people on the planet, an iconic concern of population pessimists since

Malthus. Then, a Sunday punch—"new technologies we've never had before, like chlorofluorocarbons."

Koppel was evidently impressed. "I don't know anybody on Capitol Hill who is more knowledgeable on the subject of environment than Al Gore. You have to take seriously what he says."

Limbaugh didn't have to and he didn't. He knew perfectly well that Gore wasn't a climatologist, he just played one on TV. "If you listen to what Senator Gore said, it is manmade products which are causing the ozone depletion. Yet Mt. Pinatubo has put 570 times the amount of chlorine into the atmosphere in one eruption than all of manmade chlorofluorocarbons in one year; and the ultraviolet radiation measured on this country's surface since 1974 has shown no increase whatsoever. And if there's ozone depletion going on, you're going to have UV radiation levels going way up, and they simply aren't. The sun makes ozone, and there's an ozone hole in the Antarctic Circle and the Arctic Circle simply because the sun is below the horizon for a portion of the year."

In 2008 Limbaugh rebroadcast part of his debate with Gore. The ex–vice president had since won an Oscar and a Nobel Prize for his environmental endeavors. He had also become an environmental businessman and investor, parlaying his high profile and Washington connections into a multimillion-dollar empire of "green" enterprises.[4] There was still no hole in the ozone layer over the United States. The world's temperature hadn't risen in almost a decade. Here and there you could still find some trees. "Sixteen years ago he was making the same arguments," Limbaugh said. Limbaugh thought global warming was a hoax in 1992, and nothing that had happened since had changed his mind.

I once asked Limbaugh what he would change if he got a career do-over. He replied that there was no major issue he had ever changed his mind about, and that he regretted nothing he had ever said or done on

---

4. In 2009, while testifying before Congress, Gore was asked if he would personally benefit from policies he was advocating for. Gore said he was proud to be in business and invest his money according to his beliefs. "If you believe the reason I have been working on this issue for thirty years is greed, you don't know me." Like all self-testimonials, this was not dispositive.

the air. But that isn't quite true. Early in his national program, Limbaugh did public course corrections on the way he dealt with the issues of abortion and AIDS.

In his "35 Truths," Rush pronounced abortion "wrong" without any qualification, and he has never altered that view. But he did give up using a "caller abortions" bit, which began in 1989 when a woman called the show to argue with Limbaugh's anti-choice position. It occurred to him that he could satirize the fraught subject through a radio theater game. Staffer Phil Latzman mixed a twelve-second recording of a roaring vacuum cleaner with a seven-second scream. Then, "for philosophical reasons," Limbaugh contacted the phone company, asked when a phone call actually begins, and was told that it becomes a call as soon as it is answered by a second party. With mock solemnity, Limbaugh raised a moral dilemma. He personally didn't answer his phone (screener James Golden did that). It would be wrong to leave the fate of each live call to the discretion of his staff. Limbaugh decreed that calls that remained on hold for twenty minutes or longer would be considered viable and could not be aborted.

Once this was established, Limbaugh offered his listeners a chance to become the first aborted call in radio history. A woman called in and was suddenly interrupted by a loud sucking sound mixed with a choked scream, and then silence.

The controversy was immediate and furious. A station in Seattle dropped the show, and others were threatening to do the same. After two weeks in which he "aborted" about twenty calls, Limbaugh announced that he would stop, although he didn't apologize. In fact, he was defiant. "If you didn't know in your heart of hearts that abortion was a savage, violent act, what I did wouldn't have bugged you so much. I took you inside an abortion mill and some of you couldn't take it. You can't handle it when it was only dramatized. Yet you're not bothered by abortion when it happens for real. Is there not a contradiction here? Think about it."

Another misstep came on the subject of AIDS. When the disease first became infamous in the United States, in the early eighties, Limbaugh was in Kansas City, which was relatively unaffected. But Sacramento was a different story. There was a large gay community there, and the epidemic was being felt. Limbaugh had reason to know this, and to empathize; one of his mentors, Norman Woodruff, was openly gay, an AIDS activist who eventually died of the disease. By the time Limbaugh arrived in New York to do his national show, HIV-AIDS was regarded as a deadly epidemic, although there was debate about who was actually threatened. The politically correct view was that everyone was vulnerable. In reality, most American victims were gay men and their sexual partners (gay or straight) and intravenous-drug users. Limbaugh (correctly) dismissed the "everyone is equally at risk" line as liberal propaganda intended to scare the heterosexual majority into putting AIDS at the top of the health agenda (a strategy that has largely been successful).

Limbaugh's views on homosexuality are not, as most people assume, similar to those of the Christian Right. In *The Way Things Ought to Be*, he wrote, "I don't care who sleeps with whom . . . I harbor no bias, per se, against the lifestyle." What he really didn't like was the fact that the gay rights movement was part of the Democratic coalition. Anything he could do to call it into question served his partisan agenda. After an ACT UP demonstration at St. Patrick's Cathedral in New York City that disrupted a mass, he chastised "militant homosexuals" for their disrespectful behavior and shortly thereafter began broadcasting irreverent and tasteless "AIDS update" segments introduced by Dionne Warwick's "I'll Never Love This Way Again." In his traveling stage show, the *Excellence in Broadcasting Tour*, he did a bit when he put a condom over the microphone to illustrate "safe speech."

The reaction to this elicited one of the very few public apologies of Limbaugh's career. "I engaged in an AIDS update that missed the mark totally and ended up being very insensitive to people who were dying," he said. He pledged not to do it again, and he hasn't.

Early in 1994 Limbaugh announced a new, updated version of his "35 Undeniable Truths of Life." These were, he said, all equally truthful and listed in no particular order. He stipulated that they didn't replace, but simply expanded, the first thirty-five. But this was a very different list. Gone were the mock serious "truths" about Rush's favorite pro-football teams and schoolboyish banalities on how Abe Lincoln saved the nation. There was also no mention of the Russians or the evils of Communism. The new "truths" reflected a shift in Limbaugh's concerns and his targets. It was a congressional election year, and he offered a set of principles that would contrast with the Clinton administration's liberal worldview and offer ammunition against Democratic congressional candidates. Here is Rush's list (and my own completely unofficial and personal commentary, in italics).

1.   There is a distinct singular American culture—rugged individualism and self-reliance—which made America great.

       As opposed to multiculturalism that wants to Balkanize the country and make it into a collection of equally valid cultural tribes. And did you ever notice that all these tribes are members of the Democratic Party coalition?

2.   The vast majority of the rich in this country did not inherit their wealth; they earned it. They are the country's achievers, producers, and job creators.

       My brother got the family law firm. I made my dough myself. And you can, too.

3.   No nation ever taxes itself into prosperity.

       In fact, the rich are the ones who provide jobs for the rest of the population. Trickle-down economics works.

4.   Evidence refutes liberalism.

       Exhibit A: The peace and prosperity of the Reagan administration. Ronaldus Maximus himself said that liberal economists first look at reality and then see if they can make it work in theory.

5.   There is no such thing as a New Democrat.

       Which is what the triangulated Bill Clinton claims to be.

6. The Earth's eco-system is not fragile.

    The earth got along fine for billions of years and it started to break the year Al Gore published a book about it?

7. Character matters; leadership descends from character.

    Churchill, Reagan, Thatcher—these are leaders with character. Liberals are horn-dogs who went to Woodstock, eat pizza in the White House, and hit on women they aren't married to.

8. The most beautiful thing about a tree is what you do with it after you cut it down.

    The world belongs to man, not the other way around. Without this essential belief, America would be an agricultural society instead of a world power, and you would be riding a horse to work.

9. Ronald Reagan was the greatest president of the twentieth century.

    For the information of every liberal historian who has written, is writing, or will write a book on Franklin D. Roosevelt and/or JFK.

10. The 1980s was not a decade of greed but a decade of prosperity; it was the longest period of peacetime growth in American history.

    Look it up.

11. Abstinence prevents sexually transmitted disease and pregnancy—every time it's tried, and

12. Condoms only work during the school year.

    Heh, heh, heh. Uncle Rush is just kidding.

13. Poverty is not the root ("rut") cause of crime.

    If it were, how come so many poor people are law abiding? In America, poverty should be an incentive to hard work, not to commit crime. Even Leonard Bernstein knew that, "I'm depraved on account of I'm deprived" is a phony excuse.

14. There's a simple way to solve the crime problem: obey the law; punish those who do not; and

15. If you commit a crime, you are guilty.

    Don't do the crime if you can't do the time. Or, as I will someday discover, at least do the probation.

16. Women should not be allowed on juries where the accused is a stud.

    This one goes out to all the empty-headed chicks who can't see past superficial good looks and always fall for the lead-guitar player instead of the funny, pudgy DJ.

17. The way to improve our schools is not more money, but the reintroduction of moral and spiritual values, as well as the four "R's": reading, 'riting, 'rithmatic, and Rush.

    Why, when I was a boy back in the '50s in Cape Girardeau, they weren't afraid to teach us the basics, including right and wrong. And by God I hated school. Ah, wait a minute . . . on to Number 18.

18. I am not arrogant.

    But, like Muhammad Ali said, "I am the Greatest." Did he really mean it? Do I? Yes, no, and you'll never figure it out.

19. My first 35 Undeniable Truths are still undeniably true.

    Except for maybe the one about the Steelers.

20. There is a God.

    This is not an original observation. It is believed by roughly the entirety of humanity, minus Ivy League social scientists, Episcopalian bishops, and the Chi-Coms.

21. There is something wrong when critics say the problem with America is too much religion.

    I am referring, of course, to old-fashioned Judeo-Christian religion, the stuff we learned in the Centenary Methodist Church—not the liberation theology practiced by hippie priests and anti-war activists in collars, or the fake piety of Democratic house pastors like The Revvvvernd Jesse Jackson.

22. Morality is not defined by individual choice.

    Take this one seriously. I mean it. Moral relativism is too easy to be real morality.

23. The only way liberals win national elections is by pretending they're not liberals.

    Which is why they start talking like tax-cutting patriots in election years.

24. Feminism was established as to allow unattractive women easier access to the mainstream of society.

    If one of your goals is (like mine) to offend and infuriate every self-respecting liberal woman in America, this one is a classic. Say it often enough and you will never be forgiven—or ignored.

25. Follow the money. When somebody says, "It's not the money," it's always the money.

    The only true thing I ever read in the Washington Post.

26. Liberals attempt through judicial activism what they cannot win at the ballot box.

    Teddy Kennedy made Judge Bork look like a member of the Ku Klux Klan. Robert Byrd, who was a member of the Ku Klux Klan, tried to turn Clarence Thomas into Bigger Thomas. They wouldn't go to all this trouble to get liberal activist judges if they had a majority.

27. Using federal dollars as a measure, some cities have not only been neglected, but poisoned with welfare dependency funds.

    This one is so true that even Bill Clinton is coming around. Thank God for Rudy Giuliani.

28. Progress is not striving for economic justice or fairness, but economic growth.

    A rising tide lifts all boats. This is true. I've seen it happen on the Mississippi River.

29. Liberals measure compassion by how many people are given welfare. Conservatives measure compassion by how many people no longer need it.

    And by how few welfare recipients vote Republican.

30. Compassion is no substitute for justice.

    O. J. Simpson. Case closed.

31. The culture war is between the winners and those who think they're losers who want to become winners. The losers think the only way they can become winners is by banding together all the losers and then empowering a leader of the losers to make things right for them.

    Even I am not sure what I mean by this.

32.   The Los Angeles riots were not caused by the Rodney King
        verdict. The Los Angeles riots were caused by rioters.

        *In any long list of truths you will find a certain amount of
        filler. This is filler.*

33.   You could afford your house without your government if
        it weren't for your government.

        *You may not believe this but someday—ten or fifteen years
        from now, into the next millennium—you will discover
        what I am talking about.*

34.   Words mean things.

        *I should know; I use ten thousand a day on the air and ev-
        eryone understands me perfectly. Double-talk and nuance
        are for people who don't want to come right out and tell you
        what they believe.*

35.   Too many Americans can't laugh at themselves anymore.

        And you humorless liberals know who you are.

A lot of the new Undeniable Truths were obviously there for shock
value or humorous effect, but at their core was a prescription for electoral
victory in 1994 and beyond. To win, the Republicans needed to revert to
Reaganism, with its belief in small government, lower taxes, less social
welfare, tougher law enforcement, and a sense of America as a great and
exceptional country with the power to keep the world safe for itself
and for its friends. "The only way liberals win national elections is by
pretending they're not liberals," Limbaugh said. It was time to go back to
the bedrock principles of capitalism and individualism that characterized
the reign of Ronaldus Maximus.

CHAPTER FIVE

THE HONORARY FRESHMAN

Everyone expected the Republicans would make some gains in 1994. The party out of power usually does. But Limbaugh saw an opportunity to seize control of the House of Representatives for the first time since the start of the Eisenhower administration. His strategy was to take the election national. Rush's audience provided the GOP with the means to reach into almost every congressional district in the country with a unified daily message. Thousands of fired-up "Dittoheads" (as Rush's fans are known) can't swing a presidential election, but they are enough to nominate conservatives and help them beat Democrats in much smaller congressional districts.

Six weeks before the 1994 election, one of Limbaugh's old friends and sometimes rival, Newt Gingrich, gathered a group of fellow conservative House hopefuls and issued a manifesto: the Contract with America. It offered a ten-point legislative program that candidates promised a Republican-led House would pass within one hundred days. These initiatives included introducing a constitutional amendment to require the federal government to balance its budget; a tough anti-crime package; a prohibition on welfare payments to mothers under the age of eighteen and a requirement that able-bodied recipients go to work; an "American Dream Restoration Act," with a five-hundred-dollar-per-child tax credit and repeal of the marriage tax penalty; a cut in financial support to the United Nations; weakening product liability laws to discourage frivolous litigation; tax adjustments and cuts for small business; the introduction of a constitutional term-limit amendment for senators and representatives; and "family values" legislation that would provide incentives for adoption, discourage abortion, increase parental control of education, and enact tougher anti-pornography laws. Finally, Clinton's 1993 tax hike on Social Security would be repealed.

These ideas had been floating around conservative circles for a long time. Many were in Ronald Reagan's 1985 State of the Union message. George H. W. Bush had set them aside. Now Gingrich was reviving them, at least as campaign rhetoric. Limbaugh had no direct role in drafting the contract, but it couldn't have happened without his vociferous cheerleading for the return of Reaganism to the Republican Party. "Rush was talking about the elements of the Contract with America before there was one," says Karl Rove.

Two months before the election, Limbaugh predicted victory. "Historians will remember 1994 as a watershed year in American politics," he said. "This was the year that modern liberalism, the ideology dominating nearly every important cultural and political institution in the country, tipped its hand, revealing its deep insecurity. Liberals are terrified of me. As well they should be."

Limbaugh had set his sites on Congress as far back as 1992, when the House Bank was caught allowing representatives to kite checks with impunity. Limbaugh dramatized the scandal with a radio skit.

Soft music. A mellifluous ANNOUNCER *intones: And now, another Capitol Hill moment.*

YOUNG TELLER: *I'm working behind the counter at the bank when in comes another freshman congressman. He puts five hundred dollars in his new checking account. Boy, you should have seen the look on his face when I told him that five hundred dollars in the Capitol Guild checking account is unheard of. Congressmen never keep that kind of money in the bank.*

CONGRESSMAN: *So this kindly teller tells me that my five hundred dollars is worth sixty to a hundred thousand dollars in check-writing privileges. Until that moment I never realized how much I was going to like living in Washington. Heh, heh, heh.*

ANNOUNCER: *Capitol Hill Bank for personal service.*

TELLER: *I like to really get involved with my customers. Why, once a congressman called me from this big drinking party he was throwing. Said he needed some more checks. So I went to the party with a box of checks. Why, he even paid for that party with one of those checks. I felt like I really made a difference.*

CONGRESSMAN: *I don't remember much about that party, but I do remember my Capitol Hill bank associate, he really saved me. You know, people like Ted Kennedy can rack up quite a bar tab. Capitol Hill Bank made me look like I had money and influence. You don't get that kind of treatment from a bank very often. Capital Hill Bank.*

ANNOUNCER: *Capitol Hill Bank, for worry-free check cashing.*

The bit took what might have been an inside-the-Beltway embarrassment and turned it into a national story everyone could understand. Eventually six people were convicted of felony charges and twenty-five more were singled out by the House Ethics Committee. All but four were Democrats.

Limbaugh also used satire on Illinois Congressman Dan Rostenkowski, one of the most entrenched and powerful liberal Democratic committee chairmen in the House. Rostenkowski was accused of using the Congressional Post Office to launder money, just the sort of arcane piece of business that powerful lawmakers had been getting away with forever. Limbaugh turned it into theater.

Soft music, ANNOUNCER *intones: The Capitol Hill Post Office, over a hundred years of service.*

OLD CLERK: *Yeah, I remember my first day behind the counter of the post office is something I'll never forget . . .* (changing to a young man's voice) . . . *Well, hello there Mister Congressman, is there something I can help you with there?*

CONGRESSMAN: *Yes, I need a couple of them there first-class stamps.*

YOUNG CLERK: *Is that all, sir?*

CONGRESSMAN: *Ah now, can you cash this check for a thousand dollars? . . . Trust me, son, you can. You see, that's just the way we do things up on the Hill.*

OLD CLERK: *Congressmen come and go, and some have retired, but some things remain the same.*

SECOND YOUNG CLERK: *Hello there, Mister Congressman, is there anything I can help you with?*

CONGRESSMAN: *Yeah, check my mailbox.*

YOUNG CLERK: *Just a check statement from your bank, sir.*

CONGRESSMAN: *What check statement!?*

YOUNG CLERK: *Ah, yessir, I'll just tear it up right away.*

CONGRESSMAN: *Good kid, good kid. Hey I need some postage stamps. Just one.*

YOUNG CLERK: *Okay, that'll be twenty-nine cents.*

CONGRESSMAN: *Here's a constituent's check for five thousand dollars.*

YOUNG CLERK: *And here's your change, Congressman.*

CONGRESSMAN: *And, kid, you keep that stamp.*

YOUNG CLERK: *Hey, thanks.*

CONGRESSMAN (*sotto voce*): *That way, if I'm indicted, he's my accomplice. Heh, heh, heh.*

The laughter proved lethal. Rostenkowski was forced to resign his chairmanship, got indicted for mail fraud, lost his seat in 1994, and served fifteen months in jail before he was pardoned by President Clinton.

Limbaugh's anti-corruption kick was not an act of disinterested good government broadcasting. He was after Democrats, who controlled the House and supported President Clinton. It was his good luck that his political opponents, grown fat and sloppy after so many years in power, gave him such inviting targets.

On November 8, the Republicans won a sensational victory. The GOP went from 176 seats to 230, enough to take control of the House. The Democratic Speaker, Tom Foley, was defeated in his own district, and Gingrich became the first Republican Speaker since Joseph Martin in 1953. Mary Matalin, who had served as a deputy campaign manager on Bush's 1992 campaign, watched in awe as Limbaugh led the Republican bandwagon. "Rush was a market force in 1994," she says. "I would go to political meetings all over the country and hear conservatives speaking the way he speaks, saying the things he says. The clarity he brought to issues got repeated back in questions from the audience. Back then, like now, along with Gingrich, he was one of the two most important conservatives in the country. Newt had come up with the plan, but Rush had sold it in every district in the country." A month after the election, grateful Republican lawmakers held a dinner in his honor. Representative Barbara Cubin, a member of the freshman class from Wyoming, told Limbaugh that 74 percent of the nation's newspapers had endorsed Democrats. "Talk radio, with you in the lead, is what turned the tide," she said. Vin Webber, a former congressman from Minnesota, cited data from pollster Frank Luntz showing that people who listened to talk radio more than ten hours a week voted Republican three to one. "Those are the people who elected the new Congress," Webber said.

The newly elected legislators presented Limbaugh with an honorary membership in the freshman class and a "Majority Maker" pin that was given out to first-term representatives.

■ ■ ■ ■

If Limbaugh was the winner of the 1994 election, Bill Clinton was the loser. For Rush, that was one of the sweetest parts of the victory.

He and Clinton were natural enemies, and like all natural enemies they knew one another at first sight. Both men came from the same part of the country—Hot Springs, Arkansas, and Cape Girardeau, Missouri, were almost equidistant from Memphis. As young guys they both burned with ambition to escape the provinces and fulfill their destiny on a great stage. But that's where the similarities ended. Clinton was gregarious, a joiner and a backslapper, emotionally intelligent; Limbaugh communicated best from an empty studio. Clinton used his brains and his charm to move up in the world, to rise above his embarrassingly outré mother, violent step-father, and trashy brother. Limbaugh had, for many years, traveled in social reverse, haunted by his father's admonition that a dropout would never have any real status. Clinton was the '60s, long hair, jeans, JFK, and McGovern, an FM kind of guy. Limbaugh, despite being five years younger than Clinton, was an older American, a product of the Eisenhower years, strictly AM.

There was never a doubt that Limbaugh would support the reelection of George H. W. Bush in 1992—he was the Republican candidate—but Rush wasn't enthusiastic. Bush struck him as a preppy, country club moderate, an Ivy League snob who, as a candidate in the Republican primaries of 1980, had dismissed Ronald Reagan's supply-side ideology as voodoo economics. Not only that, Bush had raised taxes.

Bush needed Reagan voters who were attracted to third-party candidate Ross Perot's Texas populism; many of these people were Limbaugh listeners. Limbaugh dismissed Perot as "not a real politician." He certainly didn't want Clinton. And so he was stuck with Bush.

Early in the summer of 1992, Roger Ailes, who was working for President Bush, made the connection. The president invited Limbaugh to accompany him to the Kennedy Center and spend a night at the White House. Bush personally carried Limbaugh's bag from the elevator of the White House residence to his room, a gesture Rush never forgot. That night he called his mother and brother from the Lincoln bedroom. "Guess where I'm sleeping tonight," he said. Bush might not be Reagan, but he was the president of the United States. Big Rush had hosted Vice President Nixon in Cape; Big George was hosting Rusty in the White House.

In August, Rush went to the Republican convention in Houston, where he wandered the halls attracting huge crowds of fans and autograph seekers. The mayor of Houston, Bob Lanier, proclaimed an official Rush Limbaugh Day. Houston was George W. Bush's home turf, but Limbaugh was the biggest celebrity in town. He sat in the presidential box when he felt like it and bonded with Bush over sports and politics. The connection was cemented, the deal struck. The president would do his best to sound like Reagan, and Limbaugh would campaign hard for him.

After Labor Day, Bush traveled to New York to address the General Assembly of the United Nations and dropped by Limbaugh's studio for a chat. "Just one more fan sitting at the table here," he chirped. But the visit had a purpose. Bush wanted to raise the issue of Bill Clinton's Vietnam-era draft dodging.

This wasn't Limbaugh's favorite topic. George H. W. Bush, like Big Rush, was a World War II combat pilot. Rush, like Clinton, sat out Vietnam. Hundreds of his classmates and neighbors from Cape Girardeau served, and twelve died, while he was skipping class at SEMO and spinning records in Pittsburgh. He had a medical exemption. He pulled a good number. Then they canceled the draft. "Simple as that," he says.

But nothing was simple when it came to the draft, as every man of Limbaugh's generation (and mine) knows perfectly well. In his freshman year of college, Limbaugh had the usual 2-S, a student deferment. In the draft lottery of 1970, he drew 152. Nobody knew if 152 was a safe number or not. The war was slightly past its peak, and troops were scheduled to begin leaving Vietnam in the fall of 1970, but there would still be more than four hundred thousand U.S. personnel there, and they had to be replenished.

Four months after the lottery, Limbaugh gave his draft board medical information that led him to be reclassified 1-Y; eligible only in case of national emergency. A 1-Y was golden, better than a 4-F medical deferment, because 4-F made it sound like there was something seriously the matter with you. In Limbaugh's case, the disqualifying malady was a pilonidal cyst, a painful, hairy cyst ingloriously located near or on the cleft of the buttocks. During World War II, pilonidal cysts were commonly known as "jeep riders disease." Limbaugh probably could have talked his way into uniform if he had wanted to serve. But he didn't. If he had been called he would have gone. But he wasn't and he didn't.

When he became a national radio commentator, Limbaugh's draft history drew attention. Reporters went out to Cape Girardeau and interviewed his mother, who spoke to them amiably but without providing much information. They talked to Rush's contemporaries, members of the draft board, and physicians, but found no irregularities. Many of them (and many of their editors) had draft irregularities of their own.

Limbaugh himself unwittingly kept the issue alive. "In 1988 or '89, I don't remember exactly, some lib called up with the usual 'you-didn't-serve-in-the-army' stuff, and I decided to turn it into a joke," Limbaugh told me. "I told the caller, 'Yeah, my father got me off. He just walked over to the draft board office, wrote them a check for three thousand dollars, and I got a 4-F.' I was still laughing my ass off when my father called screaming and cursing. 'Son, they'll believe you,' he said. He was just devastated at the thought that someone would take it seriously. The next day on the air I had to tell the audience I had been kidding." That episode taught Limbaugh two important broadcast lessons: "First, you have to close the loop on satire. That means you can't end a show with a joke. And second, you can fix your mistakes, but you have to apologize as soon as possible."

The issue of Limbaugh's draft status flared up again after Bush's appearance. Bill Clinton's draft dodging had been blatant, especially for someone who wanted to be commander in chief. Accusing a hawk like Limbaugh of the same thing might, the Democrats thought, take some sting out of the accusation. It didn't. Limbaugh dutifully bashed Clinton as a draft dodger through election day, but his heart wasn't in it. In a 1992 appearance at Manhattan's 92nd Street Y, a bastion of left-wing sentiment, he was asked why he hadn't served his country. "I did not want to go—just as Governor Clinton didn't," he replied.

Bush was the only candidate Limbaugh had, and he pumped hard for him on the air all through October and even introduced him at a rally in New Jersey. "The issue in this election is character," he said. But he saw defeat coming, and when it did he was ready to frame it. On the day after the election, he pointed out that Bush had lost, but Clinton, who got just 43 percent of the vote, had no mandate. "Six out of ten people in this country did not vote for Bill Clinton," he said. Limbaugh vowed to be the voice of the "loyal, honest, well-intentioned monolithic power which will descend on Washington, D.C." He was, of course, being facetious—he had no plan to lead a march on the capital. His arena was the studio, not the barricades. It was behind the EIB microphone that he had become the most influential conservative spokesman in America. Any doubt about his status was removed by Ronald Reagan himself, who wrote to Rush after the election. "Thanks for all you're doing to promote Republican and conservative principles," Reagan said. "Now that I've retired from active politics, I don't mind that you've become the number one voice for conservatism." Limbaugh proudly read this to his audience. He hadn't met his idol (and never did), but he had the next best thing, a coronation in writing.

The GOP's situation after the 1992 defeat was similar to the aftermath of the 2008 election. The Democrats had a young, attractive leader in the White House, and they controlled both houses of Congress. President Bush had been discredited and gone home to Texas, leaving his party with no obvious leader. Bob Dole of Kansas, the senate minority leader, was a saturnine, sharp-tongued deal maker. House Minority Leader Bob Michel of Illinois was an accommodating hack who believed that the GOP would be an eternal minority in the House and that it might as well learn to get along and enjoy life in D.C.

This sort of fatalism and passivity infuriated Limbaugh, and energized him. Did the Republicans lack charisma and fighting spirit? He would supply both.

Rush called the day before Clinton's inaugural "the last day of freedom for most Americans," and after Clinton took the oath of office he began each day with a portentous "America Held Hostage" takeoff on *Nightline*'s intro during the Iranian hostage crisis. Rush mocked the ceremony itself as a second Woodstock. In response to poet Maya Angelou's free-verse tribute to the president, he had call screener James Golden, aka "Bo Snerdley," recite a counterpoem about Clinton's alleged slovenly habits. Nor did Rush forget old scores. Ron Silver, still a liberal at the time, remarked that when he first saw fighter jets overflying the Lincoln Memorial, he felt that a military show of force was inappropriate, but on second thought he realized that "those are our planes now." "Those are American planes, Ron," Limbaugh corrected him.

Bill Clinton wanted to shut Limbaugh up from the day he reached the White House, but he lacked a legal means of doing it. Until 1987, the 1949 Fairness Doctrine required licensed broadcasters to present public issues in a manner that the Federal Communications Commission regarded as "honest, equitable and balanced." Since liberalism was the consensus view of the American elite, the commission generally regarded expressions of liberal opinion as the essence of honesty, equity, and balance. But the Reagan administration had a different view of balance and honesty. Reagan believed that the Fairness Doctrine was not only prejudicial but a limitation of the First Amendment right to free speech, and in August 1987, the FCC abolished it. One year later, and not coincidentally, Rush Limbaugh began his national program.

Lacking legal recourse, Clinton decided to delegitimize Limbaugh as a racist, and to do the job personally. On May 1, 1993, the president was the featured speaker at the White House Correspondents' Association Dinner at the Washington Hilton. The dinner was held in the shadow of the killing, by federal agents, of fifty-one members of the Branch Davidian cult in Waco, Texas. The massacre was unintentional, but women and children had burned to death, and the country was in an uproar. Congressman John Conyers of Detroit, who is black, attacked Attorney General Janet Reno's mishandling of the entire affair. On the air, Limbaugh came to her defense.

"Do you like the way Rush Limbaugh took up for Janet Reno?" Clinton asked the twenty-four hundred guests at the Correspondents' Dinner. "He only did it because she was attacked by a black guy." Clinton laughed in a good-natured way. "He's here tonight, isn't he?"

Limbaugh was there and he was livid; he was still angry sixteen years later when we discussed the incident with me in Florida. "If they can successfully tar you as a racist, you are David Duke," he told me. He demanded an apology from the White House and got one, but Clinton's attack, seen nationally on C-SPAN, stayed in the air. The last time a president had gone after a commentator in such a personal way, at a formal event, was at the 1934 Gridiron Club Dinner in Washington when FDR ambushed H. L. Mencken by reading Mencken's own contemptuous comments about American journalists as he sat on the dais.[1]

The attack on Limbaugh inspired him to even sharper anti-Clinton invective. He centered his criticism on the new administration's signature legislative proposal, universal health care. In September 1993, in a joint speech to the House and Senate, Clinton called for action:

> Millions of Americans are just a pink slip away from losing their health insurance, and one serious illness away from losing all their savings. Millions more are locked into the jobs they have now just because they or someone in their family has once been sick and they have what is called the preexisting condition. And on any given day, over 37 million Americans—most of them working people and their little children—have no health insurance at all. And in spite of all this, our medical bills are growing at over twice the rate of inflation, and the United States spends over a third more of its income on health care than any other nation on Earth.

Limbaugh insisted that the president was greatly exaggerating the number of uninsured and praised the American health care system as the best in the world. He charged that the Clinton plan was merely a way for the federal government to gain control of a large segment of the economy and seize the authority to force citizens to lead what "the smartest people in the room" regarded as healthy lives. (These same talking points, often framed in the same language, reemerged in Limbaugh's critique of the Obama health care reform effort in 2009.) When the Clinton administration launched a bus tour to campaign for the reforms, Limbaugh ran a parody of the Who's "Magic Bus" and updated his audience on the tour's itinerary, enabling them to assemble and protest. He also read the Clinton

---

1. Mencken never forgave Roosevelt for the humiliation. When FDR died, Mencken wrote in his diary that Roosevelt had "every quality that morons esteem in their heroes."

plan on the air. When the bill was defeated in 1994, Limbaugh could take a major portion of the credit.

Clinton found such opposition infuriating. On June 24, 1994, bound for St. Louis aboard Air Force One, he aired his grievance in an interview with radio station KMOX, which carried Limbaugh's show. "I'm not frustrated about [Limbaugh's criticism] exactly, but I tell you I have determined that I'm going to be aggressive about it. After I get off the radio today with you, Rush Limbaugh will have three hours to say whatever he wants, and I won't have any opportunity to respond. And there's no truth detector. You won't get on afterward and say what was true and what wasn't." Limbaugh scoffed loudly at this display of presidential petulance—since when did a liberal deconstructionist like Clinton even believe in "truth"?—and dubbed himself "America's Truth Detector."

The spectacular Republican gains of 1994 had an obvious influence on the Clinton agenda. The Democrats no longer controlled Congress, and both the president and the Congress had to consider the election of 1996 in light of what had happened. Clinton's liberal agenda slid toward the center. Even before the 1994 election, he signed the Limbaughesque Violent Crime Control and Law Enforcement Act, which built prisons, expanded the death penalty to dozens of federal offenses, and provided funding for one hundred thousand local cops. He went on to sign a welfare reform act aimed at forcing people back into the labor market, which he trumpeted as legislation that would "end welfare as we know it." He also signed the Defense of Marriage Act, which formally defined marriage as between a man and a woman. The Congressional Black Caucus and gay Democrats were respectively dismayed and outraged by these bills, but Clinton was clearly following the advice of his campaign theme song: "Don't Stop [Thinking About Tomorrow]."

Limbaugh was thinking about it, too. In 1993 he told *Playboy* that he didn't intend to get caught up in selecting Clinton's opponent. "I don't involve myself in primaries," he said. "After the party and the people have chosen the candidate, then it's a different ball game."

Would he endorse Dole?

"Well, who knows what Bob Dole's going to learn," Rush said airily. "It's a long time till 1996."

Dole did get the nomination, mostly because he was blessed with one of the least inspiring fields of rivals in the annals of modern American politics—inflammatory reactionaries Pat Buchanan and Alan Keyes and bland mediocrities such as Steve Forbes, Lamar Alexander, Richard Lugar, and Arlen Specter. In this group, Dole seemed like a towering figure. But he never had a chance to beat Clinton. The president was young and attractive. The economy was doing well. The Cold War was over and the country was enjoying a peacetime holiday. With the help of his adviser Dick Morris, Clinton had triangulated himself into the center of the political spectrum. Ross Perot was running again, but he was a spent force, and whatever votes he did pick up would probably be at the expense of the GOP. Even a terrific Republican candidate would have had a hard time winning.

Dole was not terrific. At age seventy-three, he was listless and sometimes disoriented. Campaigning in Chico, California, he lost his balance and toppled off a stage. He praised pitcher Hideo Nomo of the "Brooklyn Dodgers" (the Dodgers hadn't played in Brooklyn since the Eisenhower administration). A reporter asked him why he was running, and he vacantly replied, "You know, a better man for a better America. That's sort of our slogan."

Dole's running mate, Jack Kemp, was also a dud. Limbaugh was favorably disposed toward him at the start of the campaign; the candidate was, after all, both a Reaganite and a former pro quarterback. But Kemp flubbed his vice presidential debate against Al Gore in what Limbaugh described as "a disaster." After Dole's second debate with Clinton, Rush opened his show by admitting that he couldn't tell if the Republican presidential candidate had won or lost. Dole himself called the show later that day and tried to do some damage control. "Rush," he said, "I think we nailed him last night on a few things." Limbaugh was polite but unconvinced.

Clinton's reelection was less impressive than it should have been. Once more the Democrats failed to win a clear majority of the popular vote, a fact that Limbaugh stressed in his postmortem analysis. But he didn't seem brokenhearted. The prospect of a Dole presidency had excited no one, not even Dole. Four more years of Clinton meant four more years of sparring with the president of the United States. And Limbaugh had a score to settle with Clinton that went back to April 19, 1995, when a massive bombing destroyed the Alfred P. Murrah Federal Building in downtown Oklahoma City. One hundred and sixty-eight people had been killed in the worst domestic terror attack in American memory. Six hundred and eighty more were injured. Clinton vowed to find the bombers and bring them to justice. Two—Timothy McVeigh and Terry Nichols—were caught and convicted. Michael and Lori Fortier pled guilty to foreknowledge. McVeigh was put to death; Nichols got life in prison.[2]

The bombers were survivalists who denied the legitimacy of the federal government. During their trial it became clear that the immediate trigger for their act was outrage at the storming of the Branch Davidian compound in Waco.

On April 24, President Clinton was in Minnesota talking to a college group when he began to speculate about the motives of the killers. "We hear so many loud and angry voices in America today," he said. Their sole goal "seems to be to try to keep some people as paranoid as possible and the rest of us all torn up and upset with each other. They spread hate. They leave the impression, by their very words, that violence is acceptable . . . Those of us who do not agree with the purveyors of hatred and division, with the promoters of paranoia, we have our responsibilities, too." Clinton identified the promoters of paranoia as people who speak "over the airwaves." *New York Times* columnist William Safire took Clinton to task for this extraordinary assertion. "The impression Mr. Clinton left, by his very words," Safire wrote, "was that the Oklahoma bombing had been incited," and that the phrase "over the airwaves" was simply a coded way of saying "conservative talk radio hosts." At this time, Limbaugh was the only significant right-wing talk-show host in the country, and he was furious at what he saw as Clinton's effort to smear him as an accomplice to mass murder. He demanded an apology, but none came.

Limbaugh bided his time. It came in early 1998, when the Drudge

---

2. Michael Fortier served for approximately eleven years and was eventually released into the FBI's Witness Protection Program.

Report Web site broke the story of Bill Clinton's affair with intern Monica Lewinsky. The president denied it, and his wife went on the *Today* show to stand by her man. The host, Matt Lauer, asked her if she had really told friends that this was "the last great battle," and that "one side or the other is going down."

"Well, I don't know if I've been that dramatic," Mrs. Clinton replied. "That would sound like a good line from a movie. But I do believe that this is a battle . . . the great story here for anybody willing to find it and write about it and explain it is this vast right-wing conspiracy that has been conspiring against my husband since the day he announced for president."

It wasn't Hillary's finest moment. She looked foolish for denying what everyone else already knew. And the accusation about a right-wing conspiracy seemed paranoid. The mainstream media was with the Clintons; *Newsweek* had refrained from even publishing the Lewinsky story, which it had before Drudge, evidently out of a misguided belief that it could keep the story from going public. Matt Drudge and Rush Limbaugh and some Republican billionaires who wanted to see Clinton humiliated might be a lot of things, but they were hardly a vast conspiracy.

In fact, Rush always saw what was charming about the president. He may even have been a little envious. He once said that Bill Clinton was the kind of guy it would be fun to chase women with or just hang out with. But the Lewinsky scandal was too good to pass up. Ever since the Gennifer Flowers "bimbo eruption" in the 1992 Clinton campaign, he had been jabbing at Clinton's extracurricular sexual exploits in a series of skits and song parodies. Paula Jones inspired "Hey, Paula" and "Mrs. Jones You've Got a Lovely Daughter," sung by a Clinton soundalike. Now, Monica got "The Ballad of the Black Beret" (*"DNA upon her dress / War's declared on terrorists / Hundreds more rolled in the hay / But only one wore a black beret"*) and "Mambo Number 5" became "Bimbo No. 5" (*"A little bit of Monica, not my wife / A little Miss America on the side"*). Hillary got a song, too, "Stood By My Man" (*"Sometimes it's hard to be Missus Bill Clinton / Cleaning up the mess behind that man"*). No political conspiracy had ever been so public, no president subjected to such cruel, relentless ridicule, three hours a day, fifteen hours a week. He embraced the conceit of the conspiracy as he always embraced accusations against him. "Vast right-wing conspiracy?" Hell yeah. He even began peddling coffee mugs with the words emblazoned on them. Bill Clinton never came close to having as much fun with Monica Lewinsky as Rush did.

CHAPTER SIX

LIMBAUGH IN LIMBO

In 1997 Rush Limbaugh moved to Palm Beach. He had been in New York for almost a decade, but it had never been a good match. The acceptance he sought from his peers didn't materialize.

After Clinton's reelection, Rush was treated by the media as a has-been. It was wishful thinking—he still had his audience—but it bothered him to be discounted. The only New Yorkers who really seemed to care about him were the tax collectors.

Florida seemed like a better location. The weather was great. He could drive his own car instead of being chauffeured around or forced to walk, which he found both tiring and frustrating. Like any entertainer, he appreciated recognition, but in the streets of Manhattan he was still relatively anonymous. When strangers did notice him they were often rude. Florida was different—a conservative state full of avid Dittoheads. Palm Beach, with its ostentatiously rich lifestyle, wasn't reminiscent of Cape Girardeau, but it felt more like home to him than New York ever had. And, there is no state income tax in Florida.

Limbaugh didn't change his act when he left New York. He still went after Clinton almost every day and continued his war against the mainstream media. But very attentive listeners could hear a change: Limbaugh seemed slightly less aggressive. It was especially noticeable in the aftermath of the 2000 presidential election. Rush was living and broadcasting from Palm Beach, the epicenter of the controversy. This should have been his moment, but strangely he didn't really seize it. He supported Bush, of course, and made fun of his nemesis Al Gore ("Algore" in Rushian), but he didn't dominate the right side of the story as he had in 1994 (and would again in 2008). There was also something different in Limbaugh's voice. Sometimes he sounded a bit fuzzy, and occasionally he seemed distracted. He was increasingly absent from his show, replaced for a day or two at a time by a rotating roster of guest hosts. His fans asked: Was Rush getting tired after all these years?

On October 9, 2001, Limbaugh provided an answer: He wasn't tired, he was almost completely deaf. His hearing had been declining for a long time, and the previous spring he had lost it entirely in his left ear. Now it was gone in the right as well. There was genetic hearing loss in his family, but he told his stunned audience, it couldn't really explain what had happened. "There's something more going on," he said. "All those times that you thought I was on vacation or playing golf, I've been in an MRI machine or getting blood drawn, or on a stress EKG machine or at a cardiologist, the hearing doctor, what have you." The diagnosis, he said, was autoimmune inner ear disease.

Limbaugh explained that he could sometimes hear people with a particular voice range, especially in one-on-one conversations, but he couldn't hear radio, including his own voice, or the sound of music. "I am," he said, "for all practical purposes, deaf."

Limbaugh had been using powerful hearing aids, but even though they no longer worked, he had continued to broadcast.

"I'm not going to explain to you how we're doing this," he said. "Put two and two together, if you wish." The answer was Dawn, a court stenographer whom he hired to type callers' questions directly into Rush's computer.

Limbaugh had no intention of quitting just because the world had gone silent on him. "As long as the passion exists to do it, then we'll find a way," he said. He had decided to gamble on a cochlear implant. "It's the last thing they do because it's irreversible," he explained on the air. "Once you do that you're finished, and if it doesn't work then there's nothing they can do to put you back the way you were. So you must wait until you are entirely deaf for approval for this. The FDA even gets involved in this because it's surgery which involves the brain . . . I've talked to a number of doctors who say that it would be an improvement over the situation I'm in now."

Limbaugh left the show in the hands of guest hosts and flew out to the House Ear Clinic in Los Angeles. Dr. Antonio De la Cruz installed the implant, which consists of a microphone capable of receiving sound and transmitting it to a speech processor. The processor converts mechanical sound into an electrical signal, which is then sent to the brain via electrodes implanted in the inner ear.

The device worked. Limbaugh was back on the air full-time by the start of 2003. "This cochlear implant will reconnect Mr. Limbaugh to his environment, and that is an important benefit to his quality of life," said Dr. De la Cruz. It did not have the same effect on Limbaugh-haters who had dared to hope that they had heard the last of him.

That hope sprung anew the following October, when the *National Enquirer* broke a sensational story: Rush Limbaugh, the voice of America, was a drug addict who might be headed for prison.

The source of the story was Wilma Cline, who worked for Limbaugh as a housekeeper between 1997 and 2001, and did some drug dealing on the side. As the *Enquirer* story reported, Limbaugh learned that Cline's husband was taking hydrocodone pills and asked if she could get him some. She could, and soon she was supplying him with thirty a month. When her husband's doctor cut off his prescription, Limbaugh told Cline to find another source, which she did. He hid his stash under the mattress (presumably a Select Comfort, one of his sponsors), to keep his wife Marta from finding out.

Over the years, Cline supplied Limbaugh with thousands of pills. This wasn't done pro bono, of course. Limbaugh paid both for the drugs and for her silence. But eventually the deal went sour, and in 2003 Cline went to the Palm Beach County State Attorney's office with documents and e-mails. The *Enquirer* reported that one ledger alone showed her bringing Rush 4,350 pills in a forty-seven-day period, enough, in Cline's words, "to kill an elephant."

The fact that Limbaugh was a drug addict came as a shock to his audience but not as a surprise to his tight inner circle. He had been abusing substances since 1996 at least. Twice before he had checked himself into detox programs but failed. At least one specialist warned him that the OxyContin was endangering his hearing. Members of his family and a few old friends planned an intervention, but it fell through when no one was willing to actually confront him. Now the entire country knew his secret.

Limbaugh-haters were jubilant. He had never been much of an anti-drug crusader, but in 1995 he had made a comment that came back to haunt him: "Too many whites are getting away with drug use. The answer is to . . . find the ones who are getting away with it, convict them, and send them up the river."

Limbaugh was busted, pure and simple, and he had nowhere to hide. On October 10, 2003, he went on air and tried to explain what had happened to his audience.

"I have always tried to be honest with you and open about my life," he began. "So I need to tell you today that part of what you have heard and read is correct. I am addicted to prescription pain medication."

According to Limbaugh, he had started taking prescription painkillers after painful spinal surgery. His back and neck continued to bother him, and he decided to deal with the problem by taking pain medication, which had proven "highly addictive." He told listeners that he would be leaving the studio and going directly to a treatment center, where he hoped to beat his drug addiction once and for all. "I am not making any excuses. You know, over the years athletes and celebrities have emerged from treatment centers to great fanfare and praise for conquering great demons. They are said to be great role models and examples for others. Well, I am no role model. I am no victim and do not portray myself as such. I take full responsibility for my problem."

Limbaugh concluded by saying that he would like to go into more detail but couldn't, because he was under criminal investigation. If he was guilty of doctor shopping, a crime in Florida, he could get up to five years in prison. His celebrity status—especially as a notorious conservative in an extremely liberal jurisdiction—made him more vulnerable than the average user. On the other hand, he was much richer. He hired Roy Black, one of the top defense attorneys in the country, to keep him out of jail.

Black sent Limbaugh to a Florida-based clinical psychologist, Steven Stumwasser, who specializes in treating addiction. They met for the first time on October 5, 2003—just as the *Enquirer* story was about to break. "I had heard Limbaugh's name and I knew what he did for a living, but I was certainly no Dittohead," Stumwasser told me in an interview (authorized by Limbaugh) in 2008. "I evaluated him and saw that he was, indeed, an addict. He knew it, too. A lot of people have a hard time taking personal responsibility, but he was ready, and he wasn't in denial. He said, 'Tell me what to do.' He knew he had a problem and he surrendered."

Stumwasser arranged for Limbaugh to be treated at the Meadows, in Wickenburg, Arizona, about an hour north of Phoenix. The Meadows is a Level I psychiatric hospital equipped to deal with celebrities who, for obvious reasons, have concerns about privacy. Stumwasser flew out to Phoenix, met Limbaugh at the airport, and personally checked him in to the hospital.

"They guarded his privacy, but other than that, he was treated like everybody else," says Stumwasser. "Group sessions, individual treatment, the entire program. He could have left anytime, but he completed the entire program. He did the work, and he did it with passion."

On November 18, Rush returned to the air and reported for action. "I was a drug addict from about 1996, 1995, or whatever, to just five weeks ago," he said. "The truth of the matter is I avoided the subject of drugs on this program for the precise reason that I was keeping a secret."

Limbaugh called his rehab "probably the most educational five weeks" he had ever spent. "I have to admit that I am powerless over this addiction that I have. I used to think I could beat it with force of will. I used to think that I would be different, but I'm not." And then he went back to business as usual.

The legal issues dragged on. Eventually, in 2006, Limbaugh was convicted of doctor shopping and given eighteen months' probation under the court-appointed supervision of Dr. Stumwasser. Only a month later, he was stopped at the Palm Beach International Airport, where authorities found and seized a bottle of Viagra in a vial that wasn't in his name. It turned out that the prescription had been written by Rush's cardiologist in Stumwasser's name, to protect Limbaugh's privacy. In the doctor-shopping case, the elected state attorney of Palm Beach Country, Democrat Barry Krischer, had authorized seizing Limbaugh's medical records—an act that prompted the ACLU to file an amicus curie brief on Limbaugh's behalf. This time the authorities decided not to try to send him to prison for the risible charge of possession of Viagra.

Needless to say, many of Limbaugh's critics didn't feel sorry for him. Hendrik Hertzberg of the *New Yorker* spoke for many when he called Rush a "Vice Versa Virtuecrat" and reminded his (presumably drug-free) readers that Limbaugh's pain medication addiction "correlates strongly with committing acts that the law defines as crimes." Limbaugh's friends on the right, such as Ann Coulter and Sean Hannity, had rallied, calling him courageous for coming clean (as though he had a choice), but the dominant tone was gleeful. Limbaugh had been brought down and exposed as a hypocrite. He might even get locked up. The man who had irritated liberals by boasting that he was "having more fun than a human being should be allowed to have" stood naked now. Evan Thomas of *Newsweek* described him as "a lonely object of mass adulation, socially ill at ease, at least occasionally depressed and, for the past several years, living in a private hell of pain and compulsion."

People who thought that Limbaugh's drug bust and rehab would cost him his career were mistaken. His audience accepted his explanation and stuck with him. He had been the number one talk radio host in the country in 2003, when the *Enquirer* article appeared, and he was number one again in 2004, after he returned from Arizona. He didn't seem chastened, either. On the air he was his usual opinionated, cocky self.

A couple years later, I asked Limbaugh directly what he had learned about drugs and the people who abuse them. Was he in favor of liberalizing drug laws? Did he see a significant difference between crack and powder cocaine?

Rush responded in an e-mail: "I have no knowledge whatsoever of cocaine or any drug other than prescription painkillers," he said. He was, he told me, opposed to letting people legally obtain any drug they wanted. "My addiction taught me that there is nothing good that can result from increasing the number of addicts in society. There is nothing useful about addiction. It is destructive and not just to the addict because no one lives in a vacuum. We all have responsibilities to others in one form or another."

At the same time, he said that he didn't think that drug use should, in most cases, be a crime. "My experience, which as you know I value greatly, informs me that incarceration is not the best road to recovery except in cases of blatant, serial offenses where people repeatedly abandon serious attempts at rehabilitation. Everyone needs a wakeup call, and for some I suppose jail might suffice."

In his own case, Limbaugh made a distinction between street drugs and prescription medication. "I would never consider cocaine, heroin, crystal meth," he said. "I was introduced to codeine [the main ingredient in prescription painkillers, which, like heroin, is an opiate] via medical procedures. My 'initiation' was not recreational. But never once did I want anything more powerful, such as heroin or other forms of opiates like morphine. The reason is that I knew what I was doing was not healthy, was not 'right' and could lead to trouble, even before the law got involved. Plus I was in pain, at times very severe. Besides, I told myself, one gets painkillers at the drug store and technically they are not illegal in the sense that street drugs are. We all rationalize. Still I had my boundaries, in part because I was experiencing severe pain episodes. And with opiates, the more you take the more you need. It is a vicious cycle, and I feel for people in bad chronic pain who cannot live without painkillers."

Like a lot of conservatives, Limbaugh has a considerable libertarian streak, which doesn't always come out on the air. He regards homosexuality as, most probably, biologically determined, and while he opposes gay marriage as culturally subversive, he has no problem with gay civil unions—which is the stance of President Obama and Hillary Clinton. He drinks adult beverages, smokes cigars, and is not exactly a shining example of Christian family values. He is not opposed to capital punishment, but he "wouldn't go to the mat over it." Bill Clinton tried to lump

Limbaugh and Jerry Falwell together, but the two men never met, and Limbaugh turned down repeated invitations by Falwell to speak at Liberty University. In 2009 he declined an offer to speak at the Liberty graduation and receive an honorary degree. Rush didn't belong to the Falwell-Robertson wing of the Republican Party and never supported its candidates. Until George W. Bush came along.

CHAPTER SEVEN

"W"

Limbaugh liked George W. Bush the first time he met him back during the administration of Bush Senior. W was taking care of political business at the White House in those days, and the two young conservatives found they had a lot in common. They were products of the 1950s, fervent believers in the values of Midland, Texas, and Cape Girardeau, Missouri. They had both set out on courses that had disappointed their revered, demanding fathers. Bush, who graduated from Andover, Yale, and Harvard, was almost as contemptuous of the Northeastern elite as Limbaugh. They were both frustrated jocks, too. Rush had worked for the Kansas City Royals and dreamed of becoming an NFL broadcaster. Bush went from his father's White House to the Texas Rangers, where he was part owner and managing partner. Later he invited Rush down to Arlington, Texas, to see the last three games of George Brett's career. Limbaugh sat in Bush's private box near the team dugout and got a standing ovation from the crowd. He remembers W as profane, cocky, and determined. "He was planning to run for governor of Texas and he told me, 'Rush, I'm gonna kick Ann Richards's ass.'"

In 2000 Limbaugh was a Bush man. Bush cast himself as a latter-day Reagan. His primary opponent, John McCain, seemed to Limbaugh to be another Bob Dole. Rush was delighted when Bush won and generally approved of his first year in office. Limbaugh didn't care much for the new president's "uniter-not-a-divider rhetoric" or his warmth toward Teddy Kennedy, who was invited to the White House and praised for cosponsoring the No Child Left Behind education reform. But Bush cut taxes, which was the highest item on Limbaugh's small-government, business-oriented agenda. And he wasn't Bill Clinton. Those weren't Rushmore credentials in Limbaugh's eyes, but they were more than enough to win his approval.

Then came the attacks of 9/11. Communism, not Islamic extremism, had been Limbaugh's lifelong foreign enemy of choice, but not even the Ruskies had bombed New York City or the Pentagon. This was war, flat-out, and he wanted it fought no-holds-barred, without nuances or nice-ties, World War II–style. Limbaugh realized, as many more sophisticated commentators did not, that the attack on America was not an isolated criminal act launched by a group of fanatics operating out of Afghanistan. If it had been, there would not be cheering on the rooftops of Baghdad, Ramallah, Cairo and Damascus and Teheran. This was the logical next step in the wild anti-Americanism that had dominated Middle Eastern political culture—pan-Arab secular and Islamic fundamentalist, Nasserite and Ba'ath, Arab and Persian, Sunni and Shia—for decades. Limbaugh didn't believe in winning the hearts and minds of these enemies; he had no respect for either. What he wanted was a victory so brutal and so decisive that it would leave the countries of the Middle East prostrate and remorseful, like the Germans and the Japanese of an earlier era. Afghanistan was a good place to start, if that's what Bush wanted, but capitulation would mean a killer punch into the centers of the enemy. Baghdad was one of those centers, and the United States had an outstanding debt to collect from Saddam Hussein. If there were weapons of mass destruction there, as the Bush administration had said, so much the better. But with them or without them, total war was justified until the Arabs cried uncle.

At first, Democrats as well as Republicans supported the war in Iraq. Even Bill Clinton and the *New York Times* were caught up in the enthusiasm for taking down Saddam Hussein. But Limbaugh thought the Democrats would go wobbly eventually, and he was right. The hard left had never liked these wars, which they saw as examples of American imperialism. They rallied under the banner "Bush Lied, People Died," a slogan that became more strident when it turned out that Saddam Hussein actually didn't have weapons of mass destruction. Clinton himself said publicly that he, too, had thought Saddam had WMD, based on the assessments of U.S. and other Western intelligence. No matter: The Democratic base had never forgiven the president for "stealing" the election of 2000, or for his Texas smirk. Charles Krauthammer, who is a psychiatrist as well as a columnist, diagnosed it as "Bush Derangement Syndrome," and it infected the Democratic mainstream in time for the acrimonious 2004 election campaign. Liberals were inflamed by Bush's "Axis of Evil" conception of the world, his demand that NATO allies contribute to the fight in Iraq, and his refusal to admit that he had made mistakes in the conduct of the war. Part of this was simple politics. Democrats saw an opportunity to make Iraq Bush's Vietnam, and they took it. Limbaugh understood this kind of hardball. What he didn't understand was the concern the left was demonstrating for the previously undiscovered civil rights of enemy combatants. He reminded listeners that the sainted FDR had ordered the execution of German spies in Long Island during wartime, not to mention the internment of Japanese American citizens.

When pictures surfaced of American soldiers mistreating Iraqi prisoners at Abu Ghraib, Rush dismissed them as examples of high-spirited bad behavior akin to hazing at a college frat house.

And as conditions at the prisoner of war camp in Guantánamo Bay became an international human rights cause célèbre, Rush countered with a commercial for "Club Gitmo, the luxury resort for terrorist wannabes . . . paradise on earth on the west coast of Cuba, overlooking the bay. Every visitor, every check-in at no charge gets a new Koran, a new prayer rug, Moslem chefs, Moslem dietary laws, five prayer sessions a day. Reserve your spot today!" He also began selling Club Gitmo gear in his online store. Items with quips like "My Mullah Went to Club Gitmo and All I Got Was This Lousy T-Shirt," "Your Tropical Retreat from the Stress of Jihad," and "What Happens in Gitmo Stays in Gitmo" flew off the cyber shelves.

Limbaugh further incensed liberals in 2006 when he took on actor

Michael J. Fox, and this time he went too far. Stem cell research was a hot issue in the off-year election. The pro-life movement saw experimenting on discarded human embryos as immoral. Liberals regarded it as a promising route to a cure for serious diseases, including Parkinson's. This was not a debate that Limbaugh had paid much attention to, until it became a partisan debate that threatened a Republican senator, Jim Talent, of Missouri, Rush's home state.

Talent was against stem cell research. His opponent, Clair McCaskill, was for it. Michael J. Fox, who suffers from Parkinson's disease, made a campaign commercial for her. He said that what happened in Missouri mattered to "millions of Americans like me."

Limbaugh denounced the ad as cynical and fake. Fox wasn't an expert on stem cell research; he was an actor. His illness, while lamentable, did not confer any authority on his opinion. Rush speculated that Fox, who shook from side to side during the commercial, had skipped his medication that day to dramatize the effect. The studio webcam picked up Rush imitating Fox's gyrations. It was a cruel and insensitive performance. To make matters worse, Fox subsequently revealed that his symptoms in the ad were actually the result of taking too much medication. Limbaugh replied that this proved his point. "I was wrong . . . he did take his medications, and now he took too much medication. The point is, he did something differently to appear in this ad." That may have been true—the ad was taped in advance and Fox does sometimes show fewer symptoms—but it didn't wipe away the ugly images of Limbaugh flopping around in his chair in front of the EIB microphone. It was a case he wasn't going to win, probably his worst public relations gaffe since he had mocked AIDS activists in the early '90s.

■ ■ ■ ■

Limbaugh stuck with Bush's wars to the end of his second term, but he parted with the Republican president in his second term on two issues of cardinal importance: the future of American jurisprudence and the threat to national sovereignty.

In October 2007, Bush nominated White House Counsel Harriet

Miers of Texas to the Supreme Court. She and Bush were old friends, and like the president she was a born-again Christian who had the support of the religious right wing of the party. Limbaugh considered her a lightweight as well as a potentially unreliable centrist. He led the charge against Miers, and this time he was not alone; cerebral right-wing commentators like George Will, Charles Krauthammer, and William Kristol were equally opposed to the choice. Bush saw which way things were going and signaled Miers to step away. She did, and three weeks later the president nominated Samuel Alito, a much more conservative and prestigious jurist.

Bush and Limbaugh clashed again, this time over immigration. What to do about undocumented arrivals was an unresolved problem going back decades. In 1986 Ronald Reagan signed an amnesty bill for illegal workers who had been in the United States for at least five years; in return, the law would crack down on employers who hired illegals and stop the flow. Reagan called it a way to "humanely regain control of our borders and thereby preserve the value of one of the most sacred possessions of our people: American citizenship." That didn't happen. In the next twenty years, millions entered the country without permission, and by 2003 the U.S. Census Bureau announced that Hispanics were now the nation's largest minority group—thirty-nine million and counting.

You didn't have to be a xenophobe to see a problem; no country can remain sovereign if it can't control its territory. At the same time, a free society can't function if tens of millions of people live, without rights, in a permanent underground. The issue came to a head in March 2006, when supporters of amnesty staged mass rallies across the country, chanting in English and Spanish and waving Mexican flags. These scenes outraged Limbaugh, who acidly noted that in Mexico itself it is illegal to protest under a foreign flag.

Both political parties realized that something had to give. Bush believed that a solution had to be bipartisan. Nobody wanted to wind up on the wrong side of this. Limbaugh had no such concern. He was appalled by the brazen nature of the demonstrations. One of his Undeniable Truths is "Words mean things." But what was the meaning of the term "illegal" when throngs of people publicly flouted the immigration laws?

In May of 2007, the Secure Borders, Economic Opportunity and Immigration Reform Act was introduced in the Senate. The bill's sole sponsor was Majority Leader Harry Reid, but it had the support of both Senator Ted Kennedy and Senator John McCain. As its name suggests, the bill was the product of compromise. Like the 1986 legislation, it promised to regularize the legal status of millions of undocumented immigrants and take strong action to staunch the flow of illegals. Reid said he wanted to pass it by Memorial Day; Bush said he had hoped to sign it by the end of the summer.

"This bill is worse than doing nothing," Limbaugh said. "The thing about this that just doesn't make any sense is that we're treating the illegals as though we are doing something wrong, as though we've been bad and we're guilty of something. We want them to forgive us!"

Limbaugh was not merely opposed to the legislation. He saw the entire immigration issue as an abdication of U.S. sovereignty and a threat to America's traditional American cultural heritage. He was adamantly opposed to the entire theory of multiculturalism. The very first axiom on his most recent list of Undeniable Truths is "There is a distinct, singular American culture—rugged individualism and self-reliance—which made America great." Rush was with Davy Crockett, not Santa Ana. As far as he was concerned, immigrants from Latin America were welcome if they came with a visa and an understanding that American citizenship was not a right but a privilege, one that entailed conforming to and blending in with the Judeo-Christian, English-speaking, capitalist, constitutionally-based Republican principles and heritage of American society as he understood it.

A lot of Republicans (and more than a few independents and Democrats) saw it Limbaugh's way. Others were concerned about the effect of cheap foreign labor on the labor market. Some African Americans didn't like the idea that Hispanics had displaced them as the largest (and potentially most influential) of the minority communities. Citizens of border states were unhappy about the stress the influx of newly arrived, largely poor immigrants placed on their social service infrastructure. Limbaugh found himself at the head of a very large, highly vocal opposition. At the start of June, a pro-reform cloture vote in the Senate lost 61 to 34. The defeat was so decisive that in debate during the Republican primaries, McCain said that he would not vote for his own bill. Bush was deprived of a legislative achievement in a second term that didn't have much to brag about.

Neither Bush nor Limbaugh took these clashes personally. Just a couple months after the defeat of the immigration bill, Rush was invited to the White House, where the president gave him dinner and a ninety-minute briefing on the state of the world. Limbaugh found him "full of class and dignity," unwilling to respond to his harshest critics on the war because he didn't want to lower the level of his office. "Bush wasn't one of our greatest presidents," Limbaugh told me several years later, "but under him there was no corruption, no Lewinskys. He didn't diminish the office of the president. And someday, after we are all gone, people will say that Bush dealt with a lot of dangerous things that had to be dealt with."

This was more than he would say for Bush's predecessor. One spring evening in 2007, Limbaugh was dining with a date at the Kobe Club in Manhattan, looked up, and saw Bill Clinton approaching. He and the ex-president have different recollections of what happened next. In Clinton's account, which he gave in a radio interview in North Carolina, going over to the table was an act of Christian forgiveness on his part. "I just decided, after all the mean things he said about us over the years, after my heart surgery, I made up my mind that I didn't have enough time left to be mad at anybody, and I went over and shook his hand, sat down, and visited with him. We had a really nice visit."

The radio interviewer informed Clinton that Rush had a different version of the meeting, in which the ex-president had used his friend, Los Angeles Mayor Antonio Villaraigosa, to distract him while Clinton flirted with Rush's date.

"Well, he ought to be ashamed of himself," Clinton replied. "She seemed like a perfectly nice woman, but I spent all my time talking to him."

Limbaugh played the clip of Clinton's interview for his audience. "*'She was a perfectly nice lady but I did all my talking to Rush'?*" he said, mimicking Clinton's accent. "I ought to be ashamed? I ought to be ashamed of myself making up a story like that? Yeah, he's a married man. How could he possibly hit on my date? Right, of course, nobody would believe this. So far out of the bounds of presidential propriety, nobody would believe that the president would do something like this . . ."

Limbaugh said Clinton had come over to the table, stayed for about thirty seconds, left, and returned with Villaraigosa, whom he didn't know and whose name he missed in the introductions. When he read the mayor's card, he slid out of the booth and stood up to shake hands. "A minute later I looked over and Clinton's face is three inches from my date's." Clinton left again, and came back again, this time with his friend Ron Burkle. Limbaugh stood up to greet Burkle, looked over, and once more caught Clinton charming his date. "Forty-five minutes later, we leave," Rush said. "He's still out there. He's on the streets chatting it up with people, and as soon as I open the front door of the Kobe Club, the flash-bulbs start going nuts. Somebody had called the media, the paparazzi, so Clinton is standing about fifteen feet up the sidewalk . . . I walked up there and he acted like he didn't know who I am. Anyway, it was a fun night."

On September 25, 2007, Limbaugh used his daily "morning update" to talk about Jesse MacBeth, who had been appearing at anti-war rallies as a former U.S. Army Ranger and combat veteran, and as an eyewitness to American military atrocities in Iraq. He reported that MacBeth was a fraud who had been convicted of falsifying a Department of Veterans Affairs claim. "Yes, Jesse MacBeth was in the army," Rush said. "Briefly. Forty-four days. Before he was washed out of boot camp. MacBeth is not an Army Ranger; he is not a corporal; he never won the Purple Heart; he was never in combat to witness the horrors he claimed to have seen. But don't look for retractions, folks—not from the anti-war left, the anti-military Drive-By Media, or the Arabic Web sites that spread his lies about our troops. Fiction serves their purposes; the truth, to borrow a phrase, is inconvenient to them."

The following day, Limbaugh got an on-air call from a man named

Mike in Olympia, Washington, who had a complaint about the main-stream media. "They never talk to real soldiers," Mike said. "They pull these soldiers that come up out of the blue and spout to the media."

"The phony soldiers," said Rush.

"Phony soldiers," said Mike. "If you talk to any real soldier, they're proud to serve, they want to be over in Iraq, they understand their sacrifice, and they're willing to sacrifice for the country."

"They joined to be in Iraq," Limbaugh said. Then he retold the story of Jesse MacBeth.

Within a short time, Media Matters, a "progressive" watchdog group founded by Democrats (including Hillary Clinton) to monitor and discredit Limbaugh and other conservative commentators, reported that Rush had referred to military personnel who objected to the war as "phony soldiers." In the Senate, John Kerry rose to brand the remark "disgusting." On the floor of the House of Representatives, Jan Schakowsky accused Limbaugh of "sliming" the "brave men and women who have served their country in Iraq, Afghanistan, and other wars."

Limbaugh saw this as a teachable moment: "I want to thank Media Matters for America for making it so easy, ladies and gentlemen, to show how the real conspiracy works . . . how the left flashes the media, who flash the left in Congress, and voilà, you have a totally wrong, false, filled-with-lies, out-of-context story that ends up in the mainstream. What the media want is to create a story that fits into their template, their reality. Then they'll go to their favorite Democrats for a comment, they'll get some stupid comments from them, and run and rerun the lies so that two years from now the truth and their lies become one and the same in the minds of people. This is how it works. I want you to know it and never forget it. Thank you."[1]

On Monday, October 12, Majority Leader Harry Reid addressed the

---

1. Media Matters tried to correct its initial mistake by saying that Limbaugh had referred to phony soldiers (plural). Limbaugh responded by posting an ABC News Report titled "Phony Heroes"; the story of Pvt. Scott Thomas Beauchamp, whose grisly first-person accounts of the war in Iraq were challenged, causing the New Republic to admit that it couldn't stand by the articles it had published; and the fact that one of the spokesmen for Vietnam Veterans Against the War had later admitted lying about his service record.

Senate. "Last week, Rush Limbaugh went way over the line," he said. "While I respect his right to say anything he likes, his unpatriotic comments I cannot ignore. During his show last Wednesday, Limbaugh was engaged in one of his typical rants. This one was unremarkable, indistinguishable from his usual drivel, which has been steadily losing listeners for years, until he crossed that line by calling our men and women in uniform who oppose the war in Iraq, and I quote, 'phony soldiers.' This comment was so beyond the pale of decency, and we can't leave it alone . . ."

Reid informed his colleagues that he had written an official letter of complaint to Mark Mays, the CEO of Clear Channel Communications, Limbaugh's syndicator. In it, he once again charged that Limbaugh had called troops who oppose the war "phony soldiers" and called on May to repudiate the comments and ask Limbaugh to apologize. Forty Democratic senators and one independent, Socialist Bernie Sanders, signed this letter.

Limbaugh was almost delirious with joy. Not since the Clinton administration had he had an opportunity like this. Reid, who boasted that he had once been a Capitol Hill policeman (which had inspired Rush to nickname him "Dingy Harry") had dragged the entire Democratic Senate into his absurd charge. Charging Limbaugh with disrespecting American soldiers was like calling the Pope an atheist. Getting all the senators to sign such a letter made it look as though Reid was afraid to take on Limbaugh without a posse. Worst of all (or, best, from Limbaugh's point of view), by sending the letter, the Majority Leader came across as a tattle-tale.

Rush wasn't in any danger. Mark Mays was his syndicator, not his boss. But that wasn't the point. Here was an opportunity not simply to dismiss Reid, but to humiliate him. Limbaugh read the letter on the air, called it a "historic document," and announced that he was going to auction it off on eBay. Bidding would last a week, and in the meantime he would keep the letter locked in a titanium case "manufactured by Halliburton." He added that he would match the winning bid, all proceeds going to one of his favorite charities, the Marine Corps–Law Enforcement Foundation. The winner would be announced on Friday, October 19, at 1:00 p.m.

At noon that day, Harry Reid took the Senate floor and capitulated. "This week, Rush Limbaugh put the original copy of [my letter to Mark May] up for auction on eBay . . . and I think very, very constructively, let the proceeds of that to go to the Marine Corps–Law Enforcement Foundation that provides scholarship assistance to Marines and federal law enforcement personnel whose parents fall in the line of duty. What could be a more worthwhile cause? I think it's really good that this money on eBay is going to be raised for this purpose." Reid then tried to take credit for the auction. "There's only a little bit of time left on it, but it certainly is going to be more than two million. Never did we think that this letter would bring money of this nature." Limbaugh read this on the air with sarcasm that would have melted Halliburton's imaginary titanium case. The letter was sold to a woman named Betty Casey, for $2.1 million. Rush matched it and sent a check for $4.2 million. It was a lot of money, even for Limbaugh, but the outcome was priceless. Dingy Harry had made Limbaugh's day.

CHAPTER EIGHT

THE SOUTHERN COMMAND

In early 2008, in midst of the primary season, the *New York Times Magazine* asked me to write about Senator John McCain's campaign. McCain was the frontrunner for the Republican presidential nomination, but his candidacy was engendering strong resistance from the Limbaugh right. His long-standing policy was to refrain from endorsing a primary candidate, but he let his opinions be known. In early January, for example, after a strong showing by Mike Huckabee in Iowa, Limbaugh dismissed him as a populist, not a conservative. Limbaugh didn't love any of the remaining candidates, either, but Fred Thompson, Mitt Romney, and Rudy Giuliani all had one great virtue in his eyes: they were not John McCain. He had been in trouble with his party's right for years. His maverick image was, after all, a repudiation of much of the GOP orthodoxy. It had made him popular with reporters and liberal colleagues in the Senate, but not with the Republican base. He knew he had to mend some fences, and he did, most famously by going down to Liberty University, in Lynchburg, Virginia, in 2006, to ask for the blessing of the Reverend Jerry Falwell, the man he had called "an agent of intolerance" in 2000. Not only did McCain apologize, he hired one of Falwell's closest lieutenants, Brett O'Donnell, the coach of Liberty's nationally known debate team, as a campaign aide.

But McCain had his limits. In the 2000 primary, Limbaugh had sided with George W. Bush, and, ever since, Rush had immiserated the senator with parodies and skits about his lack of conservative principle. In one of these, Limbaugh intimated that McCain and Senator Lindsey Graham were gay lovers. In another he mocked McCain's incendiary temper and impugned his honesty. McCain, raised on the Annapolis Honor Code (formally, the Cadet Honor Code), was incensed by such personal attacks and refused to reach out to Limbaugh. He thought he could get nominated and elected without the enthusiastic support of the party's conservative base—which turned out to be correct in the first instance and a serious miscalculation in the second.

My plan was to fly out to Wisconsin to meet and interview McCain during a campaign stop, and then fly down to Florida to talk to Limbaugh. I was at New York's LaGuardia Airport waiting for a flight to Milwaukee when McCain's office called. The interview was off. The candidate was too busy. Scheduling conflicts. Last-minute hitches. They were very sorry. Don't worry, they'd call me with another date.

I flew directly to Palm Beach, checked into an airport hotel, and went to bed. The next morning I awoke to a front-page story in the *Times* about the relationship between McCain and a lobbyist, Vicki Iseman, that strongly implied they had had an affair. Now I got it. The McCain campaign had found out about the article in advance, tried to keep it out of the paper, and, failing, declared war on the *Times*. My interview was just collateral damage.

Limbaugh's chief of staff, Kit Carson, had sworn me to secrecy before giving me the address of the studio. On the air Limbaugh refers to it, with mock grandiosity, as a fortified underground bunker. It turned out to be the top floor of a modest, nondescript office on a broad boulevard lined with palm trees. The lobby was unmarked and unguarded. A small elevator took me up to a deserted, antiseptic waiting room with a gleaming wood floor, leather armchairs, and an American flag in the corner. The only decoration was a small, framed photograph of Limbaugh, captioned "America's Anchorman."

I was buzzed in to the control room by Brian, the broadcast engineer, who shares the narrow space with Dawn, a court reporter from Pittsburgh hired by Limbaugh for transcription duties after he went deaf, and James

"Bo Snerdley" Golden, a large, powerfully built man who wore a Huey Newton–style beret and matching attitude. "Are you the guy who's here to do the hit job on us?" he demanded in a deep voice.

"Absolutely," I said.

"That's what I figured." He glared at me, gave it a second, and then broke into raucous laughter.

"Don't pay attention to him," said Dawn. "We don't get many reporters here."

"None I've ever seen," said Brian.

"The media doesn't know about this place," said Dawn. "They don't know where we are. Even during Rush's big drug story, when they staked out the whole town, including his house, they never found us here."

"I'll never talk," I said. Golden snorted with what I took for good-natured skepticism.

For the next three hours we sat and watched *The Rush Limbaugh Show*. Radio studios are Limbaugh's natural habitat. He has probably spent twenty thousand hours in front of a microphone since he first went on the radio as a teenage disc jockey. Today's show was typical—ten thousand words of live, unscripted comedy and commentary, interspersed with commercials. During breaks Limbaugh scanned the Drudge Report and other Web sites for fodder, read e-mails from friends and experts who follow the show and offer advice, and spoke on the phone with staffers in New York.

After the broadcast, Limbaugh waved me into his studio and offered me a seat directly across from him. The show is webcast live to subscribers, but there is nothing particularly video friendly about it. Limbaugh was dressed for audio, in a golf shirt, shorts, and loafers without socks. His cochlear implant was clearly visible. Before the interview, his staff told me that the acoustics in the studio make it easy for him to hear but that he also reads lips.

On the air, Limbaugh had been animated, bouncing in his chair and waving his arms for emphasis. Now he was he was polite and subdued. I couldn't tell if he was drained from the performance or merely resigned to getting grilled by a stranger with a notebook.

I started by asking Limbaugh what he thought about that morning's article in the *Times*, but he waved it away. "This isn't personal between us," he said. "I've never even met McCain. I'd probably like him if I met him."

"What would you want to ask him?"

"Well, I'd be curious to know about his experiences at the Hanoi Hilton. Then I'd ask him: Senator, how could you vote to limit free speech?" This was a reference to the Bipartisan Campaign Reform Act, commonly known as the McCain-Feingold Act, which Limbaugh believes is an unconstitutional abridgment of the First Amendment and a boon to Democrats. "Next, I'd ask him: Senator, how could you have so badly misread the public on the amnesty bill? Why do you want illegal immigrants in the country? Is it because of pressure from the agriculture lobby? Or because you think they will become Republican voters?"

Partly due to Limbaugh's opposition, McCain had recently repudiated his own pro-immigration bill, something that would undoubtedly hurt him with Hispanic voters. Limbaugh made it clear that he didn't really care. He would prefer a Republican victory in the fall, but he wasn't deeply invested in it. "It's like the Super Bowl," he told me. "If your team isn't in it, you root for the team you hate less. That's McCain." The analogy made me laugh. I later learned that Limbaugh had told Charlie Rose the same thing about George H. W. Bush in 1992. Limbaugh, who began his career spinning golden oldies, has a weakness for recycling his own.

McCain and Limbaugh (like Bush) had father issues. McCain's father, a four-star admiral, was a famously domineering and difficult man whose personality problems were exacerbated by alcoholism. McCain, like Limbaugh (and Bush), had been a school-hater; he proudly finished 894th of his 899 class at the Naval Academy. Limbaugh and McCain both cultivated a maverick style. But that's where the similarities ended.

"I don't look at McCain and see elements of myself," Rush said. "I don't think that way. If we met, I'm sure I'd find him genuine, but I'm not saying I would love to be friends with him. I think he's too intense. Too intense to be president."

Limbaugh's idea of a sufficiently relaxed president is Dwight Eisenhower. "Ike was great. When he found out he couldn't shoot Congress like he had Germans, he went to Augusta and played golf." Of course, Eisenhower had been exactly the kind of moderate, compromising Republican that Rush despised, but I didn't mention that. Sometimes you don't want to let logic stand in the way of a good line.

I was aware that Senator McCain might not forgive the *Times* soon enough for me to write the article I had been assigned to write about him, and freelancers abhor (unpaid) vacuums. But talking to Limbaugh I saw an opportunity. He hadn't been written about seriously in a national publication for almost ten years. As we were wrapping up our conversation, I asked if he would consider cooperating on an article about himself.

"In the *New York Times*?" Limbaugh said incredulously. "That, my friend, will never happen. Believe me, I know these people like I know every square inch of my glorious naked body." He rose and extended his hand. "I enjoyed meeting you and I don't mean to offend you, but if you think the editors of the *New York Times Magazine* are going to do a story on me that isn't a hit job, you are naive."

Brian the engineer offered to drop me off at my hotel, and I was waiting for him outside the control booth when Limbaugh came out of the studio. "I'll bet you two tickets to a Yankees game, best seats in the house, that the *Times* will never agree," he said.

"I don't think I could afford the two best seats at Yankee Stadium," I said.

"If I'm right, I'm right. If I'm wrong, you get the tickets. Don't worry, I won't be."

"That would be unethical," I said. "I can't make a one-way bet with you." At least not in front of witnesses.

"Fine, if they say no, you owe me a box of cigars."

We shook on it.

On the way back to my hotel I asked Brian if he happened to know what kind of cigars Limbaugh smoked. "No," he said, "but I wouldn't be surprised if they cost more than Yankee tickets."

Luckily for me, Limbaugh was wrong. I sent Rush an e-mail (because of his deafness he rarely uses the telephone): "You owe me a ballgame. The magazine wants a full-fledged Limbaugh profile, 5,000 words at least, even more if the material justifies it."

Limbaugh responded in character: "5,000 words won't begin to cover it!"

I returned to Palm Beach in mid-March. By then the nomination of John McCain was a fait accompli. Limbaugh had never had the power to pick a Republican candidate, and 2008 was no exception. On the other side, though, the race between Hillary Clinton and Barack Obama offered possibilities for mischief, ratings, and, perhaps, even affecting the outcome. The campaign had been contentious. In one of their debates, Obama had called Clinton "likable enough" in a dismissive tone some Clintonites found patronizing. In South Carolina, when Bill Clinton compared Obama's victory to Jesse Jackson's in 1984 and 1988, he was accused of making an invidious racial comparison. The longer the campaign went on, the more acrimonious and potentially harmful to the Democrats these disputes would become, and Limbaugh took it upon himself to prolong the agony.

His vehicle was Operation Chaos.

On February 7, Limbaugh had suggested holding a fundraiser for Hillary Clinton, who was trailing Barack Obama. He toyed with the notion for the next few weeks. Then, on March 3, the day before the Texas and Ohio primaries, he instructed his listeners in those states to go out and vote for Senator Clinton.

"The strategy," he explained, "is to continue the chaos in [the Democratic] party. Look, there's a reason for this. Our side isn't going to do this. Obama needs to be bloodied up. Look, half the country already hates Hillary. That's good. But nobody hates Obama yet. Hillary is going to be the one to have to bloody him up politically because our side isn't going to do it. Mark my words. It's about winning, folks!"

The next day, Hillary Clinton won Ohio and Texas (although Obama took the caucus and won the delegate count, 99 to 94). The national media, which hadn't paid serious attention to Limbaugh for years, was shocked by the result, especially in Texas, which Clinton won by 100,000 votes. Various exit polls had contradictory findings, but Karl Rove, who knows more about Texas politics than anyone on earth, told me that 120,000 or so Republicans had crossed over in the open primary and won it for Clinton. The candidate herself didn't seem to disagree. After the vote was announced, reporters asked her how she felt about Limbaugh's role in the election. "Be careful what you wish for, Rush," she replied jauntily.

Unlike Texas, Ohio is not an open primary. Voting is theoretically restricted to registered party members. Unregistered voters who turn up at the polls are required to sign a pledge of party affiliation to participate. Hillary beat Obama by more than 200,000 votes, winning 53.5 percent to 44.8 percent. Obama activists charged that Limbaugh's crossover voters had tipped the scales. They also said that it was illegal—they hadn't officially changed their party membership, as the law required them to do. Michael Slater, the executive director of Project Vote—Obama's community-organizing alma mater—demanded action. "I think this is Rush and others inspiring people to commit voter fraud," he said. "They should be brought under investigation."

Chaos was working beyond Limbaugh's (always high) expectations. The media were now full of stories and speculations about his influence on the Democratic race. Democratic calls for an investigation into how people voted sounded dire and un-American. The vote, after all, had been conducted by secret ballot. Maybe some of the crossovers had voted for Obama (or Hillary) for reasons that had nothing to do with Limbaugh. What were the authorities supposed to do, track down citizens and grill them on their party loyalties and determine whom they voted for?

Limbaugh wrung a week's worth of hilarity out of this situation. On March 11, Mississippi held its primary. Obama won, but Clinton got far more votes than predicted. Once more the media reacted with alarm. Writing in the *Huffington Post*, John K. Wilson said that the Limbaugh Effect was saving Hillary. "Rarely in American politics have so many people ever intentionally voted for a candidate they hate so much. Approximately 40,000 Republicans in Mississippi decided to vote for Hillary Clinton in order to help her destroy the Democratic Party this year with a divided convention . . . The only hope for Hillary Clinton is that Republican voters will help her reduce the gap against Obama, and that the super delegates will somehow be convinced to obey the will of Rush Limbaugh and his acolytes by stealing the election from the legitimate voters."

Limbaugh was, of course, triumphant. I was sitting in his studio on March 19 when he opened his show with news from the battlefield. "Operation Chaos headquarters, I am commander Rush Limbaugh, here at the Excellence in Broadcasting Network, the Limbaugh Institute for Advanced Conservative Studies. Operation Chaos, we can safely say, is exceeding all objectives." Limbaugh then read a selection of responses to Chaos, including one from author Marianne Williamson, an Obama supporter, who said that she, for one, would not "vote with my vagina."

A Reuters-Zogby poll had just been released, showing Obama's big national lead over Hillary Clinton evaporating. The pollsters thought that Senator John McCain was benefiting from the lengthy campaign battle between Obama and Clinton. "Well, yes," Rush said. "That's the primary purpose of Operation Chaos."

A lot of seasoned political reporters thought that Chaos was more about ballyhoo than ballots, but the Obama campaign understood how much it was being hindered. Obama's campaign manager, David Plouffe, described the Limbaugh Effect in his postcampaign book, *The Audacity to Win*. "If Rush Limbaugh had not encouraged Republicans to vote in the Indiana primary for Hillary as a way of extending our race, we would have won outright . . . Over 12 percent of the Indiana primary vote was Republican and Hillary carried it, despite her through-the-roof unfavorable numbers with these voters. Limbaugh's project worked in Indiana—it cost us that victory—but it didn't matter. The die was cast."

Limbaugh saw what Plouffe saw; Obama was going to win. Chaos had created turmoil in the enemy camp, but all good things had to end eventually. He had always known that either Clinton or Obama would win out, and he was pretty sure that the winner would also be the next president. It didn't look like 2008 would be the Republicans' year, but that didn't mean it couldn't be a good one for Limbaugh.

Operation Chaos was not only an act of partisan harassment; it was also a piece of interactive political performance art. By enlisting his audience, he turned them from sullen conservatives without a real Republican candidate to support into merry pranksters. "Rush is a master at framing an issue and creating a community around it," said Susan Estrich, who ran Michael Dukakis's 1988 presidential campaign.

Rush's most famous venture in community building came in 1993 when a young guy from Fort Collins, Colorado, Dan Kay, called the show and said he didn't have the money to subscribe to the newly founded *Limbaugh Letter*. Rush saw an opportunity to score a political point against Bill Clinton, whose administration was encouraging schoolchildren to symbolically help pay down the national debt with the proceeds of bake sales. Limbaugh said that maybe Dan should do the same to raise enough for a subscription. Listeners began calling the show to say that they wanted to attend Dan's bake sale. An advertising company in Colorado offered to put up fifteen billboards to promote it. Brennan's, one of the most famous restaurants in New Orleans, sent a chef to prepare and serve eight thousand orders of bananas Foster. Limbaugh flogged the event on the air. On the appointed day, at least thirty-five thousand people gathered in Fort Collins, where Limbaugh personally welcomed them to "the conservative Woodstock."

Chaos was a national bake sale. It drew a crowd, got people laughing at the Democrats, and infuriated liberals—a Limbaugh trifecta. The goal was never to determine the winner of the primaries, just to keep the audience involved. He kept it going until Hillary Clinton suspended her campaign in mid-June, at which point Rush, speaking as commander in chief of Operation Chaos, grandly declared "mission accomplished." Chaos even enabled Limbaugh to turn an extra buck. He started selling Operation Chaos gear, including a T-shirt that proclaimed its objectives: "Crossover to vote in Democrat primaries. Prolong the Democrat primary battle. Allow the Clintons to bloody up Obama politically, since our side won't do it. Enjoy liberals tearing each other apart. Drain the DNC of campaign cash. Annoy the Drive-By Media . . . And WIN IN NOVEMBER!" The gear became the biggest seller since the Club Gitmo Collection.

CHAPTER NINE

THE RUSH LIMBAUGH SHOW

"Do you know what bought me all this?" Rush Limbaugh asked, waving his arm in the general direction of opulence. We were sitting in his study in Palm Beach, puffing on La Flor Dominicana Double Ligero Chisel cigars from his walk-in humidor. There are five houses on Limbaugh's ocean-front estate in north Palm Beach. He lives in the largest, a twenty-four-thousand-square-foot mansion that he renovated and decorated; the other houses are for guests.

This is a lot of space for a man who was, at the time, living alone with his cat. When I pointed this out, Limbaugh frowned. I was the first journalist he had ever invited over, he told me, and I could see him wondering if it had been a mistake. He told me that the house was actually quite modest by Palm Beach standards. If I wanted to see really ostentatious living, I should go to south Palm Beach, where Donald Trump and other genuine plutocrats lived.

I never got to south Palm, but Limbaugh's neighborhood seemed plush enough. On the way from the studio he had pointed out some good-sized estates, one of which was on the market for $81 million (and sold shortly thereafter). Rush had been offered $65 million for his place, but turned it down. He was comfortable; why move?

Limbaugh drives himself—at least he did in Palm Beach—in a black Maybach 57 S, $450,000 fully loaded. When we got to his house I saw that he had a garage full of them. "Anticipating a question," he said, "why do I have so many cars? Two reasons. First, they are for the use of my guests. And two, I happen to love fine automobiles."

I actually hadn't been wondering why he had so many cars. Rich people tend not to stint on transportation. What I did wonder is why all of them were black. He told me that he likes black cars, which made a kind of sense. Limbaugh is old-fashioned, even elegant, in his personal furnishing. Flashy cars are for hip-hop artists and arrivistes; professional men of substance ride in dignified black automobiles. It's what Rush's grandfather would have driven if, for some reason, he had been faced with the question of what color Mercedes he should own.

There was no visible security at the gates of Limbaugh's estate. We were greeted at the kitchen door by two members of Limbaugh's domestic staff, which includes a chef he hired away from a local hotel. It was hard to look at these women without thinking of Wilma Cline, the drug-dealing housekeeper who turned Rush in. Limbaugh is known as a very generous boss, but Cline was an object lesson in the limits of loyalty.

Rush Hudson the First was a man who shunned conspicuous consumption, but his grandson is no Veblenite. Limbaugh's house is, in the phrase of his close friend Mary Matalin, "aspirational." Largely decorated by Limbaugh himself, it reflects the things and places he has seen and admired. A massive chandelier in the dining room, for example, is a replica of the one that hung in the lobby of New York's Plaza Hotel. The vast salon is meant to suggest Versailles. The main guest suite, which I didn't visit, is an exact replica of the Presidential Suite of the Hotel George V in Paris. There is a full suit of armor on display, as well as a life-size oil portrait of El Rushbo. Fragrant candles burned throughout the house, a daily home-from-the-wars ritual.

Limbaugh led me into his inner sanctum, the two-story library that is a scaled-down version of the massive library at the Biltmore Estate in North Carolina. Cherubs dance on the ceiling, leatherbound collections line the bookshelves, and the wood-paneled walls were once, he told me happily, "an acre of mahogany." We sat at an onyx-and-marble table in a corner of the study with a view of the patio, a putting green, and the private beach beyond.

There was a brochure on the table for Limbaugh's newest version of *EIB One*, a Gulfstream G550, powered by two Rolls-Royce BR710 engines. It can fly at fifty-one thousand feet for as long as it takes to get wherever he's going. One of his Web sites shows photos of the plane's interior (which is tastefully luxe) and gives specs, including "armaments: CLASSIFIED." He told me that it would run him $56 million. Owning such a plane is a convenience, obviously, and a status symbol, but it is also an homage to his father, an aviation bug who subscribed to flight magazines and flew his own Cessna 182 out of the Cape Girardeau airport.

"One of the saddest things, one of the most regretful things I have is that my father died before we acquired *EIB One*," he said one day on his show. "He would have not believed it. I would not have been able to get him out of the cockpit jump seat. He would have tried to go get his jet rating. He wouldn't have been interested in sitting back in the passenger cabin with the flight attendant serving adult beverages and food." When I visited him in the summer of 2009, he had a picture of the plane as his screensaver on his Mac.

Limbaugh was in a very good mood during my visit. Not only was Operation Chaos keeping him in headlines, but he was on the verge of finishing negotiations on his new contract. His payday from his radio show would be $400 million for eight years, with a signing bonus of $150 million. When this figure was announced it elicited howls of indignation from journalists, many of whom were losing their jobs in the great media contraction of 2008. CNBC asked *Vanity Fair*'s Michael Wolff if Limbaugh was worth the money. "I think it's a monster error," Wolff said. "I'm sitting here saying, 'What are these people smoking?' You know, the truth is that Rush Limbaugh has ridden the rise of conservatism for twenty-five years and . . . Maybe nobody quite—quite has been following the news, but that's coming to an end. It's going to be over, and Rush Limbaugh, in a relatively short period of time, is going to look like a kind of really-out-of-it oddity. And I cannot, for the life of me, imagine how someone could have made this deal."

As predictions go, this one wasn't especially accurate. *Talkers Magazine*, the nonpartisan industry trade magazine, estimated that Limbaugh's weekly audience grew by a million listeners from the time he signed the deal with Clear Channel through the spring of 2009. A vexed-sounding Wolff wrote, "The most elemental fact about the Limbaugh career might be that, outside of seriously corrupt dictatorships, nobody has made as much money from politics as Rush Limbaugh."

Limbaugh considers this kind of analysis amateurish. "Do you know what bought me all this?" turned out to be a rhetorical question, the answer to which is: capitalism.

"First and foremost, I'm a businessman," he said. "My first goal is to attract the largest possible audience so I can charge confiscatory ad rates."

The average AM radio station devotes about five minutes per hour to news, reserves eighteen to twenty for advertising, and uses the rest for content. Limbaugh supplies that content on a barter system. For every hour of gross airtime, he owns around five minutes. Since he is on three hours a day, five days a week, on about 588 stations (in most places, he is number one in his time slot), that adds up to about forty-five hours a week.

Limbaugh sells these minutes. Some buyers are advertisers who simply run their usual ads. Others use Limbaugh as their pitchman, which costs them a premium and a long-term commitment. And lately he had created a new option: at double the normal rate card he will weave a product into his monologue.

To sell ads to a radio audience, first you need the audience, and nobody has one like Rush's. "Rush Limbaugh saved AM radio," I was told by Michael Harrison, the editor and publisher of *Talkers*. "He created the modern talk format. He's Elvis and the Beatles combined. He's been number one in the ratings for the past twenty years, and if he stays on the radio for another twenty years, nobody will ever surpass him." *Talkers* puts Limbaugh's weekly listenership at fourteen million; after 2008, it rose considerably. Nobody else was (or is) close. Sean Hannity, the number two talker, trails by more than a million listeners. Michael Savage was listed at number three. "Savage isn't even in my rearview mirror," Limbaugh told me.

Limbaugh is not effusive about most of his fellow talkers. Sean Hannity and Mark Levin are protégés, and he has defended Glenn Beck from attack by the Obama administration, but he doesn't really consider them, or anyone else, in his league. When we met in March, Bill O'Reilly still had a syndicated radio show that competed directly with Limbaugh in his afternoon time slot.

I asked Rush what he thought of O'Reilly and, after a moment's reflection, he said, "He's Ted Baxter. Sorry, but somebody's got to say it." He claimed he has never listened to Don Imus or Laura Ingraham. Garrison Keillor? "I wouldn't even know how to find NPR on the dial."

"I never mention others on the air, and I don't engage in contrived rivalry crap. That's bad business; it encourages people not to hear the station you are on." He has made an exception for Larry King, who he truly doesn't like. "He never had nice things to say about me, from 1988 to the present. He was working midnights [on the radio] when I started and demanded that his syndicator move him to afternoon drive when my success was obvious. He bombed and quit radio for CNN exclusively."

Democrats have attempted over the years to find a liberal radio talker to counteract Limbaugh, but they haven't found one. Mario Cuomo, Jim Hightower, and Gary Hart all tried and failed. "They all did two-hour Saturday shows to combat me, and the media gave them publicity out the ass . . . as though they were the Great White Hopes," says Limbaugh.

In the spring of 2004, Air America was launched to great fanfare, as the progressive alternative to Limbaugh and his fellow conservatives. The talent included Al Franken, Janeane Garofalo, and Randi Rhodes. But the venture was ill starred. It was discovered that the network received $875,000 in no-interest loans from a nonprofit Boys and Girls Club in the Bronx; the money was returned. Air America attracted a small audience, few stations, and fewer advertisers. Less than two years after its grand launch it filed for bankruptcy protection. Limbaugh celebrated the fall, calling Air America, "an embarrassing, blithering, total bomb-out of a failure." Liberals, he said, can't compete in the open marketplace of ideas, because they don't really want to spell out what they actually believe. "There's no hiding on talk radio," he said. "When your ideas sound stupid, it's out there to be exposed for one and all, and that's why Air

America and liberal talk radio doesn't get an audience—because it's not worth listening to!"[1]

But more than ideas are behind Limbaugh's broadcasting success. His innovation was to bring top-40 radio's energy to political issues, and over his career it has won him four Marconi Radio Awards for Syndicated Radio Personality of the Year from the National Association of Broadcasters and membership in both the Radio Hall of Fame and the National Association of Broadcasters Hall of Fame.

"Rush is just an amazing radio performer," says Ira Glass, the host of *This American Life*. "Years ago, I used to listen in the car on my way to reporting gigs, and I'd notice that I disagreed with everything he was saying, yet I not only wanted to keep listening, I actually liked him. That is some chops. You can count on two hands the number of public figures in America who can pull that trick off."

Glass compares Limbaugh to another exceptional free-form radio monologist, Howard Stern. "A lot of people dismiss them both as pandering and proselytizing and playing to the lowest common denominator, but I think that misses everything important about their shows," he told me. "They both think through their ideas in real time on the air; they both have a lot more warmth than they're generally given credit for; they both created an entire radio aesthetic.

"Like everyone, I'm a sucker for the smart-ass outsider, which he plays with such glee. That's what's great about him at his best: it's such a happy show! And the idea that he'd just sit there, not take calls, not have guests . . . is as radical an invention as Howard Stern's format. Rush is a lone figure. Talking to us in that peculiar way you can over the radio—where he's our buddy, leaning in for a joke, tugging on our sleeve as he tells us something nobody else knows, but he's also a preacher, delivering the good news to the masses. When I first heard him, I was surprised to hear this tone work in the middle of the day. I'd always

---

1. In 2007 Air America was bought by progressive politician Mark Green and his brother Stephen. It didn't help much. In the spring of 2008, the network's New York station, WWRL, had a 0.5 Arbitron share of the audience, which comes pretty close to radio silence.

thought of that solitary sort of radio as something that works better in the dark, late at night. Something about Rush's upbeat, triumphal, braggy joy—the happiness of the show—is what makes it play when the sun is still up."

On-air joyfulness has always been the default persona for top-40 disc jockeys; it is something Limbaugh has been honing ever since he was Rusty Sharpe. The skits and parodies he runs, mostly written or cowritten with comedian Paul Shanklin, are a part of the jollity. So is the expert use of rock and roll. What other right-wing (or left-wing) talker would have known the spoken B-part of Bo Diddley's 1962 song "You Can't Judge a Book by Looking at the Cover" (*"Come in closer baby, hear what else I got to say / You got your radio turned down too low. Turn it up!"*) and thought to use it as bumper music?

Bombastic intros and cutaways to commercials are another Limbaugh trademark. There are more than seventy of these, and they rotate with the mood of Rush and his chief engineer, Mike Maimone, who works out of Limbaugh's Sixth Avenue studio in Manhattan. Maimone sent me a very partial list:

> An Army of One
> America's Beacon of Freedom
> The Center of the Radio Universe
> The Leader of the Pack
> Members of the media—do not panic. Your show prep will
>   continue.
> Rated the number one radio personality of all time
> On a roll with lunch
> Redefining where the center really is
> A Weapon of Mass Instruction
> The Wonder of Rush
> America's Anchorman
> They used to get away with it, but not anymore.
> Unfiltered and unstoppable
> Annoying the left from coast to coast

Sometimes the cutaways are connected to current events—"insider information you can legally use," in a segment on Martha Stewart's trial, for example; or "drilling for truth" after an item on the fight to extract oil from protected lands in Alaska. From time to time Limbaugh adds something new, just to keep things fresh.

A lot of what makes Limbaugh's show fun is his irreverence toward subjects that conservatives customarily discuss, in public, with extreme reverence or not at all. Like sex. I was in the studio when Limbaugh decided to take on the prostitution scandal that had just brought down the governor of New York, Eliot Spitzer, and the admission by his successor, David Paterson, had he, too, had engaged in adulterous conduct. Conservative commentators were bashing both men in harsh language, but Limbaugh took a different approach. He laughed at them.

There is a format to this kind of satire. Limbaugh first introduces the most ridiculous liberal take he can find on the matter at hand. Today's text came from an article on LiveScience.com, "Are Humans Meant to Be Monogamous?" Then he reads it in an imitation of how he imagines the author of such a ludicrous article would speak. For scientific pieces, he usually employs a smug, supercilious Oxbridge tone. "Social monogamy is a term referring to creatures that pair up to mate and raise offspring but still have flings," Limbaugh quoted. "So a cheating husband who detours for a romantic romp yet returns home in time to tuck in the kids at night would be considered socially monogamous."

Now El Rushbo steps in to frame the issue. "Snerdley! Do you realize the great thing this is for mankind? This story has lifelong application for all of us, guys, thanks to Eliot Spitzer and David Paterson. Just keep a copy of this story in your pocket . . . get out there and do whatever, and then when you're called on it, say, 'No, no, no, look, science says I'm still monogamous . . .'"

Snerdley and Dawn exchanged looks. Rush has his unpredictable side and it wasn't clear where he was taking this. Alarmingly, he was now reading another article about a Senate candidate in Idaho who had tried to change his name to "Pro-Life" because election authorities wouldn't let him put his full name, Marvin Pro-Life Richardson, on the ballot. The phones were ringing. "Angela from Raleigh, North Carolina, Angela, thank you for waiting, you're next, the EIB Network. Hello."

"Rush, monogamous dittos," said Angela, using the standard jargon of Limbaugh fans to voice their agreement with what has already been said on the show before their call.

"Thank you," Limbaugh replied courteously. "Socially monogamous dittos, yes."

"Socially?"

"Well, that's what the story was, if I go out and cat around and get home in time to put the kids in bed, it's social monogamy."

Angela didn't think it was funny. "The reason I called, I talked to your screener and I told him that my belief is that the family is the fabric of this nation, it's what makes us great, and because it's what fuels everything that we do . . . And I just feel like this is—these attacks on the family, I wonder if these people know what they're doing."

Limbaugh, faced with a humorless caller, headed for indignation. "Hell, yes, they know what they're doing. Look, Angela, this is serious stuff. There are a lot of people in this country who want to do away with traditions and standards like you have discussed here . . . they want no standards, and in order to have no standards where they can live guilt free by doing what they want, they have to wipe them out for everybody, and they have to attack them . . . I did not mean to have my flippant attitude indicate to you that my devotion to such traditions and standards has wavered in any way, shape, manner, or form. I am Rush—Protector of Motherhood, Supporter of Fatherhood, Defender of Children—other people's."

That "other people's" caused Snerdley and Dawn to exchange another look. This is the sort of W. C. Fieldsian aside that Rush sometimes can't resist. He gets away with it largely because of the demographic of his audience. The vast majority of Dittoheads are men—72 percent according to a Pew Survey in 2008. This is much higher than any other non-sports talk show on radio or television.[2] This gender gap is the mirror

---

2. The disproportion of male consumers of talk and satire does not appear to be ideological. *The Daily Show* audience had a 2-to-1 male-to-female ratio; *The Colbert Report*, 62 percent to 38 percent; and NPR, 58 percent to 42 percent. *The O'Reilly Factor* audience is only 53 percent male.

opposite of the *Oprah Winfrey Show*, whose audience is 72 percent fe-male and 28 percent male.[3] There are obvious differences between Rush and Oprah, but also some striking similarities. They are both innovators who have built and kept vast audiences who idolize them. Rush and Oprah are cultural and political figures as well as entertainers, courted and embraced by candidates and presidents. And both use their personal stories and travails to forge emotional bonds with their listeners. Oprah often discusses her troubled teenage years and her battles with weight. Rush happily recounts (and usually overstates) the number of times he was fired, alludes sometimes to his marital failures, jokes about his ciga-rette habit, and talks about his own struggles with weight.

Oprah is a touchstone for women who see her as a wise and empa-thetic counselor. Limbaugh dispenses a fair amount of advice, too, usually on how to achieve success in a capitalist society and on the value of pas-sion in choosing a profession. On more emotional questions, he lacks Oprah's gentle touch. One of my all-time-favorite caller exchanges was with a guy named Jerry from Ohio, who wanted to know about matri-mony. "I know nothing is perfect, but I go, 'Damn, if Rush has trouble making marriages work, I think I would have even more trouble because of your situation and everything.' What do you think about that?"

Limbaugh told Jerry never to compare himself to others, least of all to him. "We had a woman call and say, 'Don't ever get married. Your work is too important to be distracted from,' and I think there are some of us to whom that applies. I don't know what you do, Jer, but I'm out there saving America and so forth, and that's a full-time job . . ."

■ ■ ■ ■

On my first night back in Palm Beach, we went to Trevini, one of Rush's favorite Palm Beach restaurants, Limbaugh at the wheel and his girlfriend, Kathryn Rogers, riding shotgun. Rush had described her as cool, and she was. He met her when she was working for golfer Gary Player, and a courtship ensued. Now she was with the NFL as an events

---

3. According to Quantcast.

coordinator for the Super Bowl. Her father, she told me, was a naval officer who had been John McCain's classmate in Annapolis. Her mother was a diplomat. Her sister went to prep school in Hawaii with Barry Obama, and she had spent part of her childhood in Guinea Bissau, a place that is not for wimps. Limbaugh, for whom the world sounds like a slightly muffled AM radio, has never heard her actual voice.

Limbaugh can't hear, but he can still do impersonations of voices he knew before he went deaf. I asked him how he pulled this off, and he touched his throat. "I know how the muscles are supposed to feel when I do the voices."

As we drove, music played on the car stereo. "If I put on oldies, I know how they are supposed to sound, and I hear them in my mind," he said. "The last song I actually heard was probably a Luther Vandross tune."

Trevini is located on the second floor of a high-end shopping center. We climbed the stairs, Kathryn in the lead, and Rush said, "This is how I like the feminist movement. From behind." It is a joke Limbaugh has been using since the early '90s. It surprised me. This was the first time he had slipped into his El Rushbo character.

If Kathryn heard the remark she didn't acknowledge it. I imagined that being Rush Limbaugh's girlfriend must present some unique challenges, starting with the fact the a great percentage of American women—especially women of Rogers's class and generation (she was thirty when we met)—consider him the worst sort of male chauvinist. Then there was the fact that Limbaugh, as he told caller Jerry, did not want to get married for a fourth time.

Rush occasionally jokes that the only people who ever hated him were his first three wives. But this isn't really true. He parted amicably from Roxy and Michelle, and both are fondly remembered by the Limbaugh inner circle. "They didn't marry Rush for his money, because he didn't have any," a close friend told me. "They left him because he basically didn't pay any attention to them. Anyone would have left him. It wasn't their fault and nobody thought it was."

The third Mrs. Limbaugh is a different matter. He met "the lovely and gracious Marta" Fitzgerald when she was still an aerobics instructor

who was married to another man. She initiated the relationship by sending him a message on CompuServe. They were married by Supreme
Court Justice Clarence Thomas in 1994, but the union ended after ten
years, and when it did, Limbaugh's family was neither surprised nor upset.
"She kept him away from Cape and she was very cold to the family," one
of his intimates told me. In the last years of their marriage, Rush and
Marta lived in separate houses on the estate, but Rush didn't let on that
there was trouble in paradise. His audience was taken by surprise when
he told them about it. "Marta has consented to my request for a divorce,
and we have mutually agreed to seek an amicable separation," he said, and
for once didn't elaborate. The terms of the divorce are sealed and secret,
and he does not mention her. After his divorce he dated Daryn Kagan,
then a CNN reporter and anchorwoman ("info-babe" in Rushian).

Trevini was packed when we arrived, but the maître d' jumped as
though he had been electrified and ushered us with great ceremony to a
corner table. The decibel level in the restaurant was loud enough to discom-
fort Limbaugh; in conversation he sometimes cupped his hand to his ear,
or asked for a repeat of a word or a sentence. All throughout dinner people
approached our table, mostly prosperous-looking men of a certain age.
"God bless you," they said, or "Keep up the fight." Rush smiled and thanked
them in a polite, good-natured way. One elderly fellow in a blue blazer and
gray slacks delivered a long spiel about his own good works on behalf of
conservative causes. Limbaugh nodded through the recitation, but when
the man left he confided that he hadn't understood a word.

Meanwhile, waiters buzzed around him. They seemed to anticipate
Limbaugh's every wish, refreshing our drinks, serving unasked-for delica-
cies, periodically checking to make sure that everything was exactly to
Mister Limbaugh's satisfaction. I had been in restaurants with celebrities
before, but this was a level of attention I hadn't seen.

Limbaugh turned the conversation to my impression of his home
and lifestyle. That afternoon in the library he had told me about his still-
unpublicized contract, and I wondered aloud what a single man with no
children could possibly do with all that money and a house the size of his.
He had frowned; it sounded to him like a hostile question, a Democrat
question, and he wanted to clarify the issue.

"When you saw my house today, you probably noticed that it isn't filled with pictures of me and famous people. That's not me. I don't have a home that says, 'Look who I know!'"

"No, you have a home that says, 'Look what I have.'"

"Why would you say that?" He sounded genuinely surprised, possibly even hurt.

"It might have something to do with that acre of mahogany you mentioned earlier."

"My home is a place I feel comfortable in, a place for entertaining my friends and family," he said.

"Mine, too," I said, or maybe I just thought it. As far as I was concerned, Limbaugh made his money fair and square, and he was entitled to live the way he liked. Maybe if I made thirty million dollars a year I'd live in an even bigger house.

Rush insisted on explaining to me that in his early years as a disc jockey, he had been poor and lived in lousy houses with noisy air-conditioners and cheap furniture, and that he simply wanted a nice place to live. He had invested not only money but effort and thought to make this a dream house where things would be comfortable and tasteful, and even the vents were quiet and unobtrusive. Later, as I was writing the profile, several of Rush's friends called me to explain once more that Limbaugh's house was not built to show off. One of them, David Rosow, told me: "He loves being able to spend his money on the way he wants to live. His home is his perception of what it means to be from Cape Girardeau and hit it big. Deep down he feels his plane is a symbol of hitting it big. But compared with others in Palm Beach, he isn't ostentatious. All he uses in the house when he is alone is his library, his home theater, and his dining room. The rest is for friends."

Many of the articles written about Limbaugh over the years have portrayed him as a solitary figure, lonely and reclusive. Newt Gingrich, with whom Rush has had a long and checkered relationship, once suggested to a Hollywood director that Rush would make a good subject for a biopic as a modern-day Citizen Kane. But I can't say I got the impression that Limbaugh is reclusive, especially given his hearing impairment. He holds a reunion for his extended family every Thanksgiving and spends Christmases in Cape with his brother. In April 2009, Julie Limbaugh, one of Rush's many second cousins, wrote an article on Salon.com about spending holidays with her famous relative. A graduate of Columbia University, she has endured a lifetime of being quizzed about Limbaugh. "What's he like? Do you know him? Is he an asshole?"

Julie Limbaugh painted a picture of a larger-than-life relative, a cousin who flies into town on Christmas Eve with a glamorous date, brings the family down to a plush Palm Beach resort for Thanksgiving, and hands out room keys that double as credit cards:

> He's fairly loud, but all the Limbaughs are. He's that one over there with the cousins singing rowdy Christmas carols around the piano . . . He's the guy who puts *March of the Penguins* on his home movie theater screen for the little cousins to watch and makes sure his candy bowls are filled with jelly beans and doesn't swear when my nephew tries to throw his antiques down the stairs. He's the guy who came from nothing to something and knows what it feels like to miss Missouri.

Julie recounted a Thanksgiving when the family gathered at the dining table, under the Plaza chandelier, and Rush apologized to everyone for making it tough for everyone to be a Limbaugh. She appreciated the sentiment. As a teacher in what she describes as a "liberal high school," she lamented the amount of hazing, taunting, and outright hostility she encounters when people hear her last name. The article made it clear that she very much disagrees with many of Rush's political views, and she also took a swipe at another of the Thanksgiving guests, Ann Coulter, but by and large it was an affectionate portrait. "He's cousin Rusty and he's okay," she wrote. It says a lot about Limbaugh's sense of privacy and his expectation of clan solidarity that he saw the article as a betrayal.

In addition to his family gatherings, Limbaugh maintains a very active social calendar. Each year he hosts a Super Bowl party for close friends and another celebration on the last day of the Masters Tournament, featuring a "sports bar" menu and very good wine. He spends a week every summer with the Rosows, takes an annual week-long golf safari to Hawaii with George Brett and a group of old friends, and belongs to several country clubs, including, recently, one in Cape.

While I was visiting Palm Beach in March, Limbaugh was busy planning his Spring Fling, a weekend he hosts every year in April. The guest list included Joel Surnow, the producer of the hit TV show *24* and one of the leading conservatives in Hollywood; Stan Shuster, owner of the Grand Havana cigar clubs in New York and L.A.; political consultant Mary Matalin; Roger Ailes; Don Ohlmeyer, the former producer of *Monday Night Football* and president of NBC, West Coast; ex–*Monday Night Football* play-by-play announcer Al Michaels; and a group of friends from Palm Beach. Naturally I asked if I could attend; the answer, unsurprisingly, was no. "I have a saying to all my guests here at my home," he wrote. "What happens here, and what is said here, stays here. They all come with that confidence assured. Our problem, my brother, is that me and my friends are into PRIVACY. Not to avoid media, but on general principles."

"'Flamboyant' describes him," Rosow says. "He's a big man and he does everything to excess. When he's on a roll, he rolls and rolls and rolls."

"Rush lives the way Jackie Gleason would have lived if Gleason had the money," says Roger Ailes. "Some people are irritated by it because they don't have the balls to live that way."

Dinner at Trevini was winding down, and I called for the check. It tickled Limbaugh to be taken out to eat on the *New York Times*. A few weeks later he sent me a copy of an interview, in *New York* magazine, with a waiter at the Kobe Club in New York named Jeremy Sullivan. A fellow Missourian, Sullivan told a reporter that Limbaugh was the biggest tipper in New York. "Several times he's left $5,000," he said. When I read this, I felt a stab of guilt toward the hyperattentive staff at the restaurant. If I had only known, I would have let Rush leave the tip.

CHAPTER TEN

INTELLECTUAL ENGINE

Shortly after arriving in New York to start his national show in 1988, Rush told Hilary Abramson of the *Sacramento Bee*, "The thing that drives me is that I have no college degree. My friends stayed [in college when I dropped out] and got their degrees and didn't have to demonstrate they were intelligent. I realized I had to demonstrate it. I became consumed by newspapers. If I stop reading newspapers, I'm in trouble in this business."

Whatever feelings of inferiority Limbaugh may have had disappeared as he became better acquainted with the work of his fellow commentators. By the time we first met in Florida, in the winter of 2008, his self-confidence was at a peak. William Buckley was gravely ill (he died just a few days after our meeting), and while Limbaugh appreciated some conservative thinkers—including Justice Antonin Scalia, columnist Charles Krauthammer, and economist Thomas Sowell—he now clearly saw himself as the thought leader of the movement. "I take the responsibility that comes with my show very seriously," he told me. "I want to persuade people with ideas. I don't walk around thinking about my power. But in my heart and soul, I know I have become the intellectual engine of the conservative movement."

Jay Nordlinger is a senior editor at *National Review*. For many years he was in charge of hiring at the magazine, and he noticed something interesting. "We'd get really bright kids, graduates of elite schools, young people with really fancy educations. I always asked, 'How did you become a conservative?' Many of them said, 'Listening to Rush Limbaugh.' And often they would add, 'Behind my parents' back.'" In the overwhelmingly liberal environment of elite American campuses, Limbaugh provides young skeptics with the vocabulary for talking back to their professors. He belongs to a fraternity of self-educated American iconoclasts such as Mencken, Ambrose Bierce, Lenny Bruce, and Eric Hoffer, subversives who challenged the certified pieties and academic orthodoxies of the day.

Like most commentators (I very much include myself), Limbaugh is not an original thinker. He belongs to a profession that toils somewhere between Plato's cave and Santa's workshop, hammering perceived Truths into interesting new shapes, wrapping them in shiny paper, and delivering them to the public. He calls himself an "instrument of mass instruction," holder of the "prestigious Attila the Hun Chair" at the (entirely fictitious) Limbaugh Institute for Advanced Conservative Studies. Despite the whimsy, he takes his role as an educator seriously. Often he turns his programs into seminars on policy issues such as cap and trade, health care reform, or budgetary restraint, or goes on about American history. Once I spent a bemused half hour in his studio as he debated the nuances of ethanol subsidies and their effects on the agricultural economy with an expert from Iowa. Not even National Public Radio subjects its audience to this kind of wonkery. No other commercial talk-show host would even attempt it. Who would have predicted that Rusty Limbaugh, who saw school as a prison, would grow up and figure out how to make it fun?

Limbaugh's audience is routinely disparaged by the national elite as a collection of dummies; civil rights attorney Constance Rice, writing in the *Los Angeles Times*, called them "a low information cohort." In fact, Limbaugh listeners have above-average education and an unusually high degree of interest in what the Pew Center defines as "hard news." They also fare better on current information tests than the readers of most elite publications, including the *Los Angeles Times*.[1]

---

1.   If anyone still needs evidence that the national press corps and the professoriate of elite universities are overwhelmingly liberal, and vote heavily Democratic, the data can be

Whatever their IQ, Dittoheads are presumed to be a collection of miserable human failures. Professor Marc Cooper of the University of Southern California's Annenberg School of Communication calls them "embittered and battered" fools who can't discern their real allies from their enemies. "Limbaugh's audience is not a happy lot," Cooper says. "They are completely convinced that an unholy coalition of liberals, homos, Feminazis, and overly entitled minorities are responsible for the mess of their own tiny, dead-end lives." Professor Cooper didn't cite a source for this conclusion. My own unscientific hunch is that the lives of Limbaugh fans are not necessarily tinier, messier, or more embittered than those of the average professor.

The Limbaugh Institute of Conservative Studies provides a daily tutorial on a variety of political, cultural, and historical issues, but no topic is visited more often or with more vehemence than the professional—ethical, ideological, and moral—imperfections of the mainstream American media establishment. The national media have constituted a Republican bête noire since the Washington press corps fell in love with JFK and Jackie. Richard Nixon famously hated journalists and put some on his enemies list. His vice president, Spiro T. Agnew, blasted the press as "nattering nabobs of negativism." Ronald Reagan was mocked by elite editorial pages and senior Washington correspondents as a dangerous fool for believing that the Soviet Union was an evil empire that should, and could, be defeated. Republican voters were caricatured as angry rednecks, religious fanatics, and reactionary idiots by an overwhelmingly Democratic press corps. (In 1972, when Richard Nixon got about 60 percent of the popular vote, the national press corps overwhelmingly voted for McGovern.)

When Rush Limbaugh came along, in 1988, the elite national media consisted of four conventionally center-left liberal television networks, three big Democratic newspapers (the *New York Times, Washington Post,*

---

found in the Appendix. The data on the comparative educational level of media consumers can also be found there.

and *Los Angeles Times*), two politically correct weekly news magazines (*Time* and *Newsweek*), two nominally objective wire services (AP and Reuters), and the unmistakably liberal PBS and National Public Radio. There was no Internet, no *Drudge Report*, no Fox News, and no conservative talk radio. Right-wing opinion could be found on the editorial page of the *Wall Street Journal*, in a couple of small magazines of opinion, and in the columns of a few token conservative pundits like Bill Safire and George Will. Limbaugh rudely shattered this soothing consensus. He was the un-Cronkite, the anti-Moyers, the Bizarro Brokaw, the inventor of back-talk radio. He wasn't fair or objective and he didn't pretend to be. His very existence on the other side of the teeter-totter provided balance. "I am equal time," he has boasted.

If Limbaugh had been all bombast, his act wouldn't have lasted long. But he proved to be not just a great broadcaster but a very astute media critic. He realized that the mainstream media's greatest vulnerability was high-handed obtuseness. News organizations acted as though their biases and interests—financial, political, and personal—were invisible to the public. Limbaugh pointed out, in the clearest possible way, that the Emperor's clothes were all tailored in the same shop, according to the same specifications, and he let his listeners in on why and how.

This was embarrassing, of course. Journalists like to think of themselves as independent thinkers and speakers of "truth to power." In fact, they work for big organizations and, like organization people everywhere, they toe the company line. To soften this reality, editors and reporters are almost uniformly recruited from a pool of like-minded people. They don't need to be explicitly told what to cover or how, any more than the Pope needs to send out memos to his cardinals about abortion. Here and there you can find editors and reporters with a certain degree of independence, but they are rare. As for editorial writers, they have all the latitude of West Point cadets.

The light Limbaugh has shined on the news business has played an important role in undermining the public's respect for it. In 1985, three years before Limbaugh went on the air nationally, only 45 percent of Americans thought the news media were politically biased. In 2009, 60 percent thought so. The number of people who said the media tend to deal fairly with all sides declined almost by half. Three quarters of Americans now believe that the media favor one side—and by a more than two-to-one margin they think the favored side is the liberal one. The majority have gone from trusting the media to be fair and reliable to believing that they are neither. Rush Limbaugh did not cause this to happen all by himself, but no single individual, with the possible exception of FOX News President Roger Ailes, Limbaugh's former producer and close friend, has contributed so much to the public's realization that "news" is not whatever the half dozen like-minded news organizations in New York and Washington decide that it is. "I *am* equal time," is not a hollow boast. At the very least he is a check and a balance on the power of the liberal media, a man willing to challenge the dominant news narrative. He is hated for this, of course, by people whose monopoly he destroyed. Some, like Professor Todd Gitlin of the Columbia School of Journalism, think the government should take Rush off the air. "Limbaugh is a liar and a demagogue, a brander of enemies, a mobilizer, and a rabble rouser," Gitlin told me. "I'm for re-instating the Fairness Doctrine [the federal policy, revoked in 1987, that paved the way for uninhibited political commentary on the radio]," Gitlin said. He conceded that this would constitute a government limitation of free speech. "The corner that right-wing radio has on the medium is a warping factor in our politics," he says. "Limbaugh is truck-driver radio. His voice is the voice of resentment, or in Nietzsche's sense, *ressentiment*—it sounds better, more venomous, in French."

When I told Limbaugh that Professor Gitlin, a prominent faculty member of America's preeminent school of journalism, had called him a liar, Limbaugh seemed amused. "Anybody who talks for fifteen hours a week extemporaneously for twenty years makes mistakes, but I correct mine as soon as I can, for a very practical reason," he told me. "If people don't trust me, they won't listen, and I won't have any sponsors. I make my living selling advertising. I have no idea who Todd Gitlin is, but he obviously doesn't know anything about the media."

He also doesn't listen to Limbaugh. Rush, like any satirist, engages in hyperbole, sarcasm, and ridicule, none of which is meant to be taken literally. Only the most oblivious or humorless critic would confuse it with lying. On reflection, and after consulting the Media Matters archive, Gitlin himself contacted me and asked to amend "liar" to "bullshit artist." In the commentary business, "bullshit" is what you call the opinions of those with whom you disagree.

"The liberals' favorite argument is that there is no argument," Thomas Sowell has written. "Nothing uttered in opposition to liberal beliefs exists, in their minds, at least nothing worthy of their intellectual engagement." This is certainly the way Democratic politicians, professors, and journalists have dealt with Limbaugh, and it has proven to be a highly unproductive strategy. For more than twenty years Limbaugh—using nothing more than ideas, words, and a microphone—has won (and kept) the hearts and minds of millions of Americans, reshaped the contours of the national media, articulated the central messages of conservatism, and helped set the Republican agenda. And, as the past year has demonstrated, he is very far from finished.

CHAPTER ELEVEN

THE BOSS

Limbaugh's central place in the national debate was on display at the end of February 2009, when eight thousand right-wingers gathered in Washington, D.C.'s Omni Shoreham Hotel for CPAC, the annual Conservative Political Action Conference of the American Conservative Union Foundation. Only a few years earlier, at the 2004 Republican National Convention, the party had fielded a dream team of popular speakers and advocates: Arnold Schwarzenegger, Michael Bloomberg, Rudy Giuliani, George Pataki, Mitt Romney, and Fred Thompson, the former senator from Tennessee who was now playing a district attorney on the TV series *Law & Order*. But they were all out of the picture now. Schwarzenegger had veered to the left on social issues and made a botch of California's economy. Bloomberg had become an independent. The primaries killed off Giuliani and Thompson. Pataki came to Iowa, opened an exploratory office, found out what he wanted to know, closed the office, and disappeared. In the posttraumatic climate of the economic meltdown, Mitt Romney reminded voters of the CEO who fired them. Jeb Bush was probably the most talented Republican politician in the nation, but for once in his life he had the wrong last name.

For a while, Limbaugh had been touting Louisiana Governor Bobby Jindal, the son of immigrants from India, as the coming man. At the age of four, Jindal had changed his name from Piyush to Bobby, in honor of his favorite character on *The Brady Bunch*, and in college he converted to Catholicism. It made a telling contrast to Obama's journey from Barry to Barack and the pews of the Reverend Jeremiah Wright's black liberation theology. Jindal was an Ivy Leaguer and Rhodes Scholar with a common touch; he won a seat in the U.S. House of Representatives at age thirty-three, got reelected with 88 percent of the vote in 2006, and at thirty-six became America's youngest governor. Best of all, from Limbaugh's perspective, he was a Reaganite—hawkish on foreign policy, opposed to big government and high taxes, and conservative on social issues. Rush thought the Louisiana governor had the intellectual firepower and GOP-style melting-pot credentials to take on Obama, and he used this influence to help Jindal land the assignment of delivering the televised Republican rebuttal to the president's first address to a joint session of Congress. But Jindal blew his chance. He came across as stiff, callow, and boring. YouTube lit up with comparisons with Kenneth, the overeager, hypernaive page on the NBC sit-com *30 Rock*. On the day after, Limbaugh spoke up for Jindal—"We cannot shun politicians who speak for our beliefs just because we don't like the way they say it," he said—but he understood that his protégé was a long way from prime time.

The delegates to CPAC 2009 wandered around the conference like political orphans, attending workshops with names like "The Key to Victory? Listen to Conservatives" and "Rebuilding the Movement Brainstorming Session." Newt Gingrich, Phyllis Schlafly, Michael Barone, Ward Connerly, Senators Tom Coburn and John Cornyn, Representatives Mike Pence and John Boehner, and 2008 primary washouts Mike Huckabee and Mitt Romney made speeches and presentations aimed at analyzing the party's postelection predicament and rediscovering its electoral sweet spot. They were received politely but, as Malcolm X once said about the civil rights leaders of his time, they neither incited nor excited anybody.

That job fell to Rush Limbaugh, who was due to give the final speech of the event on Saturday at 5:00 p.m. As the hour grew near, the mood in the hotel grew lighter and more boisterous. El Rushbo was coming! Finally there would be some action. By 3:00 p.m. the five-thousand-seat Diamond Room was packed to capacity, and ushers began leading the spillover—a couple of thousand people, at least—into adjacent rooms where they could see the speech on huge television screens.

This was my first visit to a CPAC, but I had read about them, and I wasn't surprised to see that men outnumbered women and there were very few dark faces. The youth of the audience was unexpected, though; close to two-thirds of the CPAC delegates were under the age of twenty-five, a great many of them students in on a free pass. I sat next to a twenty-year-old named Jake, a student at Gardner-Webb, a Christian college in Boiling Springs, North Carolina. In the 2008 primaries Jake had worked hard for Ron Paul, and he thought his man should be getting the Defender of the Constitution Award, which Limbaugh was slated to receive after his speech. "Rush is a defender of the Constitution," Jake conceded, "but two years ago he laughed at Ron Paul."

The elevated press platform in the center of the ballroom bristled with television cameras. FOX News was planning to broadcast the speech live and in its entirety, and CNN carried a large part of it as well. Reporters roamed the halls, asking the kinds of questions reporters ask at conservative gatherings and nodding vigorously at the answers to demonstrate that they didn't think the people they were interviewing were imbeciles. Before Limbaugh arrived, CPAC published the results of its annual straw poll. In presidential primary years this poll is considered an important symbolic test of the relative strength of GOP candidates with their core constituency. This year it dealt mostly with policy. Delegates were asked to pick their main priority from among three choices. Seventy-four percent chose "promoting individual freedom by reducing the size and scope of the government and its intrusion into the lives of its citizens." Only 15 percent picked "traditional values" by which they mainly meant opposition to gay marriage and abortion. Ten percent mentioned national security—a subject on which George W. Bush had won reelection four years earlier. The delegates were hawks and social conservatives, but, like Limbaugh himself, their first priorities were economic and ideological.

The poll included a second question: "Who is your favorite conservative media personality on either TV or radio?" Limbaugh won in a walk, outpacing Glenn Beck by 26 percent to 17 percent, and garnering more votes than Sean Hannity, Bill O'Reilly, and Mark Levin combined. When these totals were announced, Jake shook his head unhappily. How could so-called conservatives give so much love to a man who had publicly laughed at Ron Paul?

At exactly 5:00, Limbaugh took the stage to the tune of his radio theme music, the Pretenders' "My City Was Gone." Limbaugh looked terrible, bloated and sweaty in a black sports coat and a black shirt open two buttons at the neck. He looked less like the avenging angel of Republican values than John Goodman playing a Vegas lounge singer.

The audience cheered wildly and chanted "Rush! Rush! Rush!" as Limbaugh pumped his arms and threw down some self-mocking rock star moves. He is a radio man first and foremost, but he is not uncomfortable on stage. In his early years in New York, he did three annual *Rush to Excellence* tours across the country, one-man shows to build his audience. The tours were a success, and his Web site touts them as examples of his "mastery of live performance on stage." Recently, though, Limbaugh has limited his live appearances to a handful each year, and his stage chops seemed a bit rusty. Still, he was obviously delighted by the reception and thrilled to be delivering what he repeatedly called "my first live address to the nation"—a bit of faux presidential bombast intended to enrage any liberals who happened to be watching.

As usual, Limbaugh was joking and serious all at once, playing his celebrity for laughs, but he was mindful of the moment. Ronald Reagan ("a two-bit actor," people once said) had occupied this very same podium at CPACs thirteen times. Now here he, Rush, was, center stage.

Limbaugh opened with a not-too-funny joke that began, "Larry King passed away, goes to heaven . . ." The story was an old one—King went to heaven, sat on the celestial throne, and was told by God that the seat belonged to Limbaugh. The crowd chuckled at Rush mocking his own pomposity. Would a guy who actually was pompous do such a thing? I later learned that Limbaugh had another motive for telling that particular joke. In 1993 Limbaugh was inducted into the Radio Hall of Fame, and Larry King presented the award. "There is a new organization being formed," King said at the time. "It's called 'Feminists, Blacks and the

Homeless for Limbaugh, and they are meeting in a phone booth in Wichita." Limbaugh didn't react at the time, but he was mortified—many of his radio idols were in the audience. It took him sixteen years but that evening he settled a score—"Larry King passed away" on national television.

Limbaugh then turned to the issue at hand. "Let me speak about President Obama for just a second," he said. "President Obama is one of the most gifted politicians, one of the most gifted men that I have ever witnessed. He has extraordinary talents. He has communication skills that hardly anyone can surpass."

There were nervous giggles, as the crowd waited for the punch line, but Limbaugh held up his hand, signaling that he was serious.

It broke his heart, he said, to see the president misuse his gifts by fighting for high taxation to promote government welfare programs that would only make citizens more dependent on Washington rather than inspiring them to individual effort in the free market. He accused Obama of suffering from the chronic liberal disease of pessimism about America. "Ronald Reagan used to speak of a shining city on a hill," he said. "Barack Obama portrays America as a soup kitchen in some dark night."

The audience cheered, and this time Limbaugh let them go on as long as they liked. He was on national television and he was in no hurry to get off national television. "President Obama, your agenda is not new," he said. "It's not change, and it's not hope. Spending a nation into generational debt is not an act of compassion." It was not, he added, the role of Obama or any other politician to remake the country, tear the country apart, and rebuild it in their own image.

Having diagnosed the problem, Limbaugh went on to the solution. "The blueprint for landslide conservative victory is right there," he said. It was Reaganism. It frustrated him that the Republican moderates didn't see this, or care. "Why in the hell do the smartest people in our room want to chuck it? I know why. I know exactly why. It's because they're embarrassed by some of the people who call themselves conservatives. These people in New York and Washington, cocktail elitists, they get made fun of when the next NASCAR race is on TV and their cocktail buds come up to them [and say]: 'These people are in your party?'

"Conservatism is a universal set of core principles. You don't check principles at the door . . . Beware of those different factions who seek as part of their attempt to redefine conservatism, as making sure the liberals like us, making sure that the media likes us. They never will, as long as we remain conservatives. They can't possibly like us; they're our enemy. In a political arena of ideas, they're our enemy. They think we need to be defeated!"

The CPAC audience cheered and cheered. This was what they wanted, full-on defiance and resistance to the wave of liberalism that had left them disoriented since November. Rush wasn't telling them anything they didn't already know (many of them had learned it from him in the first place). They were applauding his clarity and his certainty.

The adoration got to Limbaugh. His speech was scheduled for thirty minutes, but he wouldn't stop, and he went on for nearly an hour over the allotted time. Later he told me that the organizers of the event asked him to continue, but his own sense of timing should have told him he had gone on much too long. In the studio he is a master of control and timing, but today he rambled. The people around me began sneaking looks at their watches. We were getting very close to dinnertime. Limbaugh finally concluded the speech, accepted his award, went directly from the ballroom to the airport, and flew back to Palm Beach, where he had left a houseful of weekend guests. He had done what he had come to do—rally the troops, cement his role as the leader of the conservative movement, and keep the media fixated on him. His plane wasn't even in the air when Bill Schneider, CNN's political analyst, said that Limbaugh had "crossed a line" by reiterating his hope that Obama failed and described the speech as "sinister."

It was just the first in a loud chorus of media indignation occasioned by Limbaugh's CPAC performance. But the White House was pleased. They still thought there was political gain in putting Limbaugh's face on the GOP. "Rush Limbaugh is the voice and the intellectual force and energy behind the Republican Party," Obama's Chief of Staff Rahm Emanuel said the following morning on *Face the Nation*. "Do you really think he is that important, that other Republicans are paying that much attention to him?" asked host Bob Schieffer.

"Well," said Emanuel, "he *was* given the keynote, basically, at the Conservative Conference, to speak . . . I do think he's an intellectual force, which is why the Republicans pay such attention to him."

That night, RNC Chairman Michael Steele, a black Maryland lawyer, went on D. L. Hughley's short-lived CNN interview program. Hughley is a comedian and former gang banger, a Blood so fearsome—according to himself—that his nickname was "Lil Rock." Steele, who fenced in college, was clearly intimidated by such enormous street cred. When Hughley said that the Republican National Convention "literally looked like Nazi Germany," Steele remained silent. But when Hughley referred to Limbaugh as a "clown" and "the head of the Republican Party," Steele spoke up.

"No he's not," said Steele. "I'm the de facto head of the Republican Party—"

Hughley said he was happy to hear that, because he had heard Limbaugh say that he wanted Obama to fail.

"Let's put it into context here," said Steele. "Rush Limbaugh is an entertainer. Rush Limbaugh, the whole thing is entertainment. Yes, it's incendiary; yes, it's ugly."

The next day, on his first show since CPAC, Limbaugh had a few words for the chairman of his party. "Okay, so I am an entertainer, and I have twenty-two million listeners because of my great song-and-dance routines. . . . Michael Steele, you are head of the RNC. You are not head of the Republican Party. Tens of millions of conservatives and Republicans have nothing to do with the RNC, and right now they want nothing to do with it, and when you call them asking them for money, they hang up on you. . . ."

Limbaugh didn't say how he knew this. It didn't matter. He wasn't reporting on the party's fundraising; he was threatening it. "If we don't want Obama and Reid and Pelosi to fail, then why does the RNC exist, Mr. Steele? Why are you even raising money? What do you want from us?" He went on to say that he had personally campaigned for Steele when he ran for a U.S. Senate seat in Maryland and that Steele was now stabbing him in the back. Knives were on his mind. "If I were chairman of the Republican Party, given the state that it's in, I would quit. I might the hari-kari knife because I would have presided over a failure that is embarrassing to the Republicans and conservatives who have supported it and invested in it all these years . . ."

It took less than one hour for Michael Steele to do what Congressman Phil Gingrey had done: crawl. "My intent was not to go after Rush," he told Mike Allen of Politico. "I have enormous respect for Rush Limbaugh. I was maybe a bit inarticulate . . . There are those out there who want to look at what he's saying as incendiary and divisive and ugly, that is what I was trying to say. There was no attempt on my part to diminish his voice or his leadership . . ."

Limbaugh was now clearly the biggest elephant in the country. Robert Gibbs, the president's spokesman, used the White House briefings to attack him day after day, alternately bemoaning his political obstruction and belittling him as merely a radio broadcaster trying to improve his ratings and make some money. Limbaugh laughingly pleaded guilty on every count. At one point, pro-Obama journalists in the press corps anxiously asked Gibbs if he wasn't making a mistake by paying too much attention to Limbaugh.

That, however, remained the Democratic strategy. Howard Kurtz of the *Washington Post* reported that Obama people were going around town bragging about how they had lured the Republicans into a trap. "The White House has decided to run against Rush Limbaugh," he wrote in a long article. It wasn't exactly a scoop. Democratic strategist James Carville bragged about it on TV (Carville is married to Republican strategist Mary Matalin, one of Limbaugh's best friends; they were among a handful of guests at Limbaugh's third marriage), and Obama's campaign manager, David Plouffe, published an anti-Limbaugh op-ed in the *Washington Post*.

Limbaugh had become a full-fledged media obsession. *Saturday Night Live* did skits about him. A *New Yorker* cover depicted eight Limbaugh-faced infants squalling. David Letterman joked about how awful Limbaugh had looked at CPAC and asked his guest, CBS news anchor Katie Couric, what she made of "this bonehead, Rush Limbaugh." Couric passed with a girlish "*Dave!* Don't do this to me."

"Every time you turn on the TV you see something about Rush Limbaugh," said James Carville, on TV.

Limbaugh, as usual, kept coming. They wanted to make him out to be the leader of the Republican Party? Great! *Reductio ad absurdum* was his game. As the "titular head of the Republican Party" he challenged President Obama to a one-on-one debate, graciously offering to send the *EIB One* to transport the president to the event. It would, Limbaugh explained, save taxpayers money. Needless to say, Obama did not respond.

Susan Estrich, who managed the 1988 Dukakis campaign, warned her fellow liberals, as Tina Brown had several weeks earlier, that they were being too clever by half. Limbaugh, she said, is not encumbered by the practical constraints and duties of real politicians, very much including the president. "Trying to beat him at his own game when your own game is played by a different set of rules is a losing proposition. He knows that," she wrote. It was smart advice, but Obama's strategists were not inclined to accept counsel from one of the masterminds of the Dukakis campaign.

Limbaugh assured his listeners that he was happy to be fighting the White House. "I was made for this. I was built for this," he said. "I admit if this were happening my first year behind this microphone, I would probably be a little panicked and I'd be backing off and I'm sure my broadcast partners would say, 'Ooooh, maybe gotta back away here, a little bit too out front there, blah, blah' . . . But don't worry, it's not my first time." Limbaugh admitted that the people close to him were concerned about the beat of criticism coming from the Oval Office and the Democratic leaders in Congress. He said that he considered it a teachable moment.

After CPAC, Limbaugh found himself fighting on several fronts. *Newsweek* columnist Jonathan Alter wrote that Limbaugh was destroying the Republican Party and that his actual influence in the country was on the decline. *New York Times* blogger Timothy Egan wrote that "sm Republicans know [Limbaugh] is not good for them." He quoted Frum, who had been a Bush speechwriter: "If you're a talk radio h you have five million who listen and there are fifty million who hate you, you make a nice living. If you're a Republican Party, you're marginalized." Limbaugh laughed at such criticism. Since when, he asked, did liberal columnists like Alter and Egan worry about the health of the Republican Party? "They only attack those they fear," he said.

Newsweek was in the process of remaking itself into a left-of-center magazine of opinion, and it assigned Frum to write a cover story entitled "Why Rush is Wrong."

"With his private plane and his cigars, his history of drug dependency and his personal bulk, not to mention his tangled marital history, Rush is a walking stereotype of self-indulgence—exactly the image that Barack Obama most wants to affix to our philosophy and our party. And we're cooperating! Those images of crowds of CPACers cheering Rush's every rancorous word—we'll be seeing them rebroadcast for a long time . . . Rush is to Republicanism of the 2000s what Jesse Jackson was to the Democratic party in the 1980s."

Rich Lowry, the editor of *National Review*, fired back: "I find the attacks on Rush from the right mostly stupid. . . . Rush is a huge benefit to the Right, and if we didn't have him, we'd have to try to invent him (and probably fail, because so much of his success is a product of his natural, can't-be-reproduced talent)."

Only one aspect of the torrent of criticism of his CPAC speech actually got to Limbaugh—the comments about his physical appearance. "Personal bulk" was comparatively kind. Timothy Egan called him "a swollen man." Begala mocked his "bloated face." MSNBC's Ed Schultz invited Limbaugh on his show this way: "C'mon, you fat pig. Let's get it on." David Letterman joked that the way he was dressed made him look like a European gangster.

Rusty Limbaugh had been a tubby kid, and Rush, in his various adult iterations, has been a fat man. At CPAC he weighed 290 pounds. "I dressed for comfort because I was overweight," he wrote me in May, "I did not want a closed collar and tie because I did not want to sweat. I did not intend to attract attention or comment with my attire. I wanted to be comfortable and not be distracted by how I felt based on my attire. Those of us who are overweight do NOT ever think of making fashion

Big Rush, the father
who always knew best.

(Courtesy of Kit Carson)

Limbaugh's mom,
Millie Armstrong Limbaugh.

(Courtesy of Kit Carson)

"Cape Girardeau royalty": three generatio
of Rush Hudson Limbaughs.

(Courtesy of Kit Carso

Rush's boyhood home on Sunset Street in Cape Girardeau.

(Courtesy of Chuck Martin)

The unsinkable Rusty Limbaugh.
(Courtesy of Kit Carson)

DJ Bachelor "Jeff Christie" and friend, in Pittsburgh.
(Courtesy of Jeff Roteman)

HEROES AND ROLE MODELS

Muhammad Ali taught Limbaugh how to draw a crowd,
pick a fight, and win with an "anchor" punch.

(Courtesy of Harry Benson/Hulton Archive/Getty Images)

Larry "Superjock!" Lujack
(with his wife, Jude): a big voice from
Chicago. Rush listened and learned.

(Courtesy of Donald Pointer)

William F. Buckley:
my "second father."

(Jan Lukas)

Ronaldus Maximus: "the greatest
president of the twentieth century."

(Courtesy of Lisa De Pasquale, CPAC)

Rush with Israeli prime minister Yitzhak Rabin in Jerusalem.
(Courtesy of Rabbi Nathan Segal)

Rush and Ahmed Karzai
in Afghanistan.
(Courtesy of Kit Carson)

Rush's first televised address to the nation. Message: "I hope he fails."

(Courtesy of Lisa De Pasquale, CPAC)

On the town: Rush (with ex-wife Martha), Gingrich and Buckley.

(Courtesy of William F. Buckley, Jr., Estate)

Rush at his White House birthday party with Ed Gillespie (left) and President Bush.
(Eric Draper, courtesy of the George W. Bush Presidential Library)

Rush with his fiancée, Kathryn Rogers: hopelessly romantic.
(Courtesy of Rush Limbaugh/Kit Carson)

statements, nor do we believe our attire will ever be mentioned one way or another. I was surprised my attire drew attention. I have never relied on looks to contribute to my 'image.' I have never tried to project an image. My mind does not operate that way. I rely on, and hope my ideas, my substance, speak for me, not the superficiality of appearance." He also started losing weight, but no diet was going to make him less visible.

In the first week of March, Pew reported that Limbaugh stories amounted to 8 percent of all the news stories in the national media organizations it monitors. White House reporters once again queried Gibbs on the efficacy of the strategy, and this time Gibbs conceded that it might be counterproductive. But ten days later, after Dick Cheney said that Obama was "making some choices that, in my mind, will in fact raise the risk to the American people," Gibbs tossed another Rush bomb. "I guess Rush Limbaugh was busy, so they trotted out the next most popular member of the Republican cabal." The Democratic National Committee announced an Internet contest to pick a national slogan to use against Limbaugh in a billboard campaign.

Vanity Fair media critic Michael Wolff marveled at the centrality of Limbaugh. A year ago, he and his fellow media mavens had written him off as a dead man talking. Now he was not only back but bigger than ever. Wolff was perplexed by this. AM radio was a dying medium, a dinosaur even when Limbaugh began to broadcast twenty years earlier. Now, on the Internet, how could one man with a microphone dominate the debate so thoroughly? "The only sensible market view of conservative talk is that it will contract and be reduced, in the coming years, to a much more rarefied format. And yet, by the end of Rush Limbaugh's fractious month of calculated outrage, his audience was back up to 20 million. That's showmanship."

When would Limbaugh peak? On March 26, NBC's Savannah Guthrie told Joe Scarborough that Limbaugh was in decline. "People here recognize that argument only goes so far. So notice the last few weeks we haven't heard too much about Rush Limbaugh."

Rush jumped on it. "Savannah," he said in his most patronizing tone, "let me just read to you what we have just received." He then recited his latest ratings. His show was number one in its time slot in New York;

Chicago; Los Angeles; Houston; Washington, D.C.; and Detroit, and second in San Francisco. The numbers were up, sometimes sharply, all across the country. The pro-Limbaugh Web site Radio Equalizer asked, "Given this blockbuster data, will the White House think twice before targeting Rush again?"

A lot of Democrats now agreed, and the attacks on Limbaugh tapered off briefly. But he was too hot to quench. Colin Powell, former secretary of State under George W. Bush and one of the leading Republican moderates Limbaugh had scored at CPAC, went on Fareed Zakaria's show and took a shot at Limbaugh. "I think the party has to stop shouting at the world, at the country," he said. "I've talked to a number of leaders in recent weeks and they understand that." Powell went on to quote columnist Mort Kondracke on Limbaugh's unfitness to act as party spokesman because of his appeal to peoples' "lesser instincts."

Limbaugh responded the following day by telling his audience that Powell was still angry because Powell had endorsed Obama during the 2008 campaign, and Rush explained it as Powell putting racial solidarity over his party and his friend, McCain.

"So, General Powell, let me explain something. The fact is, Republicans did not listen to me. They listened to you. They have not been listening to me for years. The Republican Party nominated your ideal candidate. They nominated a moderate who's willing to buy into an endless array of liberal causes . . ."

Round two of Powell-Limbaugh started in May, on *Face the Nation*. Dick Cheney was asked who was a better Republican, Limbaugh or Powell. "If I had to choose in terms of being a Republican, I'd go with Rush Limbaugh," the former vice president replied. "My take on it was Colin had already left the party. I didn't know he was still a Republican."

A few days later, Powell delivered a speech to a crowd of business leaders in Boston. "Rush Limbaugh says, 'Get out of the Republican Party.' Dick Cheney says, 'He's already out.' I may be out of their version of the Republican Party, but there's another version of the Republican Party waiting to emerge once again," Powell said.

Limbaugh was palpably bored by the controversy. He had made his point—Powell was an Obama Democrat and a political nonentity, and it was now time to turn the whole thing into a joke. With mock seriousness he announced that he was resigning from the position of "titular head of the Republican Party" that had been bestowed upon him by President Obama and the media. "There, frankly, is someone far more qualified and capable and more in tune with today's Republican Party than I, to be not only its titular head but its real head, and that would be General Colin Powell. So I now pass the baton to General Powell. . . . I now today pronounce and proclaim General Colin Powell as the titular head of the Republican Party. From now on out, those of you who want to know what the party should do to win elections, to beat back the onslaught of Obama-ism, ask General Powell."

A few weeks later, *USA Today*–Gallup published the results of a poll question: Who is the main person who speaks for the Republican Party? Limbaugh finished first, with 13 percent, followed by Cheney, at 10 percent. McCain and Newt Gingrich tied for third at 6 percent. Among Republicans only, Limbaugh and Gingrich tied at 10 percent. George W. Bush got less than half a percentage point. Colin Powell wasn't even mentioned.

CHAPTER TWELVE

THE MAGIC NEGRO

Rush Limbaugh's "I hope he fails" stance toward President Obama and his skirmishing with Powell over the nature of the party were bound to embroil Rush in charges of racism. He wasn't surprised. When Obama first appeared as a viable Democratic candidate, Limbaugh saw that a great many moderate Republicans would be wary of taking on an attractive, charming, soft-spoken, intellectually gifted, young black candidate. The idea of voting for an African American was attractive; nobody wanted to be on the wrong side of history. Besides, it would be dangerous to stand against Obama. In the course of Hillary Clinton's Democratic primary campaign against Obama even Bill Clinton, the darling of black America, a man whom author Toni Morrison famously called "our first black president," was accused by the Obama camp of playing the white race card. In a different climate such a bogus charge would have been hooted down by the press corps, but in the campaign of 2008, mainstream reporters functioned as Obama bodyguards. Playing a role in the victory of the first African American president was a thrilling personal and professional opportunity, and the media seized it with undisguised enthusiasm. Limbaugh, of course, did not. He was a conservative and a Republican, Obama a liberal and a Democrat. Of course he would take on the Democratic candidate. That was his job.

One of Limbaugh's favorite techniques is to take liberal words and turn them on their authors. In March 2007, the *Los Angeles Times* gave Limbaugh a gift in the form of an article by a black, liberal film critic, David Ehrenstein, entitled "Obama the 'Magic Negro.'" Ehrenstein wrote that Obama was running for an unelected office that exists in the popular white imagination—the "Magic Negro." This term, he explains, is not meant as a compliment; it is a white fantasy, a black man who "has no past, he simply appears one day to help the white protagonist." Part of the help consists of allowing the white man to accept the Magic Negro, demonstrating tolerance at no real cost and separating himself from the legacy of slavery and segregation. In other words, the Magic Negro is a racial enabler. Ehrenstein said that Obama was being protected by white critics because they needed Obama to be perfect to fulfill their own fantasies of racial redemption. "The only mud that momentarily [sticks to him] is criticism (white and black alike) concerning Obama's alleged 'inauthenticity,' as compared to such sterling examples of 'genuine' blackness as Al Sharpton and Snoop Dogg."

Limbaugh knew what he had right away. His goal was to stir problems in the Democratic camp (just as it was in Operation Chaos a year later) and to knock the halo off Obama's head. He didn't give a damn about the racial subtleties of the Magic Negro construct or any similar theoretical speculation. This was politics. That same day he read the *Los Angeles Times* piece on the air, in its entirety. Two days later he introduced a parody song, sung by a dead-on Al Sharpton soundalike, to the tune of "Puff, the Magic Dragon."

> *Barack the Magic Negro lives in D.C.*
>
> *The L.A. Times, they called him that*
>
> *'Cause he's not authentic like me.*
>
> *Yeah, the guy from the L.A. paper*
>
> *Said he makes guilty whites feel good*
>
> *They'll vote for him, and not for me*
>
> *'Cause he's not from the hood.*

See, real black men, like Snoop Dogg

Or me, or Farrakhan

Have talked the talk, and walked the walk

Not come in late and won!

Oh, Barack the Magic Negro, lives in D.C.

The L.A. Times, they called him that

'Cause he's black, but not authentically.

. . .

Some say Barack's "articulate"

And bright and new and "clean."

The media sure loves this guy,

A white interloper's dream!

But, when you vote for president,

Watch out, and don't be fooled!

Don't vote the Magic Negro in—

'Cause I won't have nothing after all these years of
    sacrifice . . .

The song worked on several levels. It attempted to set the Sharpton Democrats (those who weren't supporting Hillary Clinton already) against Obama. It mocked Democratic candidate Joe Biden's observation that Obama was "clean" and "articulate," and the liberal pretense that only Republicans engage in negative racial stereotyping. It mentioned Farra-khan, always a hot button for Jewish Democrats. And it was funny—even Sharpton admitted that. "I despise his ideology," he told me, "but Rush is a lot smarter and craftier than Don Imus. Limbaugh puts things in a way that he can't be blamed for easy bigotry. Some of the songs he does about me just make me laugh."

The media, which reflexively squawk at any politically incorrect use of racial language, couldn't stop talking about it. Two years later, with Obama safely in the White House, the *Today* show was still asking Limbaugh to defend the song. No wonder it became Rush's all-time-favorite parody.

The Magic Negro controversy was a year old when I first met Limbaugh. It appeared that Obama would very possibly get the Democratic nomination, and we discussed the problems it would pose for Limbaugh as a conservative satirist. A couple days later I was at home listening to his show when he said, "Ladies and gentlemen, I had a conversation with a friend Wednesday afternoon after the program, and he said, 'Nobody's criticizing Obama. How are you going to do this? How are you going to handle criticizing the first black American to run for president?'"

It took me a few seconds to realize that Limbaugh was talking about me. I was surprised to hear myself described as a friend. Limbaugh said that he was going after Obama as he did all his political opponents, "fearlessly." He had used that word with me, too, and I realized that this was one part of our interview that wasn't going to remain exclusive.

"I'm not going to bow to political correctness," Limbaugh said.

"I'm going to do it with humor. I'm going to focus on the issues. I'm going to react to what he says. Simple. I'm going to do it just like if it were any other case—he's a man, right? He's a liberal. How do I criticize liberals? I criticize them."

That's indeed what Limbaugh had said to me, almost word for word. But he wasn't finished. "I have devised, ladies and gentlemen, an even more creative way of criticizing Obama. I have, just this morning, named a new position here on the staff. The EIB Network now has an Official Obama Criticizer. He is Bo Snerdley . . . When Obama needs to be criticized, our official criticizer, Bo Snerdley, will do so."

The previous night there had been a candidates' debate in which Obama recounted a conversation he had with an army captain whose platoon in Afghanistan was badly understaffed and underequipped because many of his soldiers and a lot of his equipment had been sent to Iraq. This was a stock complaint of Obama's during the campaign; Afghanistan, the right war, was being slighted by concentration on Iraq, the bad one. It was, he said, a typical example of Bush's poor leadership, which he proposed to reverse once he got to the White House.

Limbaugh played a clip of Obama saying this, and then turned the microphone over to James Golden, who introduced himself as "Bo Snerdley, African-American-in-good-standing-and-certified-black-enough-to-criticize-Obama guy." Snerdley said he doubted Obama was accurately portraying the situation and asked for the name of the captain. Switching into dialect he said, "On behalf of our EIB brothers and sisters in the hood, we're asking you, Mr. Obama, what's up with that, yo? You got proof? On behalf of our Hispanic brothers and sisters, we're asking, *Señor Obama, es verdad?*"

Limbaugh's intention was not to question Obama's veracity. It had very little to do with Obama. He was taking the challenge of opposing a black candidate and turning it into an opportunity to make fun of the Democratic Party's convoluted racial coalition building and the racial authenticity tests of the American left. In June, Charles Steele, the former president of the Southern Christian Leadership Conference, Martin Luther King's old group, claimed that Obama was getting an easy ride from white people because he wasn't really black. "Why are they attacking Michelle Obama, First Lady Michelle Obama, and not really attacking, to that degree, her husband?" Reverend Steele wondered aloud. "Because he has no slave blood in him. He does not have any slave blood in him, but Michelle does." It wasn't hard to figure out Reverend Steele's meaning—that Americans have an easier time dealing with blacks whose ancestors were not chattel for four centuries—but expressing it in terms of blood levels conjured up the old Jim Crow "one drop" criterion. Limbaugh, who sometimes reminds his audience that Democrats (including Bill Clinton's mentor, Senator William Fulbright of Arkansas) were historically the party of racial discrimination and segregation, knew what to do. He turned the microphone over to Golden once more, who went on the air as Bo Snerdley, "Official Barack Criticizer for the EIB Network, certified black enough to criticize with a blend of imported and domestic one hundred percent fortified slave blood."

Throughout the campaign, Obama sent mixed messages about his cultural identity. When Jesse Jackson and Al Sharpton ran for president, they sounded unmistakably like themselves, black preachers. Obama's self didn't sound like that. Black English was not his mother tongue. For national audiences he spoke in the flat, Midwestern tone of the Kansan grandparents who raised him. When he appeared before black audiences, in churches or at venues like the convention of Al Sharpton's National Action Network, he slowed and softened his speech and dropped in South Side Chicago expressions (but never any South Side attitude).

Linguistic flexibility is common political practice. Al Gore spoke Southern in Tennessee and Northern above the Mason-Dixon Line. In the campaign of 2004, Bostonian John Forbes Kennedy went to a store in rural Ohio and asked, "Can I get me a hunting license here?" And who can forget candidate Hillary Clinton at a civil rights meeting in Selma, Alabama, trying to channel the gospel style of the Reverend James Cleveland ("I don't feel no ways tired / I come too far from where I started from / Nobody told me that the road would be easy"). But in Obama's case there was a special significance to his changing dialects.

During the campaign, a black waitress at Ben's Chili Bowl in Washington, D.C., asked the candidate if he wanted change, and Obama replied, "Nah, we straight." A Politico reporter, Nia-Malika Henderson, explained that this exchange was conducted in black code. "The phrase was so subtle some listeners missed it. The reporter on pool duty quoted Obama as saying, 'No, we're straight.' But many other listeners did not miss it. A video of the exchange became an Internet hit, and there was a clear moment of recognition among many blacks, who got a kick out of their Harvard-educated president sounding, as one commenter wrote on a hip-hop site, 'mad cool.'"

"Mad cool" in the barbershop in Harlem plays differently at the Varsity in Cape. Same with the famous fist-bump that Barack and Michelle shared at the Democratic Convention. Something seemed to be going on that white middle America didn't get, a change of cultural signals they failed to decode. Such changes had happened before, in music and other forms of popular entertainment, and eventually they were accepted and adopted. The high-five was once considered a radical greeting; today parents teach it to their two-year-olds. "Right on" and "Uptight" and "Do your thing" went from 125th Street to Sesame Street as an enrichment of the English language. Go to any Elks Club in Michigan on a Saturday night and you will find baby boomers dancing a flat-footed variation of the Watusi to the sounds of Motown. In a few years, these same Elks will be fist-bumping and saying "Nah, we straight," without giving it a thought. But meeting these innovations for the first time in a presidential campaign was jarring; a lot of people were suspicious that they were a form of secret black communication, something that has animated the white American imagination since drumming was banned during slavery.

This concern was fueled by Obama's longtime relationship with the Reverend Jeremiah Wright, his pastor and mentor in Chicago. Trinity United Church of Christ, Obama's longtime congregation, preaches black liberation theology. According to its Web site, the church is "Unashamedly Black and Unapologetically Christian. . . . Our roots in the Black religious experience and tradition are deep, lasting and permanent. We are an African people, and remain 'true to our native land,' the mother continent, the cradle of civilization. God has superintended our pilgrimage through the days of slavery, the days of segregation, and the long night of racism. It is God who gives us the strength and courage to continuously address injustice as a people, and as a congregation. We constantly affirm our trust in God through cultural expression of a Black worship service and ministries which address the Black Community."

Video clips of Reverend Wright's heated anti-American sermons about "the USA of KKK" and American chickens coming home to roost on 9/11—shown first on FOX News and then, grudgingly, on other networks—made it clear who Obama's minister thought was the source of injustice. Such rhetoric is the stuff of the black liberation church, and Obama may very well have ignored it, as many candidates have ignored the sermons of their pastors over the years. But white America heard the congregation cheering Wright and found it disconcerting. The fact that

Obama had dedicated one of his books to Wright added to a general sense that there was something deeply different and alienated about the senator from Illinois and his exclusionary brand of religion.

Michelle Obama compounded the problem during the election campaign when she called the United States a "mean" country and said that her husband's candidacy had made her proud, for the first time, to be an American. Obama's advisers realized that these remarks were too blatantly honest and revealing, and with the candidate's approval, they scheduled appearances that would enable Michelle to walk them back and show the country that she was just as sweet and friendly as the nice (white) girl next door.

Limbaugh had been concerned about Obama's view of America for a long time. From his perspective, he was right to be. Obama did not share Limbaugh's veneration of the founding fathers or the conviction that the Constitution was a near-perfect document. He saw the United States as a deeply flawed nation whose international behavior was often aggressive and self-aggrandizing. He ran as a revolutionary, someone who would alter and improve precisely those things about America that Limbaugh most wanted to preserve. Rush had always been a master of ambiguity—Is he serious? Is he kidding?—and he saw that Obama had a similar skill, to be Harlem or Harvard, Hawaii or Kansas, a man of the world or a bro from the hood, as the occasion demanded. Limbaugh wanted to make the point that Obama was a shape-shifter, but the candidate was too good at it. His wife, who had less practice, made a better target.

Michelle Obama opened the Democratic National Convention with a major speech. Obama's team worked with her on a talk that would showcase her as a patriotic mom from the Midwest who happened to be African American. They came up with a template: The upscale, non-threatening, good-natured cast of the *Bill Cosby Show*. The media, briefed in advance on the message, prepped the country. "Michelle Obama has to make this the Huxtables," said NBC's Norah O'Donnell. "Present the Huxtable image of the Obamas," urged Eugene Robinson of the *Washington Post*. "The challenge is making the Obama family into the Huxtables," said Rachel Maddow on MSNBC. Her colleague Chris Matthews begged Michelle to show the country, "This is the Bill Cosby family!"

The future first lady stayed on script, and the next day Rush un-leashed his Official Criticizer. "It was evident, my dear, that you have been handled," James Golden said. "We did not see the real Michelle. . . . [Y]ou papered things over with a nondescript presentation that could have come from Martha Stewart's America."

Golden then slipped into his Bo Snerdley persona.

What was up with you last night, girl? The big lights all up on you and you come out frontin' instead of breaking it down, yo? Ever since you broke about being proud for the first time, you've been taking heat. Last night was your chance, yo. You said Amer-ica was mean, everybody went off on you. Last night you coulda explain it, okay . . . you coulda told 'em like, yo, listen, yeah sometimes I'm mad, check it out, if you came from where I came from you be mad, too, okay? Schools all messed up, brothers can't get no jobs. . . . Yeah I'm mad. You all be mad, too, if this was going on in your neighborhood, okay, criminals running all up and down the street, come on, yo, it ain't like that up in white land where Hillary live, okay?

    . . . look, you are a strong black sister, yo, come from our culture, you were out there fronting like you Michelle Partridge, everything is cute. Come on, you coulda told them, for instance, Fourth of July, yo man, we ain't down with that, June 15th is when we're free, but that don't mean we don't love America, ev-erybody is down with this, you know? Okay, look, Michelle, you Obama's shorty, you got the slave blood, he don't. You supposed to understand what it is, and you are supposed to break it down for us. What did you do? You were fronting, girl. Fake.

Limbaugh himself concentrated his fire on the Drive-By Media, which he accused of attempting to throttle criticism of Obama by enforc-ing a code of acceptable commentary:

When Obama started out, we couldn't talk about his big ears 'cause that made him nervous. We've gone from that to this: Not only can we not mention his ears. Now we can't talk about his mother. We can't talk about his father. We can't talk about his grandmother unless he brings her up as a "typical white person."

We can't talk about his wife, can't talk about his preacher, can't talk about his terrorist friends, can't talk about his voting record, can't talk about his religion. We can't talk about appeasement. We can't talk about color; we can't talk about lack of color. We can't talk about race. We can't talk about bombers and mobsters who are his friends. We can't talk about schooling. We can't talk about his name, "Hussein." We can't talk about his lack of experience. Can't talk about his income. Can't talk about his flag pin. We can't call him a liberal. It started out we just couldn't talk about his ears. Now we can't say anything about him.

After the election, the Washington press corps took to writing about Obama in heroic terms, comparing him with the great figures of American history. Limbaugh regarded this as a blatant dereliction of duty. During the campaign, Hillary Clinton had mocked her opponent's ethereal style, and now, taking a page out of her playbook, he began calling Obama "the Messiah."

Limbaugh was quick to notice that, despite his reputation for eloquence, Obama was not much of an extemporaneous speaker. In fact, the new president rarely spoke without a teleprompter. After Obama accidently read the speech of his guest, the Irish prime minister, instead of his own, Limbaugh developed the conceit that the teleprompter, not Obama, was in charge.

"Teleprompter, do you have a name?" he asked. "In your opinion, how is President Obama doing so far? Did he convey the level of anger you hoped for regarding what you told him to say about AIG? Teleprompter, is the president ever argumentative with you, or is he compliant with your instructions? Are you dating anybody, Teleprompter? Mac or PC?" This bit caught on, and when the wind blew over the teleprompter during a speech by Vice President Biden, he cracked, "What am I going to tell the president when I tell him his teleprompter is broken? What will he do then?"

The mainstream comics and satirists were protective of the new administration. David Letterman attacked the teleprompter gimmick as "nitpicking," and ran "Teleprompter vs. No Teleprompter," a segment that contrasted an eloquent passage of Obama's address to Congress with George W. Bush's awkwardly extemporizing at a press conference. It took almost an entire year for *Saturday Night Live* to run a critical skit, based on the premise that Obama had accomplished nothing in office. Jon Stewart followed a few days later with a similar routine. This was so unusual that it made news. "Is President Obama in trouble with his late-night comedy base?" asked *New York Times* reporter Mark Leibovich, who, with considerable understatement, noted that late-night comedy had been "relatively gentle" on the new president. "Mr. Obama has of course been a puzzle to comedians for some time," he wrote. "They agonized during the campaign about how his low-key and confident manner did not lend itself to edgy caricature. The challenge was made greater by the sensitivities inherent to lampooning a black candidate."

In fact, the president and his administration—like all presidents and administrations—produced a daily menu of comic possibilities, from pompous declaration to incompetent execution. But liberal satirists (on the networks and Comedy Central there is no other kind), like nervous parents at a high school play, watched with crossed fingers and scowls for anyone rude enough to giggle at the performance. There was nothing funny here! This fine young man was doing his very best! And, of course, there were those "special sensitivities" to consider.

This left the field pretty much to Limbaugh, who had no trouble at all discerning and mocking the new president's narcissism, his bowing and scraping to Third World dictators, his frequent changes of mind, and the pretense that he wanted a bipartisan government. Not all his jokes were funny; many were crude. But they demonstrated that the nation's comics, like its serious journalists, weren't doing their jobs.

Four months into Obama's presidency, the guns were turned around, as the White House Correspondents' Association held its annual gala dinner at the Washington Hilton Hotel. The WHCA is a venerable Washington institution founded in 1914, during the administration of Woodrow Wilson. Presidents since Calvin Coolidge had been guests. During

World War II, the banquet was one of the rare public social events Franklin D. Roosevelt allowed himself to attend.

The WHCA Dinner is a black-tie affair that has gone show-biz in recent years. Journalists invite celebrity guests and a comedian-MC delivers political jokes. In 2006 Steven Colbert eviscerated George W. Bush in his routine, telling the president not to worry about poor poll numbers because statistics merely reflected reality, and reality "has a well-known liberal bias." The takedown made Colbert a hero to Democrats, but some members of the WHCA thought it was too rough. The following year the anodyne impersonator Rich Little was brought in to make amends.

This time the comedian-in-residence was Wanda Sykes. It was an interesting choice. Sykes is a black, openly lesbian comedienne who works in the misanthropic style of the great Jackie "Moms" Mabley. Obama's presence on the dais with her was a sign to his African American base— much louder and bolder than "we straight"—that the president was not dropping hot sauce for mayonnaise.

Traditionally the master of ceremonies skewers the president, but Sykes tossed a few softballs at him and then turned to her real target. "Mr. President, Rush Limbaugh said he hopes this administration fails . . . like, 'I don't care about people losing their homes, their jobs, or our soldiers in Iraq.' He just wants our country to fail. To me, that's treason. He's not saying anything differently than Osama bin Laden is saying. You know you might want to look into this, sir, because I think Rush Limbaugh was the twentieth hijacker, but he was just so strung out on OxyContin he missed his flight."

The crowd laughed, and Obama, after hesitating a moment, broke into a grin. Sykes turned to him and said, "Too much? You're laughing inside, I know you're laughing. Rush Limbaugh—'I hope the country fails.' I hope his kidneys fail, how about that? He needs a waterboarding, is what he needs." At this point Obama stopped grinning; Sykes had finally gone too far. He saw the humor in hooking Rush up to a broken dialysis machine, but waterboarding was nothing to joke about.

Atypically, Limbaugh didn't say a word on the air about Sykes's routine, or the fact that the president of the United States had smiled broadly, in front of the entire country, about the prospect of his death. He was disconcerted, though, and he was right to be. He was in first place on the enemies list of the president of the United States. The day after the correspondents' dinner he sent me an e-mail: "I know I am a target and I know I will be destroyed eventually. I fear that all I have accomplished and all the wealth I have accumulated will be taken from me, to the cheers of the crowd. I know I am hated and despised by the American Left."

CHAPTER THIRTEEN

THE GUNS OF AUGUST

Two weeks after the WHCA dinner, President Obama nominated Judge Sonia Sotomayor to the Supreme Court vacancy left by the retirement of Justice David Souter. The appointment of the first Hispanic to the High Court was warmly welcomed by liberals as a harbinger of the change that Obama had promised in the campaign.

Limbaugh was not so welcoming. Ten years earlier, when Sotomayor had been appointed to the Federal Court of Appeals in New York, Rush predicted that she was being groomed for a seat on the Supreme Court and urged Republicans to oppose her nomination. Sotomayor had been confirmed and served as an appellate judge, without any special distinction or particular controversy. Her power was in her biography, that of the daughter of a poor Puerto Rican widow, raised in a Bronx housing project, who, by dint of hard work—and affirmative action—made it to Princeton and Yale Law School. Sotomayor was also important to the Obama coalition, which is premised on a solid black-Hispanic alliance. Appointing Sotomayor was good politics, especially since it also made a lot of Democratic women, still smarting from Hillary Clinton's primary defeat, feel included.

To Limbaugh, Sotomayor symbolized all that was wrong with the liberal, multicultural approach to jurisprudence. She had once remarked publicly that she hoped a "wise Latina" judge would make better decisions than a white man. Limbaugh demanded to know what would have happened to a white man who made such a statement about Hispanic women. The question, of course, was rhetorical. No male candidate could have survived it. Limbaugh and Newt Gingrich accused her of reverse racism.

At a White House briefing, a reporter asked spokesman Robert Gibbs about the charge. Gibbs responded with something that sounded like a threat: "I think it is probably important for anybody involved in this debate to be exceedingly careful with the way in which they've decided to describe different aspects of this impending confirmation," he said.

"Robert Gibbs at the White House yesterday warned people like me to be very careful about what we say about Sonia Sotomayor," Limbaugh said the following day. "So, ladies and gentlemen, I want you to turn your radio up because I'm going to have to whisper this so that they don't hear [it] at the White House. In fact, those of you who can, if you're in your cars, roll up your windows. Those of you who are at home, take your radios to the bathroom, close the doors. Make sure that no one else hears what I'm about to tell you about Sonia Sotomayor." No sensational material was forthcoming. The "warning" was theater, a way of mocking the White House press office's effort to dampen what appeared to be effective criticism of Sotomayor.

It failed, of course. Republicans continued to dig and, eventually, came up with a video clip of a speech that Judge Sotomayor delivered at Duke Law School in 2005, in which she said that the Court of Appeals "is where policy is made, and I know, this is on tape and I should never say that because we don't make law, I know, I know . . ." The audience laughed nervously; the accusation that judges legislated from the bench is at the heart of the conservative critique of liberal jurisprudence. Limbaugh played the tape again and again, adding his own legal commentary. Big Rush would have been proud to hear his son expounding with such passion on issues of constitutional law.

Limbaugh went after Sotomayor especially hard over her opinion in the case of *Ricci v. DeStefano*. In 2003 the city of New Haven, Connecticut, gave written and oral examinations to firefighters for promotion. There were nine vacancies for captain, and they went to the nine highest scorers—seven whites and two "Hispanics" who may or may not have been "white" (the Census Bureau doesn't regard "Hispanic" as a racial category). Whites also scored highest on the lieutenant exam and filled all eight available slots. The city of New Haven invalidated the results of the tests. The white and Hispanic firefighters sued, claiming their rights had been violated. A law suit followed. The district court upheld the city's decision, which had been based on the argument that blacks are a protected minority and were unfairly impacted by the results of the test. The Court of Appeals, which included Sotomayor, upheld the lower court's decision. But, in a fluke of timing, the decision was reversed by the Supreme Court right in the middle of Sotomayor's nomination, and it became a cause célèbre. Limbaugh once again saw it as an example of reverse racism and linked it to President Obama's remark that he wanted judges who were "empathetic." Limbaugh understood that empathy is in the eye of the beholder. He (and his mostly white, male listeners) had no trouble imagining how the doctrine of multicultural empathy might affect them in a court of law.

In the end, Judge Sotomayor was confirmed easily. She was not, despite some ill-considered remarks, a radical, as her Senate hearing made clear. In any case, the Democrats had an insuperable majority in the Senate, and many Republicans didn't want to go back home having voted against a qualified Hispanic woman.

Besides, Sotomayor wouldn't tip the balance of the Court. Limbaugh knew he would lose this one, but he was laying down a marker for Obama. No future liberal nominee to the Court, no matter how personally virtuous, experienced, intellectually accomplished, or ethnically attractive, would get a free pass. In Limbaugh's view, judicial liberalism was its own disqualifier.

Limbaugh's opposition to Judge Sotomayor was a gift to Democrats courting the Hispanic vote. President George W. Bush won almost half these votes in 2004, and while Obama had received a comfortable majority in 2008, Latinos, especially the Mexican American community, were still up for grabs. But Limbaugh didn't believe that the GOP could beat the Democrats at the game of ethnic pandering. "The Republican Party, when it wins, does not do identity politics," he told an interviewer. "We don't have one policy for Hispanics, another for blacks, and another for whites. That's not how Republicans win; it's how Democrats win." As proof he pointed to the poor showing that McCain, the champion of immigration reform, had made among Spanish-speaking voters in the 2008 election.

Limbaugh himself became an issue in that election when the Democrats aired Spanish-language TV ads featuring an alleged comment he made about "stupid and unskilled Mexicans" and another in which he supposedly told Mexican Americans to "shut your mouth or you get out." "John McCain and his Republican friends have two faces," says the narrator in Spanish. "One that says lies just to get our vote . . . and another, even worse, that continues the policies of George Bush that put special interests ahead of working families. John McCain . . . more of the same old Republican tricks."

ABC's Jake Tapper, one of the few network journalists who retained a modicum of professional distance from the Obama campaign, checked the ad and reported that it was bogus.

The first "quote" was from a 1993 monologue on NAFTA in which Limbaugh said that the bill would cause "unskilled, stupid Mexicans" to take the place of "unskilled, stupid Americans." And "shut your mouth" had nothing to do with immigrants. It was part of a bit on Limbaugh's Laws of Immigration: "First, if you immigrate to our country, you have to speak the native language. You have to be a professional or an investor; no unskilled labor." No government business would be conducted in a foreign language, he said, and the schools would not offer bilingual education. "If you're in our country, you cannot be a burden to taxpayers. You are not entitled to welfare, food stamps, or other government goodies . . . if you want to buy land, it'll be restricted. No waterfront, for instance. As a foreigner, you must relinquish individual rights to the property. And another thing: You don't have the right to protest. You're allowed no demonstrations, no foreign flag waving, no political organizing, no bad-mouthing our president or his policies. You're a foreigner: shut your mouth or get out! And if you come here illegally, you're going to jail."

There was a punch line to this rant: These are Mexican laws.

"That's how the Mexican government handles immigrants to their country. Yet Mexicans come here illegally and protest in our streets!"

I asked Limbaugh how he felt to be demonized in a language he doesn't speak. It gave him an idea. "Maybe I should start broadcasting my show in Spanish," he said. "Of course, I'd have to find a broadcaster who could do it with my charisma and showmanship, but you never know. Maybe I can find one. It's a thought."

■ ■ ■ ■

Just as the Sotomayor controversy was dying down, another racially charged incident made headlines. Harvard Professor Henry "Skip" Gates, a black man in his late fifties, was arrested in Cambridge by a white policeman who had received a report that someone had been seen breaking into a house. That someone was Gates, and the house was his. He had been abroad, returned home from the airport, and found his door jammed. He and his driver jimmied the lock, which is what set off a neighbor's call to the cops. Gates took umbrage at the officer's request for some form of identification and an argument ensued. Professor Gates wound up handcuffed and booked for disorderly conduct.

That evening, during a press conference, a reporter asked President Obama about the incident. Obama, who is a friend of Gates, said he didn't know the facts or what role race played in the event, and added, "I think it's fair to say, number one, any of us would be pretty angry; number two, that the Cambridge police acted stupidly in arresting somebody when there was already proof that they were in their own home; and, number three, what I think we know, separate and apart from this incident, is that there is a long history in this country of African Americans and Latinos being stopped by law enforcement disproportionately. And that's just a fact."

Shooting from the hip like that was a rookie presidential mistake. The cop, it turned out, was neither a racist nor stupid; in fact, he was a highly regarded veteran of the Cambridge force who taught courses in racially sensitive policing to new officers. And Professor Gates hadn't been an entirely innocent figure in the argument that led to his arrest. In fact, it was alleged, he had made some unflattering comments about the cop's mother. Obama, who had come to office promising to heal racial rifts, invited Gates and the officer to the White House for a beer, a handshake, and a photo op. Limbaugh dismissed it as "two guys with an attitude" who had jumped all over a cop and didn't even apologize.

It wasn't a great moment in Obama's presidency, but he was certainly right about one thing: there is a long history of blacks being stopped by the police for no good reason. Limbaugh thought that the remark, coming from the country's chief law-enforcement officer, was extreme and inappropriate, a sign of what he saw as Obama's basic disaffection with the country he had been elected to lead. In an interview with Greta Van Susteren on FOX News, he said, "Let's face it. President Obama is black, and I think he's got a chip on his shoulder."

■ ■ ■ ■

Rush and I were both raised at a time of racial optimism and naïveté, when the goal of decent white people was an integrated society. We were taught that skin color shouldn't matter, that we were all basically the same, that we should judge others not by their color but the content of their character. And if we didn't achieve this in practice, or even try very hard—and most of us didn't—it was, at least, the ideal that decent people subscribed to.

But things changed. Malcolm X introduced a compelling analysis of the black condition in America that included a historical counternarrative leading to a doctrine of racial nationalism and separatism. In one of his most famous metaphors, he compared black integrationists like Martin Luther King to "house Negroes" who loved the slave master more than the master loved himself. The black masses, he said, were "field Negroes" who caught hell every day and hated white people. "When the master's house caught on fire, the field Negro prayed for a wind, for a breeze. When the master got sick, the field Negro prayed that he died . . . He was intelligent." The militancy of Malcolm X begat the Black Power movement (just as Marcus Garvey and W. E. B. Du Bois begat Malcolm) and encouraged African American intellectuals to see themselves not as Americans but as people of color whose interests and sympathies were properly aligned with the (anti-American) Third World.

White America was baffled by this. At the very moment the United States was passing landmark civil rights, black people (still known in polite circles as "Negroes") were rioting in the streets and kicking well-meaning whites out of the civil rights movement. How could that be? Then Dr. King was murdered, more rioting followed, and more white reaction. Efforts to integrate schools by enforced bussing were violently opposed in Northern Democratic cities like Boston and my own home town of Pontiac, Michigan. The Republican Party capitalized on white fear and disaffection with the "southern strategy" that brought Richard Nixon to office. Blacks left the Republican Party en masse and became a permanent wing of the Democratic Party. Meanwhile, the American intelligentsia stopped talking in terms of an integrationist, national melting pot and adopted a tribal model, in which righteously disaffected minorities (blacks, women, gays, Hispanics, and Native Americans) made group identity the basis for their politics.

While all this was going on, Rush Limbaugh was in the studio spinning oldies or selling tickets for the Kansas City Royals. When he emerged, blinking, into the harsh light of political combat in the mid-1980s, he came armed with the belief in color-blindness that had been in vogue twenty years earlier. Mort Sahl once said that anyone who maintains a consistent position in America will eventually be tried for treason. Or racism.

Race was on Limbaugh's mind when I went down to Palm Beach to see him in the summer of 2009. By then we had spent hours together talking and exchanged more than a hundred e-mail messages; and, of course, I had listened to his show almost daily for several years. I had a pretty good idea of what he did and didn't think on a range of matters. Including race. I told him that I thought he had a blind spot on the subject.

Limbaugh asked me what I meant by a blind spot, and I mentioned his unwillingness to see why American blacks didn't share his narrative of America as a uniquely virtuous nation.

"The Constitution defined Negroes as property. They counted as three-fifths of a human for the purpose of the census. You can see why that might be a problem," I said.

"The Framers had to accommodate slave states," Limbaugh said. "Those were the actual politics of the situation. And the Constitution set up a process to gradually end slavery. That stuff legally has been washed away and dealt with."

"Sure, but a lot of the early founders were slaveholders. Washington, Jefferson. Imagine how a black kid feels going to a school named after a man who owned slaves."

Limbaugh was incredulous. "The founding fathers were not oppressors," he said. "And at some point, you have to let go. We fought a war. And we've done what we can to level the playing field."

"So, you don't feel guilty?"

"No, not in perpetuity. That keeps the races divided. I plant myself firmly in reality. I want everyone to experience the greatness of this country. And they can. We have a black president now. We have Oprah. I'm bullish on America as it exists today. Negative people make other people sick. Stop thinking of yourself as a hyphenated American. We all have obstacles. I have, because of my size and my opinions. But I believe in individuals, everyone succeeding. I have never kept anyone back or subjugated anyone."

The following day I got to the studio early and dropped in on James Golden. He was sitting in his office going over some mail, but he didn't mind being interrupted. Since our first Huey Newton meets the Mainstream Media moment, we had developed an easy connection. We're about the same age, like the same kind of music, and have some experiences in common. And I admired Golden for his willingness to stand up for his views. "After you've been called an Uncle Tom for the two millionth time, it loses its meaning," he told me. "I'm a conservative, okay? That's how I see the world. My mother is part of the Democrat machine in New York—she couldn't understand how I could be a conservative, but I am one. And I was one before I went to work for Rush. I was already in the radio business in New York, and I saw a lot of so-called liberals who were real racists. And I can tell you, Rush isn't."

Golden has been screening Limbaugh's calls and acting as his alter ego going back to the start of the national show. "When he came to ABC in 1988, the in-joke was that AM radio was going to be Muzak at the Hilton Hotels. Howard Stern was on FM. Imus was on WNBC, but he wasn't even syndicated. Everybody ABC tried, all the big DJs from around the country, bombed. I wasn't happy at ABC and I quit, which is when Rush hired me for his show. He had no idea what my politics were and he never asked."

One day, early on, Limbaugh walked into the studio and found Golden in tears. He was broke and couldn't pay his bills. The next day, Limbaugh handed him an envelope with five thousand dollars in it. "Rush wasn't rich then," says Golden. "Five thousand was a lot of money to him. He told me, 'This is a gift, not a loan,' and didn't mention it again. At that moment I decided, anything I can do for the guy, I'm in. I hear people call him every name in the book, especially on race. They have no fucking clue who this man is."

Golden is a voracious reader of history, and we were chatting about World War I when Limbaugh walked into the room. "James," he said, "I want to ask you a question. We were talking yesterday and, let me put it this way, would it ever bother you to go to a school named George Washington or Thomas Jefferson because they were slave owners?"

Golden laughed. "Well, I can tell you that when I was in school, I was the one who stood up in English class and gave a speech about why the Black Panthers are needed."

Limbaugh look befuddled. "But James, you're a conservative," he said.

"That's right, I am."

"You're an American patriot."

Golden nodded. "I am. Absolutely. But I don't celebrate the Fourth of July—that's not my Independence Day. That's white people's Independence Day." Something clicked, and I remembered Golden, as Bo Snerdley, riffing on how Michelle Obama was "frontin'" in her speech at the Democratic National Convention when she didn't tell the nation that blacks don't consider the Fourth of July to be their Independence Day. Evidently Limbaugh hadn't been listening, or maybe he thought Golden was just kidding. Now he seemed shocked to discover that Bo Snerdley, the Official Obama Criticizer, Rush's sidekick for two decades, a conservative in the very best kind of standing, didn't celebrate the nation's birthday. Limbaugh has an expressive face, and I could see him turning the matter over in his mind.

Our talk about race obviously made an impression. A few weeks later Rush brought it up on the air. "There's a guy writing a book about me and the last time I sat down and did an interview with him, it was down here in Florida, and he said, 'I don't think you get it about race.'" Limbaugh described our conversation about the Constitution and slavery and his own experiences. "I told him some stories about growing up," he said. "I told him about our maid that came in two or three times a week named Alberta. We called her Bertie. She was like a grandmother to my brother and me, and my mom and dad. My mother took her home and I'd drive in the car. I'm six or seven years old. I saw where Bertie lived and it made me sick. I talked to my parents about it. I said, 'Why does this happen?' They sat me down and they talked to me about the circumstances. It was my father that enabled Bertie to buy a house outside of that neighborhood and get her a job at . . . I think it was at Woolworth's. I'm telling this author all this stuff and I don't know if it's registering at all—and I'm, frankly, angry I have to tell it. I'm angry that I have to say this stuff. Here's a guy doing a book on me who I don't know if he thinks [I'm a racist] or if he's just asking the question because he thinks readers are going to want to know it."

It was cringe inducing to hear Limbaugh defend his lack of bias by mentioning his housekeeper. Sophisticated people don't say such things. Race talk in America is carried out in euphemism and politically correct code, a point Attorney General Eric Holder had made earlier that year when he said that Americans are cowards when it comes to candidly discussing race. Limbaugh has been conducting that sort of conversation, from the perspective of a traditional white integrationist. He regards black nationalism and black liberation theology as separatist, opposes affirmative action as a racial quota system, and sees multiculturalism as an effort to undermine a national American identity. These views are conservative, but they are not racist, and he sees the accusation that he is a racist as a form of liberal Kryptonite. "I didn't become a racist until somebody called me one when I started this radio show," he said. "I wasn't a racist up until 1988, and then somebody called me one—and ever since I was called a racist, I've been one, according to the media. And yet I never was one and I'm not one now." But Limbaugh is not quite as innocent as he sounds. He has known from the start that mocking Al Sharpton and Jesse Jackson as racial shakedown artists ("the Justice Brothers") or calling the NAACP a wholly owned subsidiary of the Democratic Party were not likely to make him a beloved figure in the black community. And he certainly knew that bits like "The Magic Negro" parody would be interpreted by his enemies as racist. Joe Biden could get away with marveling, during the 2008 primary campaign, that Barack Obama was "clean" and "articulate"; Senator Robert Byrd could muse publicly about "white niggers" without losing his honored place in the Democratic Party. Their reputation as liberals entitled them to racial get-out-of-jail-free cards. Limbaugh didn't have one of those. He didn't know it yet, but he would need one.

CHAPTER FOURTEEN

WELCOME TO THE NFL

From his early boyhood, Rusty Limbaugh has been sports crazy. Baseball was his first love, but his experience with the Kansas City Royals cooled his ardor. Besides, in Pittsburgh, in the 1970s, he fell for the "the greatest team of all time," the Steelers. Football back then was the sport of Republicans. The anti-war left despised the NFL, with its long bombs and ground attacks and martial values. Richard Nixon, a frustrated college player, diagrammed plays in the Oval Office and sent them over to the coaching staff of the Washington Redskins. His successor, Gerald Ford, had been a football star at the University of Michigan, good enough to have received contract offers from the Detroit Lions and the Green Bay Packers (which he turned down). Ronald Reagan, another college player, starred in a biopic about Notre Dame football hero George Gipp and, in the White House, sometimes channeled the character.

Limbaugh was no Gipper. After his sophomore years on the Central High team, the closest he came to playing was in touch games organized by George Brett in Kansas City. But Limbaugh loved pro football, and as his fame and wealth grew, he was able to attend games all over the country, sit in owners' boxes, chat with coaches and players, and discuss intricacies with analysts. Monday through Friday he devoted himself to the political area, but he had weekends off, and the thought of spending them combining his two loves, broadcasting and football, appealed to him. In 2000 he discussed the possibility of joining ABC's *Monday Night Football* media team, but nothing came of it.

Three years later, ESPN hired Limbaugh as an analyst for its flagship show, *Sunday NFL Countdown.* The broadcast team also included Chris Berman and three former NFL stars, Tom Jackson, Steve Young, and Michael Irvin. There was plenty of professional football expertise in the group. Rush was hired, as ESPN itself said, to stir debate and bring in viewers. He did his job. In the first month he was on the show, ratings went up 10 percent. On his fourth (and as it turned out, final) appearance, *Sunday NFL Countdown* had its biggest audience in more than six years.

The discussion on that last broadcast focused on Philadelphia Eagles quarterback Donovan McNabb, an all-star who was in the midst of one of his weakest pro seasons. Up for discussion was the question: Is Donovan McNabb regressing?

Limbaugh didn't accept the premise. "Sorry to say this, I don't think he's [McNabb] been that good from the get-go. I think what we've had here is a little social concern in the NFL. The media has been very desirous that a black quarterback do well, black coaches and black quarterbacks doing well. There is a little hope invested in McNabb, and he got a lot of credit for the performance of this team that he didn't deserve. The defense carried this team."

Tom Jackson and Steve Young disagreed with Limbaugh's assessment of McNabb's ability, which was, obviously, a matter of opinion. But neither they nor Irvin disputed that the league and the football media (much of which is a mouthpiece for the NFL and its teams) were working for racial diversity. At the start of 2003, Commissioner Paul Tagliabue actually announced a policy, known as the Rooney Rule, requiring teams looking for head coaches to include black candidates among those they interviewed.

The only guy on a football team more visible than the coach is the quarterback, and for decades quarterback was considered a white position. Even the great Warren Moon had to play in Canada for six years before finding a team that would take him. By the 1990s this was an embarrassment to the NFL, as well as a marketing problem. More than half the players and a great many fans were African Americans. The league wanted and needed black quarterbacks, but there wasn't much of a supply, mostly because promising black high school quarterbacks had been routinely converted into running backs, pass receivers, or defensive backs at the college level. But there were black quarterbacks at traditionally black colleges. In 1995 Steve McNair of Alcorn State was selected number three in the draft by the Houston Oilers; by 1997 he was the starting quarterback. His success opened the way for others. In 1999 McNabb was the first black quarterback to be taken number two in the draft; two others, Akili Smith and Daunte Culpepper, were selected in the first round. Michael Vick was the first overall pick in 2001. By the time Limbaugh addressed the McNabb issue, there were ten black quarterbacks in the NFL, seven of them starters.

Like all football fans, Limbaugh was aware of the racial change in the premier position. He was a social commentator and he made a social comment. It hadn't been off the cuff, either. Limbaugh later said on the air that he had planned it. "I weighed it, I balanced it, but you know what I decided? Look, they brought me in to be who I am. This is what I think. It's a sports issue. It's a sports opinion."

At the time, Limbaugh's opinion didn't seem to disturb or surprise his fellow analysts. Only Jackson questioned him: "So, Rush, once you make that investment though, once you make that investment in [McNabb], it's a done deal," he said.

"I'm saying it's a good investment," Limbaugh replied. "Don't misunderstand. I just don't think he's as good as everybody says he has been."

"Rush has a point," said Michael Irvin, who, like Jackson, is black.

"Well, [McNabb] certainly hasn't matured," said Steve Young, who is white.

That was Sunday. On Tuesday, the *Philadelphia Daily News* published an interview with McNabb. "It's sad we've got to go to skin color. I thought we were through with that whole thing," he said.

At first, ESPN Vice President Mark Shapiro defended Limbaugh. "Rush was arguing McNabb is essentially overrated and that his success is more in part due to the team assembled around him," he said. "Rush is also arguing that McNabb has been propped up because the media is desirous to have successful black quarterbacks, much the same as others have claimed the media is desirous to have Chris Simms succeed because of his father [ex-quarterback Phil Simms]. We brought Rush in for no-holds-barred opinion. Early on, he has delivered."

Shapiro spoke too soon. Three Democratic presidential candidates—Howard Dean, Wesley Clark, and Al Sharpton—called for Limbaugh to be fired. So did the National Association of Black Journalists. Tom Jackson said that he would no longer appear with Limbaugh. ESPN decided that it didn't want controversy if it was going to be so controversial. On Wednesday the network issued another statement: "Although Mr. Limbaugh today stated that his comments had 'no racist intent whatsoever,' we have communicated to Mr. Limbaugh that his comments were insensitive and inappropriate." Limbaugh resigned and ESPN expressed its relief in a press release: "We believe that he took the appropriate action to resolve this matter expeditiously," the league said.

When the controversy first burst, Limbaugh snapped back against his perennial adversary, the liberal media. "If you don't say what the appointed, anointed superiorists and those who think that they are at the top of judgmentalism—if you don't say what they want to hear, if you don't say what they think is right, then not only are they going to disagree with you, then they're going to demand that you not be allowed to say it, that you not be given a position or forum to say it because they don't want to hear it. Now, that is discriminatory in itself." But veteran Limbaugh listeners sensed that he wasn't counterpunching with his usual ferocity. This impression was confirmed on Wednesday, when he left ESPN. Since when did El Rushbo throw in the towel? Mike Lupica of the *New York Daily News* thought it showed that Rush was all talk and no heart. "He did it because he couldn't take the heat . . . He wants to be the rough, tough, truth-telling conscience of America. But the very first time he gets hit, he quits on his stool. Even some of the Democrats he hates so much can take a punch better than that."

But there was something happening that Lupica and the other commentators knew nothing about. On the day he resigned, Limbaugh learned that the *National Enquirer* was about to publish a sensational scoop: Rush Limbaugh was a drug addict. Suddenly he had no time for football skirmishes. He faced personal, legal, and professional challenges that were far more important than the NFL. His destination was rehab. One thing it didn't cure was his football jones. Five years later, he was still itching. After he negotiated his massive new contract, in 2008, he told me that he might want to get involved with the game again, although not as a broadcaster. "I'm more interested in owning a team," he said. "Maybe I'll buy the Eagles and make Donavan McNabb my quarterback." I thought he was kidding but I mentioned his ambition in the *Times* profile.

Less than a year later, in May 2009, Limbaugh was approached by Dave Checketts, the former president of the New York Knicks and the founder of Sports Capital Partners Worldwide, which owns, among other properties, the St. Louis Blues hockey team. Checketts was putting together a group, with the aid of Solomon Brothers, to buy the St. Louis Rams. He invited Limbaugh to become one of the partners in the group.

"I was intrigued," Limbaugh wrote in an op-ed in the *Wall Street Journal*. "I invited him to my home where we discussed it further. Even after informing him that some people might try to make an issue of my participation, Mr. Checketts said he didn't much care. I accepted his offer."

Limbaugh's warning was an understatement. When his connection to the Checketts bid was leaked, penalty flags fell all over the place. Al Sharpton and Jesse Jackson, who Limbaugh had been mocking for years as racial shakedown artists, struck back. Sharpton sent a letter to NFL Commissioner Roger Goodell asking him to block Rush.

Jackson agreed, adding that Limbaugh had gotten rich "appealing to the fears of whites" (which, considering Jackson's own corporate scare tactics, was a bit much).

The head of the NFL Players Association, DeMaurice Smith, piled on. Smith, like Jackson and Sharpton, is a Democrat—in fact, he was a member of the Obama transition team. He wrote to his members that ". . . sport in America is at its best when it unifies, gives all of us reason to cheer, and when it transcends. Our sport does exactly that when it overcomes division and rejects discrimination and hatred." A few black players said they would refuse to play for a team owned by Limbaugh, and Smith cheered their heroic stand. "We also know that there is an ugly part of history and we will not risk going backwards, giving up, giving in or lying down to it," he said. "Our men are strong and proud sons, fathers, spouses and I am proud when they stand up, understand this is their profession and speak with candor and blunt honesty about how they feel."

Limbaugh knew going in that there would be opposition. But even he hadn't anticipated the lengths to which some members of the media were willing to go. *St. Louis Post-Dispatch* columnist Bryan Burwell called Limbaugh a racist and proved it with a damning quote: "Slavery built the South, and I'm not saying we should bring it back . . . I'm just saying that it had its merits. For one thing, the streets were safer after dark." Dave Zerin, the sports editor of the *Nation* magazine repeated this on MSNBC, and CNN anchor Rick Sanchez did the same on his show. At least a half dozen writers, including Michael Wilbon of the *Washington Post*, cited the slavery remark in print.

It got worse. Karen Hunter, an assistant professor of journalism at Hunter College, went on MSNBC and claimed that Limbaugh had lauded James Earl Ray, the murderer of Martin Luther King. She quoted Limbaugh: "You know who deserves a posthumous Medal of Honor? James Earl Ray. We miss you, James. Godspeed."

Limbaugh never said these things or anything resembling them. They were inventions, pure and simple, taken from a book by Jack Huberman, *101 People Who Are Really Screwing Up America*. Grudging apologies followed. Rick Sanchez, for example, reread the "quote," mentioned Limbaugh's denial, and said, "Obviously that does not take away that there are other quotes that have been attributed to Rush Limbaugh that many people in the African American community and other minority communities do find offensive."

In Boston, Commissioner Goodell told sportswriters that he, too, had a problem with Limbaugh getting into the game. "The comments that Rush made specifically about Donovan, I disagree with very strongly," Goodell said. "They are polarizing comments that we don't think reflect accurately on the NFL or our players. I obviously do not believe that those comments are positive and they are divisive. That's a negative thing for us. I disagree with those comments very strongly and I have told the players that."

Limbaugh had never said McNabb was a bad man or even a bad quarterback. He said that McNabb was overrated (a debatable sports observation) and the recipient of the goodwill and support of some journalists who were rooting for a black quarterback (which was perfectly true and in accordance with the NFL's own expressed hope for racial diversity in all positions).

Checketts folded under the pressure and asked Limbaugh to drop out of the ownership group. Limbaugh refused; if Checketts wanted him out, he would have to fire him. So Checketts did. On October 16, Limbaugh told his audience the story. "I still love professional football. I'll still love the people that play it and admire them, and I'll probably end up remaining the biggest nonpaid promoter of the sport. . . . I am more sad for our country than I am for myself."

That was debatable. Limbaugh was deeply hurt—you could hear it in his voice. As a capitalist he conceded that nobody has the right to buy a football team. And he should have known that there wouldn't be much sympathy for a man who lives in a twenty-four-thousand-square-foot glass house. Still, it stung. Twenty years had passed since he had been rejected in New York by the elite fraternity of broadcasters he had once dreamed of joining. It had been a long time since he had put himself out there again, and now that he had, he had been rejected again. All his success, wealth, and power weren't enough to get him in the door of the new club he wanted to belong to. Not only that: the blackballing had been public and cruel. Sharpton and Jackson and DeMaurice Smith (and, he believed, the White House) had successfully branded him a racist, while the media spread the slander and the men he thought of as friends, rich men like himself whose owners' boxes he had shared over the years, sat by and let it happen. The NFL had been his church on every given Sunday of his adult life. Now he found himself excommunicated.

CHAPTER FIFTEEN

FORWARD TO THE PAST

In August 2009, when I saw Limbaugh in Palm Beach, he was in an upbeat mood. He had lost eighty pounds and was actually swimming laps, although he didn't like admitting that he was exercising. He still thought he had a shot at buying the Rams. He was making more media appearances than he had in years—the following week he was scheduled to fly out to California to tape an episode of *Family Guy*, and he was booked to be one of the first guests on the new prime-time Leno Show. And he had a secret—he was in love.

Professionally he was at the top of his game. The *Atlantic* named him the second most influential commentator in America, preceded only by *New York Times* columnist Paul Krugman, a man with whom he shares a pugnacious, partisan style. A recent Gallup Poll reported that 40 percent of Americans now identified themselves as conservative, 35 percent as moderate, and just 21 percent as liberal. And politically, his just-say-no strategy was bearing fruit. Thanks to Rush, the president and his party were left alone as champions of a very unpopular health care reform initiative. Obama and the Democrats had been shrinking in the polls for months, but members of Congress, home for summer vacation, were shocked by the outrage that greeted them at town hall meetings. Irate constituents demanded to know why the federal government, which was trillions of dollars in debt, wanted to take over health care and provide "free" medical coverage to forty million uninsured citizens. These questions came directly out of Limbaugh's daily talking points.

House Speaker Nancy Pelosi attacked the demonstrators as "un-American," a characterization that the White House itself stepped away from ("I think there's actually a pretty long tradition of people shouting at politicians in America," Deputy Spokesman Bill Burton told a group of reporters). *New York Times* columnist Frank Rich said the meetings were violent and compared the protestors to the militant right-wing anti-government movement. (It later emerged that there were a dozen or so reports of violence, mostly for shoving and pushing, at the more than four hundred town meetings. The worst casualty was a Republican whose pinky was bitten off by an Obama supporter.) A number of pundits began referring to the tea party crowds as "tea-baggers" a term that describes an esoteric form of oral sex that requires dexterity and a considerable amount of courage. Most people had no idea what tea-bagging actually was, but it caught on as a pejorative term. MSNBC turned it into an inside joke. David Shuster said that the protestors wanted to give President Obama "a strong tongue lashing and lick government spending" and that "if you are planning simultaneous tea-bagging all around the country, you are going to need a Dick Armey." On CNN, Anderson Cooper noted that "it's hard to talk while you're tea-bagging."

Limbaugh, who once coined the term "addadicktome" for female-to-male sex-change operations, was not at all offended by this sort of crude humor. On the contrary, he saw it as a sign that the left was once again playing on his court. He hadn't started the tea party movement, but he had done as much as anyone to fuel it and to provide the protestors with ammunition. He argued that health care was simply a socialist Trojan horse that would allow the government to assume control of a large part of the economy and serve as a pretext for bureaucrats butting into the personal lives of citizens in the name of promoting healthy behavior. And even before Sarah Palin began talking about "death panels," he was pointing out that any government-controlled health system necessarily winds up making decisions about life and death based on cost effectiveness. All summer he had been playing a taped exchange between the president and the daughter of a 105-year-old woman whose request to be fitted with a pacemaker, at the age of 100, had been refused by her doctor. Luckily, she said, a second surgeon had performed the procedure, and her mom was still alive. "Outside medical criteria for prolonging life for somebody who is elderly," asked the daughter, "is there any consideration that can be given for a certain spirit, a certain joy of living, the quality of life, or is it just a medical cutoff at a certain age?"

Obama had answered honestly. "I don't think that we can make judgments based on people's spirit," he said. "I think we have to have rules that say that we are going to provide good quality care for all people. End-of-life care is one of the most difficult sets of decisions that we're going to have to make. But understand that those decisions are already being made in one way or another. If they're not being made under Medicare and Medicaid, they're being made by private insurers. At least we can let doctors know and your mom know that, you know what, maybe this isn't going to help. Maybe you're better off not having the surgery but taking the painkiller."

Obama was at a town meeting in New Hampshire that day, and his televised town meeting took place at the same time as the *Limbaugh Show*. Rush provided a real-time fact check. When someone asked about end-of-life care, Rush once more played the exchange about the hundred-year-old mom. "You know what 'give your mom the pain pill' means, folks," he said. "It means loop her out, let her die . . . you may be deciding it yourself about your grandmother, you may—or your mother—you may be deciding it with your doctor, but the United States government, the president of the United States is not issuing the guidelines yet." Then he played a parody of Randy Newman's "Short People," sung by a faux Obama.

> *Old people got no reason*
>
> *Old people got no reason*
>
> *Old people got no reason*
>
> *To live*
>
> *They need lots of drugs*

New hips

After fallin' down

Just a couple of steps

They need pacemakers,

The cost is out of sight

I give 'em a pain pill

And just say good-bye . . .

Don't want no old people

'Round here.

. . .

Fat people got big bodies

Fat people got big bodies

Fat people got big bodies

And bad luck

They don't exercise

They move too slow

They got heart disease

And cholesterol

They'll need those expensive machines

That go beep beep beep

Hospital tests that don't come cheap

Gonna tax everything they eat

Every greasy bag of chips,

Every single treat . . .

While the song played, James Golden said, off the air, "He's full of shit, this stuff about letting you keep your insurance."

"He's a fucking liar," said Limbaugh.

"If I could lie like this I'd have any woman I wanted," said Golden.

Meanwhile, in New Hampshire, a member of the audience rose and asked if Obama supported a universal, single-payer system. "I have not said that I was a single-payer supporter because frankly we historically have had an employer-based system in this country . . ." he began, but that was enough for Limbaugh, who hollered at his engineer, "Roll the tape, 2003, AFL-CIO conference, Obama campaigning for the U.S. Senate." Sure enough, there was candidate Obama saying, "I happen to be a proponent of a single-payer universal health care plan."

"Mr. President," Limbaugh said, cutting back in. "You can't do this and have people trust you. The power of your cultlike appeal is gone . . ."

Limbaugh almost never has guests in his studio, but he had two today, college-age brothers from Arizona who were such big Dittoheads they had invited Rush out to attend an Arizona State football game. Limbaugh had made a counterinvitation, to visit him at the Southern Command. The brothers, both finance majors, were wide-eyed as they watched their hero perform at the EIB microphone ("It really is golden" one said to the other in awe) through the glass of the control booth. They listened in silence until Obama began talking about the cost benefits of preventive care for illnesses like diabetes. "But if that same diabetic ends up getting their foot amputated, that's $30,000, $40,000, $50,000, immediately, the surgeon is reimbursed. So why not make sure that we are also reimbursing the care that prevents the amputation? Right? That will save us money."

One of the brothers whipped out his cell and called his father, a surgeon, in Arizona. At the top of the hour, they informed Rush that a surgeon's standard charge for a foot amputation, including three months of aftercare, was a thousand dollars. Anything more went to the hospital. Back on the air, Limbaugh quoted this figure, crediting his guests and their father. The boys were now a part of EIB history.

As they were exchanging high-fives, Kathryn Rogers walked in. I hadn't seen her since our dinner at Trevini, when her relationship with

Rush was still more or less secret. Since then they had been photographed together, and the media were calling her Rush's girlfriend. Kathryn rarely comes to the studio, but she was there today to look after Rush's guests from Arizona. Like a lot of diplomats' kids, Rogers has an easy way with strangers; the brothers were very obviously charmed by her.

We chatted for a while about Rush's diet, which she had arranged with a local weight-loss clinic, and how arrangements were going for the next Super Bowl. As we spoke, I noticed (couldn't help but notice, actually) that she was wearing a gigantic rock on the third finger of her left hand.

"Do you need to get congratulated?" I asked.

She laughed and said, "It's not real." Which didn't exactly answer the question.

After the show, Rush and I sat in his studio alone, and I mentioned the ring on Kathryn's finger. Since his last, acrimonious, divorce, he had insisted that he was through with marriage; he often told friends that if he ever even mentioned matrimony, they should tie him up and drop him in the ocean. He said something similar to me the first time we met. I was expecting to hear something like that again, but he said, "If Kathryn and I were to get married, I know they'd go after her," he said. "I'm always going to be a villain. I learned in rehab that you can't control what people who don't know you think of you. But Kathryn—I don't know how it would be for her, all the gossip and the nastiness. I worry about it."

The animosity level was indeed exceptionally high, not least because of Limbaugh's unrelentingly harsh attacks on the president. The president had recently hosted a "beer summit" between Professor Gates and the Cambridge cop who arrested him; I asked Rush if, in that conciliatory spirit, Rush would be interested in reaching out. "You guys are both golfers," I said. "Would you play a round with the president and show the country that there are no hard feelings?"

Limbaugh thought it over and said, "He's the president of the United States. If any president asked me to meet him, or play golf with him, I'd do it. But I promise you that will never happen. His base on the left would have a shit-fit."

"You never know," I said. "After all, you thought the *Times* wouldn't run a profile of you." I wanted to add that I still hadn't seen my Yankees tickets, but I thought it would seem small. "How about letting me ask?"

"Go ahead," Limbaugh said. "Nothing will come of it."

"What's your handicap, just in case?"

"Eighteen, nineteen," he said. "What's his?"

I had no idea, but I promised to check in the event the president agreed. In the coming days I tried several times to reach David Axelrod, whom I know slightly, but he didn't return my calls. I spoke to a very senior Democratic activist with whom I'm friendly, and he said he would convey the message. A day or two later he got back to me with the answer: "Limbaugh can play with himself."

On November 3, the voters went to the polls. The main attractions were the gubernatorial races in Virginia and New Jersey, and in both places the Democrats were, as Virginia senator Mark Warner said, "walloped." Just a year before, Virginia had been hailed as a bellwether of the new political demography when a coalition of African Americans and idealistic young voters and white suburbanites gave Obama a large majority—the first for a Democratic presidential candidate since 1964, when Lyndon Johnson carried the state. In 2009 the Obama coalition disappeared. A conservative Republican, Bob McDonnell, beat a moderate Democrat, Creigh Deeds, by a landslide, 17 percent. Democrats said that Deeds was not a good candidate. Maybe not, but in 2005 he had lost to McDonnell for attorney general by just 323 votes. Either the Republican had undergone a remarkable improvement in the intervening five years, or something else was going on.

New Jersey was even worse for the Democrats. Chris Christie, a conservative Republican, unseated Democratic incumbent Governor Jon Corzine in a three-way race, by a comfortable 5 percent margin. New Jersey hadn't elected a Republican governor for fifteen years. Obama won it by 16 percent in 2008. The president came to the state three times to campaign for Corzine and told voters how much he needed Corzine in the state capital, Trenton, to help him carry out his agenda. On the Sunday before the election, they appeared together at a rally at the Prudential

Center in Newark, where they didn't even draw a capacity crowd. Corzine, Democrats said after the election, was unpopular. That much was obvious, but it didn't explain his loss to a not especially attractive or dynamic Republican conservative in one of the bluest states in the country.

The Democratic leadership tried hard to put a positive spin on these results. They blamed the bad economy, which they argued was George W. Bush's fault, and emphasized that gubernatorial elections always turn on local issues. House Speaker Nancy Pelosi went so far as to declare the November 3 elections a victory for her party, staking her claim mostly on the outcome in the 23rd congressional district of New York, where a Democrat, Bill Owens, was elected to the House of Representatives for the first time in more than a hundred years. The 23rd—a normally obscure stretch of upstate New York that runs up to the Canadian border—became the focus of national attention in 2009. It began when Obama named the very popular incumbent congressman, Republican John McHugh, to the post of secretary of the Army. The seat was vacant, and a special election was scheduled. Local party bosses, animated by the fear that only a moderate-to-liberal Republican could win in the post-Obama climate, picked State Assemblywoman Dede Scozzafava.

Limbaugh, Sarah Palin, the Club for Growth, and other movement and media conservatives were incensed by the choice. Scozzafava was far from their notion of what a Republican should be, and with the notable exception of Newt Gingrich, they decided to back Conservative Party candidate Doug Hoffman, an unknown accountant who hadn't even lived in the district. A few days before the election, it became apparent to Scozzafava that she had no chance. She suspended her campaign and threw her support to the Democrat, making the conservative's point that she wasn't really one of them. Campaigning with Owens on the weekend before the election, Vice President Biden declared that his candidate was up against an opponent who had been "handpicked by Rush Limbaugh." When Owens won, with just under 50 percent, Biden, Pelosi, and other Democrats said that El Rushbo and his fellow conservatives had cost the GOP a seat in the House and confirmed their thesis that hard-liners were electorally passé anywhere outside the South.

Limbaugh didn't read election night that way. To him the results in Virginia and New Jersey were the result of the pounding Obama had taken from the GOP guns of August. The following day he practically burst into song. "I'll tell you what, folks, the results last night tell us one certain thing and that is that the Democrat Party is in trouble. It is led by a radical, it is stuck with extreme leaders in Congress who continue to defy the public and advance an extreme agenda that will undo that party . . . the Virginia victory is massive because it's only the second time one party has swept all three statewide races. Combine Virginia and New Jersey and what you have is a blowout."

As for the 23rd, Limbaugh pointed out that Doug Hoffman had come from nowhere and received more than 46 percent of the vote as a third-party candidate up against both the Democrat and the Republican. Owens won with 48 percent and change. Limbaugh confidently predicted that the seat would return to the GOP the following year and that it would be part of a national trend. "The worst has yet to come for the Democrats," he said. "The exit polls say that the economy is number one and jobs and taxes, I mean if that isn't about Obama, I don't know what is. Do you think they're still voting against George Bush out there? I don't think so, folks. How is that hope and change working out for you?"

■ ■ ■ ■

Shortly after Sarah Palin's book, *Going Rogue*, went platinum, callers to Limbaugh's show began asking if he would support her for the Republican presidential nomination. Limbaugh cautioned that it was much too early to be thinking about 2012. "What we need to keep our eyes on now is 2010," he said.

Congressional elections are Limbaugh Time, and he made it clear that he wanted not just Republican victories but victories by the right kind of Republicans. This is both an electoral prescription—"real conservatism works every time it's tried"—and an antidote to what he sees as the dangerous temptation of RINOs (Republicans in name only) to pander to the elites. His far enemy in 2010 would be the Democrats, but the near enemy was "blue-blood, country-club, Rockefeller Republicans" embarrassed by the party's unsophisticated "Billy Bobs" and consumed with the need to be popular in Washington and the Northeast Corridor.

The ballots were hardly counted in New Jersey and Virginia when Limbaugh began his onslaught on these heretics by announcing his list of the "Top Ten Republican Moderate Moments," which included George H. W. Bush's loss to Clinton in 1992, Bob Dole's defeat in 1996, Gerald Ford's failure against Jimmy Carter in 1976, McCain's loss in 2008, and Colin Powell's endorsement of Barack Obama. "Do you see a pattern here, folks?" he said. "Every one of them took us where? Backwards! Every damned one of them. These are the people and these are the things that should define the Republican Party?"

There were plenty of Democratic strategists and pundits who were delighted by Limbaugh's demand for ideological purity. "The more right-ists who win G.O.P. primaries, the greater the Democrats' prospects next year," wrote Frank Rich just before the 2009 election. He pointed out that John McCain lost every demographic group in the country ex-cept for white senior citizens and rural voters, and applauded this as a permanent shift in the nation's political demography. According to him, there was once an American majority of conservative, middle-class, white, Christian voters. "That America was lost years ago, and no national po-litical party can thrive if it lives in denial of that truth," Rich wrote. "Most Americans like their country's 21st-century profile."

Moderate Republicans, the kind Democrats approve of, like Senator Lamar Alexander of Tennessee, former Virginia Congressman Tom Davis, California Governor Arnold Schwarzenegger, and GOP Chairman Mi-chael Steele, all call themselves conservatives. But they accept the idea that the GOP can't win without reaching out to liberal-leaning independents and ethnic and racial minorities with focused messages. This theory of politics is known as being inclusive, a use of language Limbaugh considers Orwellian. He made the point in an interview with Chris Wallace two days before the 2009 election—the same day, in fact, that Obama was rallying his base in New Jersey and Frank Rich's column ran in the *New York Times*. Wallace asked if Limbaugh wanted a small tent party, as his detractors said.

He replied that he wanted a big tent.

"But you sound like you're kind of saying to the moderates, particularly on social issues, 'If we lose you, too bad,'" Wallace said.

Limbaugh shook his head. "The conservative message is not, 'Okay, Hispanics, we have this plan for you. Women, we have this plan for you.' Why be Democrat lite? Let them handle that. Let's go after the big tent that is the country, and let's go get every person in this country—I don't care what their race is, what their gender is, what their sexual orientation. If they are told that there is somebody . . . who is actually going to strengthen them, give them the tools, get out of their way and let them make this country work, the Republican Party can attract a majority like they haven't seen since the 1980s."

The outcome in 2009 strengthened Limbaugh's hand. He and his allies demonstrated in the 23rd District that, whatever else they could do, they were able (and willing) to keep a moderate Republican from winning. And in Virginia and New Jersey, exit polls found that a large majority of independents voted not for the Obama-approved candidate, but for the Old American conservatives. This was bound to have a sobering effect on anyone running for reelection in 2010 outside the most Democratic districts in the country. Nancy Pelosi, Barney Frank, and Maxine Waters are as safe as Ba'athist candidates in Damascus, but they are a fortunate minority.

The vote on the House's America's Affordable Health Care Choices Act of 2009, in early November, made the Democrats' dilemma clear. Congressman Bill Owens of the 23rd took the oath of office just in time to support the bill. So did 218 of his fellow Democratic Representatives (and one Republican, Anh Joseph Cao of New Orleans). But thirty-nine Democrats voted no, and others raised their hands in favor of the legislation only after the Stupak Amendment—which banned public funding for abortion in any new health care system—was added. This amendment enraged liberal feminist groups and highlighted the ideological fault lines in the Democratic party. Mainstream pundits had, for months, been touting a Republican civil war between the forces of GOP reason in the center and the Limbaugh extremists. But the internal contradictions among Democrats were acute. On paper they had overwhelming margins in both the House and the Senate, but they were finding it nearly impossible to translate them into coherent legislation. The Progressive caucus of the House, which represents the party's left-wing base, had seventy-nine votes. On the other side, there were fifty-two Blue Dog moderates, Democrats who represented moderate to conservative constituencies. Most of the Blue Dogs had voted for Obama's stimulus bill and had been hearing about it from disgruntled voters ever since. On health care, even with the addition of the Stupak Amendment, almost half the Blue Dogs voted with the Republicans.

The problem of moderate Democrats in the era of Obama became clear in the Senate when sixty Democratic senators were unable to come up with a bill that included the heretofore critical "public option." Half a dozen Democratic senators up for reelection in red states began to re-evalutate their prospects. Limbaugh would make them all targets, but he had a special bull's-eye reserved for Dingy Harry Reid.

Thanks to Limbaugh's refusal to accept the concept of "bipartisan-ship," the Democrats owned a whole agenda of unpopular spending measures—not just health care reform (which got just one Republican vote in the House and none in the Senate), but cap-and-trade (just eight Republicans in the House, one of whom subsequently resigned to work for Obama) and the stimulus bill (no votes in the House, three in the Senate—one of which belonged to Arlen Specter of Pennsylvania, who later left the GOP and became a Democrat). For months, pundits had been promoting the idea that Republican moderates and conservatives were engaged in a civil war. If so, Limbaugh was Grant at Appomattox.

The Obama administration thought it was scoring points when it claimed that Limbaugh was the de facto head of the Republican Party. In 2009, they discovered that the ploy had backfired. Limbaugh really *was* the dominant Republican voice. It is easily possible to visualize the Republican Party without Mitch McConnell, John Boehner, Michael Steele, Colin Powell, or even George W. Bush (whatever happened to him, anyway?). But not without Limbaugh. As long as he is on the air, his program is the most audible voice of the party, and 12:00 EST will be the hour that the GOP's rank and file get their marching orders and their talking points.

Those talking points rest on the unchanging principles of Limbaugh's conservative worldview. His seventy "Undeniable Truths" are still in effect, although the emphasis has shifted and become more focused over the years. They can be condensed, I think, into ten absolutely absolute Limbaugh beliefs (my list, not his):

1. The world is governed by the aggressive use of force. American security and prosperity rest on its unquestioned military superiority and the will to use it.

2. There is a God who has endowed humans with freedom and moral precepts. Morality is not a matter of individual choice and it is not relative; it is absolute and found in the tenants of the Judeo-Christian tradition.

3. America is an exceptional nation because of its Constitution. It is a unique force for good in the world and an example to the rest of mankind.

4. There is a distinct American culture based on individualism, self-reliance, capitalism, and a common language. Immigrants should accept and embrace this culture.

5. Economic prosperity flows from free markets, low taxes, and a minimum of government regulation.

6. When the virtues of equality and freedom clash, generally speaking, the latter trumps the former.

7. Freedom of speech is absolute.

8. The earth and its ecosystem are not fragile, and they cannot be ruined by human effort. Those who claim to be saving the planet are actually motivated by schemes to get rich, redistribute wealth, weaken America, or establish a one-world government.

9. In government, character and a conservative philosophy are the most important qualities in a leader, and Ronald Regan is the model for presidential greatness.

10. All Democrats are liberals. The worst Republican candidate is better than the best Democrat.

Any GOP candidate who wants Rush Limbaugh's support in 2010 (or beyond) will have to agree to these principles and the ways in which he translates them into specific policies. The specific agenda is easy to predict. It will begin with Limbaugh's belief that Obama is not only a failed economic chief executive but a dangerous one. Rush sees this administration, with its appetite for control and regulation, and its ownership, via bailout, of major American industrial and financial companies, as uniquely unfriendly to the private sector. Bush-era spending and fiscal policies may have done serious damage to the economy—Limbaugh really doesn't dispute that—but this president, Rush believes, has intentionally exacerbated crises in order to step in with new central control.

There is a limit to how far Limbaugh can go with his economic critique. Bad economic news is a slippery commodity. Blaming Obama and the Democrats for high unemployment, inflation, the falling value of the dollar, and the size of the national deficit is standard GOP operating procedure; the Democrats, in a similar situation, would do the same. But by emphasizing negative economic markers and pessimistic forecasts, Limbaugh risks sounding like he's cheering for higher unemployment or a continuation of the recession. At the height of the Iraq War he often said (correctly) that bad news from the battlefield was treated as good news by the left. That's a charge that can easily be reversed on the economic front and turned on Republicans.

The same applies to Afghanistan. In late November 2009, in a speech at West Point, President Obama announced that he was ordering thirty thousand additional troops to Afghanistan—and that he would begin to withdraw forces in 2011. Limbaugh had been attacking Obama for months for failing to give the generals the reinforcements. He could have followed Newt Gingrich's lead and praised the president for finally coming around. Instead, he accused Obama of being too late with too little and attempting to appease his anti-war base with the withdrawal pledge. Here he was staking out a position. By Election Day 2010, the president's surge will be in full swing. In the nature of military operations, it will probably succeed in some areas, fail in others, and leave a good deal unresolved. But nothing short of Osama bin Laden's head on a stick in the White House Rose Garden will stop Limbaugh from deriding the president's efforts and charging Blue Dog Democrats who back the president's war policy with supporting a commander in chief who doesn't really believe in victory and whose real goal is to get out of Afghanistan in time for the 2012 presidential election.

Obama's foreign policy offers a lot of opportunity for Rushian mockery. The president is very popular around the world, and American popularity abroad is extremely important to some of his key supporters—especially those in the entertainment industry, whose business plan depends on the goodwill of foreign consumers. But Obama's good standing overseas is less critical to average Americans, who are apt to wonder with whom Obama is popular and why. Jocular photo ops with the anti-American Hugo Chavez, or kowtowing to the Emperor of Japan and the King of Saudi Arabia, are not likely vote getters in most of the country.

The policy of engagement hasn't shown many results, either. The reset button with Moscow jammed. The Iranians are building their nuclear weapons undisturbed. Obama went to China and got a cool reception; its leaders even warned him not to endanger the value of their dollar by inflating U.S. currency with profligate spending. During the presidential campaign, he promised to remove U.S. troops from Iraq and close the prison at Guantánamo Bay during his first year in office, but did neither. His appeal to the Arab world in Cairo, in which he went so far as to equate the plight of the Palestinians to that of the Jews after the Holocaust, got him nothing in return. Obama went to the UN Global Climate summit in Copenhagen and brokered an obviously meaningless deal. His only foreign policy success was winning the Nobel Prize, an honor even he admitted was undeserved.

A poll published by *Vanity Fair* in its January 2010 issue found that 26 percent of Americans think that Limbaugh is the most influential conservative in the country. Glenn Beck was a distant second, with 11 percent. Dick Cheney and Sarah Palin tied for third place with 10 percent. Sean Hannity got 8 percent. The highest-scoring currently serving

Republican official was House Minority Leader John Boehner, with 4 percent. In 1994 Rush came out of right field to sell Newt Gingrich's Contract with America. This time, the election is Limbaugh's to win or lose. If the results of 2010 resemble the landslide of 1994, Limbaugh will want more this time than to be named an Honorary Freshman.

The momentum of 1994 was squandered in 1996 by the nomination of Bob Dole, a moderate Limbaugh viewed with disdain. Rush didn't have a candidate of his own that year, but he won't make that mistake again. He will be backing somebody next time. It won't be Mike Huckabee, whose "Club for Greed" slams at the corporate wing of the GOP have made him Rush's idea of an irresponsible populist. It won't be Gingrich, either; Newt has gone soft in Rush's opinion. And it very likely won't be Bobby Jindal. Limbaugh has stopped referring to the Louisiana governor as "the next Ronald Reagan" and scarcely mentions him at all these days.

Minnesota governor Tim Pawlenty is a possibility. Rush said good things about Pawlenty when he was being considered for the vice presidential nomination in 2008; and in 2009 he took note of Pawlenty's endorsement of conservative candidate Doug Hoffman. Limbaugh respects Mitt Romney, but probably not enough to push hard for him. Right now, the frontrunner for his support is Sarah Palin, whom he calls "the most prominent, articulate voice for standard, run-of-the-mill, good old-fashioned conservatism." When Palin's autobiography was published Rush gave it a rave review in the *Limbaugh Letter*, and spent an hour with her on his show—the sort of gesture he usually reserves for Republican presidents and special friends. In that interview, Rush noted approvingly that Palin was unpopular with the Republican Party establishment, by which he meant the McCain-Steele moderates. Listeners came away with the impression that if the nomination were being decided tomorrow, she would be his candidate.

It isn't, of course; 2012 is a long way off. New candidates, perhaps including some Limbaugh conservatives, will emerge from the 2010 congressional elections. Palin may turn out to be the conservative Geraldine Ferraro and disappear, or wind up with a lucrative career in the private sector. She might prove to be the lightweight her critics, in the Republican Party and beyond, take her for. On the other hand, she might get herself nominated and even elected. If a washed up, elderly movie actor like Reagan, or a black man raised in Hawaii and Indonesia named Barack Hussein Obama, can be elected president, anything can be imagined. And it would be undeniably ironic if the first woman president owed her job to Rush Limbaugh, the bête noire of feminism.

President Obama was unpopular at the start of 2010, but he still has plenty of time to recover. Even if the midterm elections go badly for the Democrats, he could still win reelection with the sort of comeback Bill Clinton staged in 1996. It is possible that Obama, as liberal pundits like Frank Rich believe, represents a new American political demography that will rule for years to come. It is also far from certain. John F. Kennedy was the herald of a new generation "born in this century" (the twentieth)— and four of his first five successors were older than he. Twenty years after Camelot, Reagan, who was born during the administration of William Howard Taft, supposedly redrew the electoral map by turning the clock back to Norman Rockwell's America. Bill Clinton moved it forward again to the Age of Aquarius. As Larry O'Brien, one of JFK's smartest aides, once observed, there are no final victories in politics.

What America has instead is a permanent argument between Federalists and Jeffersonians, progressives and traditionalists, conservatives and liberals. This is an essential argument about human nature, and the balance between personal freedom and collective responsibility. The presence of this debate is one of the vital signs that a society is open and free. Those who decry Limbaugh (or, on the other side, relentlessly partisan liberal Democrats like Frank Rich or Paul Krugman) "polarizing" ignore the fact that only totalitarian states are unipolar. Democracies are adversarial, and you don't get to choose the other side's advocates. Limbaugh isn't interested in putting himself in the shoes of the Other. He doesn't want to make a deal, split the difference, or strike a blow for civility. "There are no books written about great moderates," he sometimes says. "Great people take stands on principle, not moderation." That's not true, of course—the founding fathers Limbaugh venerates compromised their way into a Constitution, and even Ronaldus Maximus knew when to bend. Politics is the *art* of compromise. But, of course, Limbaugh is not a politician or even a political strategist. He is a polemicist and, as polemicists since Cato the Elder have known, moderation doesn't draw a crowd.

On December 22, 2009, Limbaugh opened his show by announcing that he had been chosen "radio personality of the decade" by *Adweek* magazine. "The man manages to stay in the headlines no matter who's in the White House or who's gunning for him," he quoted approvingly. A few days later he flew out to Cape for Christmas with the Limbaugh family, and then on to Hawaii for a golf outing, and promptly made headlines once again. On the afternoon of December 30 he was rushed to the Queens Medical Center with a severe chest pain he thought was a heart attack. The ambulance was still on its way when Wikipedia flashed a bulletin to the world: Rush Limbaugh is dead.

The news of Limbaugh's death, like that of his fellow Missourian Mark Twain, proved premature. Within fifteen minutes Wikipedia corrected its report. Limbaugh was alive, resting comfortably, and, as it turned out, all right. Like Tom Sawyer, he had been given a preview of his own funeral. His fans deluged him with e-mail prayers followed by joyful messages. Limbaugh-hating bloggers expressed their delight at his demise and then their deep disappointment. Soon rumors raced through cyberspace that Limbaugh was using drugs again and had overdosed. To counter them, a fit-looking Rush held a press conference with his cardiologist, Doctor Joana Magno standing by, and explained that an angiogram had turned up no heart problem at all. A reporter asked if Limbaugh was once more using pain pills for his back, to which he responded with a grin. "No. Prednisone," an anti-inflammatory cortiscosteroid.

At the press conference Limbaugh lavishly praised the hospital for the outstanding care he had received and remarked that as far as he was concerned the American health care system was just great. This provoked a political storm, with commentators on the left charging that Limbaugh had taken a swipe at Obama's health care initiative. Limbaugh was perfectly well aware that it would, too. "That little comment, we're going to get three days out of this," he told Kathryn Rogers. He was wrong. He got a week.

Like all originals, Rush Limbaugh contains multitudes. There is some Sunday School boy in him, left over from the Centenary Methodist Church, and a fair amount of Hugh Hefner; Bo Diddley's swaggering guitar, and Bill Buckley's drawing-room harpsichord. He is an introvert with forty guests for dinner on Thanksgiving, a cynical romantic who doesn't understand women but keeps on trying (in December he sent out save-the-day notices to his friends for a June wedding to Kathryn Rogers), a polite, soft-spoken listener who, on the radio, shouts rude, sometimes vulgar personal insults at his ideological enemies. Limbaugh is a biting and sophisticated political satirist whose own taste in humor runs to mother-in-law jokes told by Borsht Belt tummlers like Myron Cohen and Professor Irwin Corey. There probably isn't another man on the planet whose heroes and role models have been Ronald Reagan, Muhammad Ali, James Madison, Gordon Gekko, superjock Larry Lujack, and Justice Antonin Scalia.

But, more than anything else, Rush is his father's son. Big Rush taught Rush and his brother, David, that being an American meant being a Limbaugh, and that a Limbaugh worth his salt was an outspoken patriot, a conservative Republican, a college-educated professional, a family man, a pillar of the church and the community, and a passionate defender of the well-established truths of the Judeo-Christian tradition as understood in Cape Girardeau, Missouri, circa 1956. Like all sons, Rush often fell short of his father's standards, but he never stopped believing in them, or trying to win Big Rush's approval by carrying his message to the world.

It has been more than twenty years since Rush Limbaugh first appeared on the scene and almost that long since Ronald Reagan passed on to him the half-serious title of "most dangerous man in America." Limbaugh took the coronation seriously. Over the years he has endeavored to carry forward the banner of Ronaldus Maximus, which he always credits as "Reaganism." But as time moves on the memory of Reagan fades. It is Limbaugh's voice conservatives identify with. For millions, conservatism is now Limbaughism.

Even after more than twenty years there are still many people who refuse to accept that Limbaugh is more than an entertainer, a pitchman, or a hot-air balloon. These are the same people who mistook Reagan for an amiable dunce. Two decades should have been enough to convince even the most obtuse that Rush Limbaugh is someone you underestimate or ignore at your peril. He can't be wished away or shouted down or sniffed into irrelevance. Smart liberals will listen to him, even if they hate what he has to say. The easily outraged, will be. Those with a sense of humor will find themselves laughing despite themselves. Presidents and politicians come and go, but Rush Limbaugh, equipped now with a clean bill of health and accompanied by a lovely new wife (and, who knows, maybe a future Rush Hudson IV), and in undisputed control of the conservative movement, is ready for the next act. He has often said that he doesn't intend to quit until he has convinced every liberal in the country. He's not in a hurry, either. His grandfather, the original Rush Hudson Limbaugh, didn't retire until he was 103 years old.

EPILOGUE

THE PARTY OF "HELL NO"

I was going to end this book at the end of 2009, but Rush just kept on rolling. On January 5, Democratic senator Byron Dorgan announced that he wouldn't run for reelection. That news was followed by Senator Chris Dodd's decision to retire (and a couple weeks after that by an announcement by Beau Biden, the vice president's son and the presumptive favorite to win his father's old Senate seat in Delaware, that he wasn't going to run). "They know what's coming in November," said Limbaugh. "And they know why . . . Don't doubt me."

The momentum kept building. Republican Scott Brown won a special election for the U.S. Senate with moves right out of Limbaugh's playbook—opposition to the Democratic plan to reform health care and a stinging critique of the administration's antiterrorism policies.

Rush compared Brown's victory to the fall of the Berlin Wall. The Democrats had lost *Teddy Kennedy's* seat! "This one's for you, Mary Jo," he said. "This one's for you, Judge Bork." He predicted that 2010 would be an even greater Republican landslide than 1994 and reminded his audience who was responsible. "A year ago [moderate Republican pundits] were telling us we had to cross the aisle, we had to hope Obama succeeded, we had to work with him, we had to show the electorate that we were for larger government . . . that's what some in our party were actually saying one year ago. There was one man, ladies and gentlemen, who stood tall and opposed every aspect of that, and I don't mind saying it was I, your host, El Rushbo." Temporarily speechless at his own prescience, he ended the riff with James Brown's "I Feel Good."

Two days later, the U.S. Supreme Court threw out major portions of the McCain-Feingold campaign reform legislation, which limited the political contributions of corporations and unions. Limbaugh had been calling for this for years; the law, which he considered a limitation of the First Amendment, was one of the first things he raised when I asked him, in 2008, what he had against John McCain. Limbaugh hailed the Court's decision as a "huge victory for freedom and liberty."

More good news was coming. The Pew Institute's annual poll of voter priorities found that Americans listed concerns about global warming dead last on a list of twenty-one issues. Not only that: The UN panel on climate change (ICCP) was forced to admit that one of its key assertions—that the Himalayan glaciers are rapidly melting—was based on nothing more than an unverified claim by an environmental lobby group. "The primary evidence that they used has been made up," Limbaugh said. To complete Rush's environmental trifecta, the AP reported that Osama bin Laden (or whoever issues audiotapes in his name these days) was warning that global warming threatened the world—and that the best way to stop it would be to destroy the American economy.

The new year rolled merrily along, Air America, the left-wing radio network founded in 2004 as the antidote to Rush, abruptly shut down. Limbaugh had predicted from the start that its staff wouldn't succeed any better than previous Great Liberal Radio Hopes such as Mario Cuomo and Jim Hightower. Now he mockingly wondered why Air America employees hadn't been among the millions of Americans whose jobs President Obama claimed he was saving with his stimulus spending—demonstrating once more that he is nothing if not a bad winner.

The demise of Air America coincided with another survey. Public Policy, a Democratic-leaning polling company, found that Fox News was the *only* television news organization trusted by a plurality of the public. The media establishment was shocked and outraged, but Limbaugh, the Godfather of the Fox approach (and an increasingly frequent guest on its air), was delighted. Fox, like Rush, had been singled out by the White

House as an unreliable source of information. The Public Policy poll was sweet vindication. Somewhere Big Rush, who had eaten his dinner cursing at Dan Rather on the nightly news, was smiling.

Meanwhile, everything seemed to be going wrong for Obama and the Democrats. Brown's victory imperiled the prospect of real health care reform along liberal lines. The terrible numbers on global warming, coupled with one of the worst prolonged snowstorms in recent American history, made the passage of cap-and-trade legislation highly improbable. Unemployment remained extremely high and Obama offered no solution. A big majority of the public disagreed with Attorney General Eric Holder's decision to read Miranda rights to the man accused of attempting to blow up a plane over Detroit. Senator Chuck Schumer, one of Obama's stalwart supporters, pushed back against the president's proposal to hold the trial of Khalid Sheikh Mohammed and other 9/11 hijackers in downtown Manhattan. The prison in Guantánamo was still open, despite Obama's promise to shut it. "The fact that Obama's agenda has totally failed this year is the best thing that could have happened to this country," he told an interviewer on Fox. "I thank God it is going down the tubes" (the agenda, presumably, not the country). In one year, Limbaugh had gone from hoping the president would fail to declaring he had.

Rush celebrated in Las Vegas, where he served as a judge at the Miss America pageant and stole the show by winning the judges' dance contest with some strenuous moves to Lady Gaga's "Poker Face." Then he flew back to the Southern Command and right into a new controversy.

White House chief of staff Rahm Emanuel, it was reported by *The Wall Street Journal*, had lashed out at liberals in his own party, calling them "fucking retarded" for their all-or-nothing approach to health care reform and the threats of some interest groups to run against Blue Dogs who weren't supporting the legislation. Sarah Palin, who has a mentally handicapped child, denounced Emanuel's use of the word "retarded" and called on him to apologize or resign. Limbaugh saw this as a fine opportunity to make fun of Emanuel. "What did the politically correct language police want from the guy?" Rush asked with mock innocence. All poor Rahm had done was tell the truth, "calling a bunch of people [i.e., liberal Democrats] 'retards,' who *are* retards."

The joke blew up in Rush's face. It sounded like he was dissing Palin as "politically correct," and using "retard" as a putdown in the same way Emanuel had. When reporters asked her why she wasn't going after Limbaugh as she had the White House chief of staff, she lamely said that name-calling is always wrong and, besides, Rush was just being satirical. Governor Palin clearly didn't want to get into a fight with the one man in America who could end her national aspirations in a few sentences. Besides, Governor Palin is a lifelong Dittohead (years ago her father ran into Limbaugh at a golf tournament and requested an autograph for his daughter).

Rush's influence on Palin was apparent in her speech to the inaugural meeting of the Tea Party movement in early February. Her talking points were orthodox Limbaughism—a call for low taxes, small government, domestic energy drilling, a muscular foreign policy based on national interest, and American exceptionalism. Even her best jibes at Obama ("a charismatic guy with a teleprompter") and his policies ("how's that 'hopey-changey stuff' working out for you?") were lifted from Rush's routine. Predictably he loved the speech and even compared the governor to Ronald Reagan.

Palin was very careful in Nashville to make clear her opposition to turning the Tea Party movement into a political party. Limbaugh adamantly opposes third parties on the right ("that's how Democrats win," he said after the speech). The conservative mission was to reclaim control of the GOP from the moderates and compromisers and then lead a unified party to victory in November and beyond.

On Super Bowl Sunday, Limbaugh hosted his annual Super Bowl party. He and his thirty-six guests sat sipping 1961 vintage Château Latour and firing up cigars from Rush's vast humidor when President Obama appeared on the giant theater screen in his viewing room for a pregame interview with Katie Couric. Obama invited Republicans to a health care summit at the White House at the end of February. "I want to come back and have a large meeting with Republicans and Democrats to go though, systematically, all the best ideas that are out there and move forward," the president said.

The next day, Limbaugh called the invitation a trap. His "I hope he

fails" rejection of Democratic outreach had been a winning political strategy for more than a year, and Rush called on Republicans to stay the
course. "Don't be afraid of the media calling you the 'party of no,'" he
counseled his listeners, who include every Republican in the country who
hopes to win election this fall. "We *need* to be the party of 'no.' We need
to be the party of *hell* no."

In mid-February, John McCain announced he intended to reprise the
1994 Contract with America with a new set of 10 Republican Promises
to American voters. Limbaugh didn't care for the idea. What kinds of
promises could a moderate like McCain make? He advised even hard-core
conservatives, including members of the Tea Party movement, to refrain
from offering ideological programs or electoral pledges on the grounds
that these would only foster internal Republican disunity and confuse
voters. Limbaugh offered a simpler formula. "My ten promises to the
voters in 2010? The Bill of Rights. The Constitution of the United States.
That's the only document we need." Specifics to come, of course, every
weekday at noon Eastern Standard Time on your AM radio dial.

ACKNOWLEDGMENTS

I have been in the book-writing business a long time, but I was amazed to discover that almost no New York publisher wanted a book about Rush Limbaugh that didn't have the word "idiot" or "liar" in the title. A friend in the business explained it to me. "I have to go out for lunch in this city every day." Luckily I found an editor, Adrian Zackheim, who doesn't care about lunch. He and his extremely talented assistant, Courtney Young, have been steady partners in this project, and I am very appreciative.

Warm thanks, as always, go to Flip Brophy of Sterling Lord Literistic. Somehow she keeps me working, which is the highest compliment an author can pay to an agent.

The world of Rush Limbaugh is not an easy one to enter. HR "Kit" Carson, Rush's executive producer, decided, for some reason, to help me and provided a portal into Limbaugh-land. He arranged my first trip to Palm Beach, got me a front-row seat at CPAC, let me hang around Limbaugh's New York studio, sent me photos and transcripts from programs past, and generally helped me understand the history and trajectory of the *Limbaugh Show*. Other members of the staff were also very helpful. Thanks to Dawn, Cathy, Brian, Michael, and James Golden, aka "Bo Snerdley." Many of the song parodies and skits on *The Rush Limbaugh Show* are written (or cowritten) and performed by comedian Paul Shanklin. I want to thank him for giving me permission to quote from his work.

David Limbaugh was extremely generous during my stay in Cape Girardeau. He took time to show me the town—and the Limbaughs' boyhood—through his eyes. He is a pundit in his own right, and I very much appreciate his insights into the conservative movement and his brother's place in it.

In the course of my research I talked with literally hundreds of people who have known Rush—boyhood friends; colleagues in Pittsburgh, Kansas City, Sacramento, New York, and Florida; members of his wide professional and personal circle; and people who have had interesting encounters with him. I can't mention them all, but I do want to give special thanks (alphabetically) to Nick Adams, Roger Ailes, Michael Barone, George Brett, Bryan Burns, Ann Coulter, Bill Figenshu, Jim and Frank Kinder, Mary Matalin, Frank Nickell, David Rosow, Karl Rove, the late Tim Russert, Dr. Jan Seebaugh, Rabbi Nathan Segal, Dr. Steve Stumwasser, and Joel Surnow. I also benefited from the advice and thoughts of Elizabeth Bland, David Brooks, Lisa De Pasquale, Charles Dunn, Susan Estrich, Ira Glass, Michael Harrison, Nicholas Lemann, Mark Jurkowitz, Mark McKinnon, Chuck Martin, Jay Nordlinger, Brett O'Donnell, Jeff Roteman, Al Sharpton, Nick Trautwein, and Vivian Turner.

Being written about is an invasive procedure, especially for someone as private and (and as media wary) as Rush. Rush had reservations about a Limbaugh book not written by Limbaugh, but he eventually came around and was cooperative and candid. I asked him hundreds of questions in person, via e-mail, and over the phone, many of which he answered promptly and (with a couple insignificant exceptions) on the record. Even more important, he never told me anything about his life that didn't check out.

Limbaugh is a man who speaks for himself, and I have tried to let readers hear his voice as much as possible. Radio talking isn't as smooth as writing, and I sometimes cut out a repeated word or irrelevant digression, often using ellipses, sometimes not. But in no case has this changed his basic message.

As always I want to thank my wife, Lisa Beyer, who is also my best friend and my best reader, and my kids, Michal, Charley, Shmuelik, Coby, and Annie for their support, forbearance, and occasional reminders that I am not the smartest man in the room.

APPENDIX

On the Informational and Educational
Level of Media Consumers

Pew reports that "readers of news magazines, political magazines and business magazines, listeners of Rush Limbaugh and NPR, and viewers of the *Daily Show* and C-SPAN are also much more likely than the average person to have a college degree." And in a "general knowledge test in which 'media consumers' were asked to identify the majority party in the House of Representatives, the U.S. Secretary of State and the Prime Minister of Great Britain," the Dittoheads scored twice the national average at 36 percent—less than NPR listeners (44 percent) but higher than the audience of the *Colbert Report*, the *Daily Show*, the *PBS News Hour*, BBC News, CNN, all three network news shows, and C-SPAN.

Pew also measures the percentage of those who are, by its definition, consumers of "hard news" (as opposed to human interest features, daily horoscopes, sports, and so forth). "Most news organizations attract a wide range of news consumers, including the hard-news core and those who are less interested in such news. But some stand out for their high proportion of hard news viewers and readers. Among the regular audiences for broadcast programs, Rush Limbaugh's radio show (56% attentive), the Sunday morning interview programs (52%), the *NewsHour* (52%), the

O'Reilly Factor (49%), and *Larry King Live* (48%) have especially large numbers of hard-news consumers."

ON THE IDEOLOGICAL LEANINGS OF ACADEMIA

One of the best studies of academic imbalance was published in 2005 by Professor S. Robert Lichter of George Mason University, who heads the Center for Media and Public Affairs, and two colleagues, Professors Stanley Rothman of Smith College and Neil Nevitte of the University of Toronto. They found that, among 1,643 full-time faculty at 183 four-year schools, 72 percent of these faculty members defined themselves as "liberal," 15 percent as conservative. Fifty percent identified as Democrats, 11 percent as Republicans. At the most elite schools, the gap was greater: 87 percent liberal, 13 percent conservative. The most liberal faculties, the study's authors found, were in the humanities (81 percent) and social sciences (75 percent). In departments of English literature, philosophy, political science, and religious studies, at least 80 percent of the faculty called themselves liberals and about 5 percent identified as conservatives. Since 1990, according to the Center for Responsive Politics, the faculties of universities, colleges, and schools have donated to Democratic candidates sums roughly three times greater than they have to Republicans. In 2008, the number was 82 percent.

ON THE POLITICAL AFFILIATIONS AND VOTING OF THE ELITE MEDIA

In 1981, political scientists S. Robert Lichter, Stanley Rothman, and Linda S. Lichter reported the results of their survey of 240 journalists at ABC, CBS, NBC, PBS, the *New York Times*, the *Washington Post*, the *Wall Street Journal*, *Time*, *Newsweek*, and *U.S. News & World Report*. Going back to 1964, the number who said they voted for the Democratic presidential candidate never went below 80 percent. In the 1964 contest between Johnson and Goldwater, 94 percent voted for Johnson. In 2001, the study was updated. Professors Stanley Rothman and Amy E. Black found that, "three-quarters of elite journalists (76.1 percent) ... voted for Michael Dukakis in 1988, and even larger percentages (91.3 percent) ... cast ballots for Bill Clinton in 1992." Neither Dukakis nor Clinton got anywhere near a majority of the general vote. The Freedom

Forum's poll of Washington bureau chiefs and congressional correspondents found similar trends. A Freedom Forum poll of Washington bureau chiefs and congressional correspondents found 89 percent had voted for Clinton in the 1992 election, compared with 7 percent for President Bush and 2 percent for Ross Perot. The *Minneapolis Star Tribune* summed it up: "In no state or region, among no race or class, did support for Clinton predominate more lopsidedly than among this sample of 139 journalists who either cover Congress or head a Washington bureau." Elaine Povich, the study's director, tried to make the case that this didn't necessarily mean the Democratic press had favored the Democratic candidates just because they all happened to be Democrats: "One of the things about being a professional is that you attempt to leave your personal feelings aside as you do your work."

ON OTHER MEDIA

The liberal consensus extends to the rest of the media as well. According to the Center for Responsive Politics, 78 percent of the political contributions of the music, television, and movie industries in 2008 went to Democratic candidates. Over the past twenty years, these industries have supported Democrats by more than a 2-to-1 margin. Presumably, this has no impact on their content.

INDEX

ABC Network, Limbaugh's national show, 44–57
Abortion
    caller abortions bit, 68
    Limbaugh on, 50, 58, 68
Abu Ghraib, 102–3
Academia, ideological imbalance in, 212
ACORN (Association of Community Organizations for Reform Now), 61
Adams, Dick, 16–17, 21
Affirmative action, Limbaugh on, 58
Afghanistan, troop surge, Limbaugh on, 199–200
African Americans, Limbaugh racial bias, 85, 179–85
Agnew, Spiro, 24, 137
AIDS, Limbaugh on, 58, 68–69
Ailes, Roger, 57–61, 81, 134, 139
Air America, 124, 125*n*
Alexander, Lamar, 88, 195
Ali, Muhammad, 7–8
Alinsky, Saul, 6
Alito, Samuel, 104
Allen, Mike, 148
Alter, Jonathan, 149–50
American Mercury, The, 62–63
Angelou, Maya, 84
Anti-Semitism, 51–53

Armey, Dick, 187
Armstrong, Millie. *See* Limbaugh, Millie (mother)
Atwater, Lee, 47
Axelrod, David, 192
Axis of Evil, 102
Ayers, Bill, 61

Barone, Michael, 142
Beauchamp, Scott Thomas, 108*n*
Beck, Glenn, 123–24, 144, 200
Begala, Paul, 9, 65, 150
Berman, Chris, 179
Bernstein, Leonard, 72
Berry, Chuck, 26
Biden, Joe, 156, 177
Bierce, Ambrose, 136
Big government, Limbaugh on, 65, 101, 144
Bipartisan Campaign Reform Act (McCain-Feingold Act), 114
Black, Roy, 96
Bloomberg, Michael, 141
Blue Dog Democrats, 197
Boehner, John, 6, 142, 197, 201
Bonneville International, 41
Bork, Robert, 74
Branch Davidians, 85, 89
Breslin, Jimmy, 58
Brett, George, 37, 39–40, 49, 100, 178

Brisker, John, 35
Brokaw, Tom, 50
Brookhiser, Richard, 57
Brooks, David, 4
Brown, Jerry, 42
Brown, Tina, 10, 149
Brown v. Board of Education of Topeka, 19
Bruce, Lenny, 136
Buchanan, Pat, 88
Buck, Jack, 22
Buckley, James, 55
Buckley, Pat, 56–57
Buckley, William F., Limbaugh's relationship with, 54–57, 135
Burkle, Ron, 107
Burns, Bryan, 38–40, 42, 46
Burton, Bill, 187
Burwell, Bryan, 183
Bush, George H. W.
    election of 1992 loss, 81–85, 195
    and Limbaugh, personal relationship, 81–82
Bush, George W., 4, 5, 12, 197
    Limbaugh during administrations of, 100–106
    and Limbaugh, personal relationship, 4, 100, 106
    Limbaugh clash with, 104–6
Bush Derangement Syndrome, 102
Byrd, Robert, 74, 177

Cao, Ahn Joseph, 196
Cape Girardeau, Missouri, Limbaugh family/background in, 11–31
Capitol Hill Bank scandal, 77–79
Caray, Harry, 22
Carnegie, Jim, 36
Carson, Kit, 112
Carter, Jimmy, 65, 195
Carville, James, 148–49
Casey, Betty, 110
Chambers, Whittaker, 54
Chase, J. Frank, 63
Checketts, Dave, 182–84

Cheney, Dick, 151, 152, 153, 200
Chinn, Tom, 41
Christie, Chris, 192
    Limbaugh as, 32–42
Civil rights movement, 172–73
Clark, Abraham, 15
Clark, Wesley, 181
Cline, Wilma, 94, 121
Clinton, Bill
    election of 1992 victory, 81–85
    on Iraq war, 101–2
    Kobe Club meeting with Limbaugh, 106–7
    Limbaugh's attacks on, 81–92, 106–7, 119
    Limbaugh's view of, 59, 65, 70–71
    remarks about Limbaugh by, 85–87, 89
    and Vietnam war draft, 82–83
Clinton, Hillary
    and Media Matters, 108
    and Operation Chaos, 116–19
    on right-wing conspiracy, 90
Clubb, Peter, 12
Club for Growth, 193
Coburn, Tom, 142
Colbert, Steven, 165
Colford, Paul, 20–21
Communism, Limbaugh on, 48, 65, 66, 101
Connerly, Ward, 142
Connor, Bull, 9–10
Conservative Political Action Conference of the American Conservative Union Foundation, 141–52
Conservative thinking
    liberal view of, 54–55, 136–37, 140
    Limbaugh at CPAC, 141–52
    Limbaugh as influence, 136–37, 143–44, 186, 196–201
    and Limbaugh family, 13–14, 16–18, 24, 28, 47–49
    Limbaugh's views. *See* Limbaugh, Rush Hudson, III

most influential conservatives, 200–201

and William F. Buckley, 54–57

Contract with America, 76–77, 201

Cooper, Anderson, 187

Cooper, Marc, 137

Coppedge, Thomas, 12

Cornyn, John, 142

Corzine, Jon, 192–93

Coulter, Ann, 97, 133

Couric, Katie, 59–60, 148

Creative Coalition, 52

Crime, Limbaugh on, 64, 72

Cronkite, Walter, 50

Cubin, Barbara, 80

Cuomo, Mario, 124

Cutaways, Limbaugh show, 126–27

Davis, Tom, 195

Dean, Howard, 181

Deeds, Creigh, 192

Defense of Marriage Act, 87

De la Cruz, Dr. Antonio, 94

Democratic Party
  Blue Dog moderates, 197
  elite media affiliation with, 212–13
  and health care reform, 196–97
  on Iraq war, 101–2
  Limbaugh's view of, 6–7, 9–10, 65, 70–71, 73–74
  and Media Matters, 108
  reaction to "phony soldiers" comment, 108–10
  view of Limbaugh, 6, 9–10, 108–10, 181–83

Dittoheads
  Florida population of, 92
  influence on elections, 76
  profile of, 128–29, 136–37, 211–12

Dole, Bob, 84, 87–88, 195, 201

Dowd, Maureen, 53–54, 56

Downey, Morton, Jr., 41–42

Drive-By Media, 5, 107, 119, 162, 177

Drudge, Matt, 90

Drudge Report, 113, 138

Economy
  Buckley (William) on, 56
  Limbaugh on, 7–8, 70
  Obama plan, Limbaugh on, 7–8

Education, Limbaugh on, 72

Egan, Timothy, 149–50

Ehrenstein, David, 155

EIB One, 122, 149

Eisenberg, Emma (grandmother), 12

Eisenberg, Heinrich, 12

Eisenhower, Dwight, 18–19, 114–15

El Rushbo, Limbaugh as, 1, 43–44, 60

Emanuel, Rahm, 65, 146–47

Environmental movement, Limbaugh on, 44, 65–67, 71

ESPN, Sunday NFL Countdown problem, 179–82

Estrich, Susan, 118, 149

Excellence in Broadcasting (EIB) Network, 1, 44, 57, 64

Excellence in Broadcasting tour, 69

Fairness Doctrine, 85, 139

Falwell, Jerry, 99, 111

Farah, Joseph, 64

Feminism, Limbaugh on, 44, 50, 73

Figenshu, Bill, 34, 38

Firing Line (TV program), 55

Fitzgerald, Marta Maranda. See Limbaugh, Marta (wife)

Flowers, Gennifer, 90

Foley, Tom, 80

Forbes, Steve, 88

Ford, Gerald, 178, 195

Foreman, George, 8

Fortier, Michael and Lori, 89

Fox, Michael J., 103

FOX News
  Limbaugh on, 5, 61
  Obama statement about, 61
  Reverend Wright broadcasts, 160

Frank, Barney, 6, 65, 196

Franken, Al, 124

Frazier, Joe, 8

Friedman, Milton, 7

Frum, David, 149–50
Fulbright, William, 54, 158
Fund, John, 61, 64

Garofalo, Janeane, 9, 124
Gates, Henry, 171–72, 191
Gay marriage, Limbaugh on, 98
Gibbs, Robert, 148, 151, 168
Gibson, Bob, 26
Gingrey, Phil, 8–9, 148
Gingrich, Newt, 57, 80, 132, 142, 153, 168, 193
    Contract with America, 76–77, 201
Gitlin, Todd, 139
Giuliani, Rudy, 111, 141
Glass, Ira, 125–26
Global warming, Limbaugh on, 65–67
Godwin, Linda, 26
Golden, James "Bo Snerdley"
    as conservative, 174–76, 190
    Maya Angelou, counterpoem to, 84
    as Official Obama Criticizer, 157–58, 162–63
    as phone call screener, 68
    and unpredictable moments, 127–28
Goldwater, Barry, 55
Goodell, Roger, 182, 184
Goodman, Walter, 62–64
Gorbachev, Mikhail, 48, 65
Gore, Al
    green enterprises of, 67n
    -Limbaugh debate, 66–67
    as Limbaugh target, 59
Graham, Lindsey, 112
Green, Mark, 125n
Green Stephen, 125n
Grossberger, Lewis, 53
Guantánamo POW camp, 102, 200

Hannity, Sean
    as influential conservative, 200
    on Limbaugh's drug use, 97
    relationship with Limbaugh, 5, 28, 123
Harrison, Michael, 123

Hart, Gary, 124
Harvey, Paul, 53
Health care reform
    Democrats against, 196–97
    Limbaugh on, 86–87, 187–90, 203–4
Henderson, Nia-Malika, 159
Hertzberg, Hendrik, 9, 97
Hightower, Jim, 124
Hirsch, Oscar, 17, 18
Hirschfeld, Abe, 52–53
Hise, Conrad, 12
Hoffer, Eric, 136
Hoffman, Doug, 193–94, 201
Holder, Eric, 175–76
Huberman, Jack, 183
Huckabee, Mike, 142, 201
Hughley, D. L., 147
Hunter, Karen, 183
Hussein, Saddam, 101–2

Immigration reform, Limbaugh on, 104–6, 170–71
Imus, Don, 41, 51, 124, 156, 175
Ingraham, Laura, 124
Iraq war, Limbaugh on, 101–2, 107–8, 199
Irvin, Michael, 179–80
Iseman, Vicki, 112

Jackson, Jesse
    dialect of, 159
    Limbaugh's view of, 2, 60, 65, 73, 177
    St. Louis Rams bid protest, 182–84
Jackson, Michael, 40
Jackson, Tom, 179–81
Jennings, Peter, 50
Jews, Limbaugh anti-Semitism, 51–53
Jindal, Bobby, 141–42, 201
Jones, Paula, 90
Jones, Van, 61
Judicial activism, Limbaugh on, 74
Justice Brothers, 177

Kagan, Daryn, 131
Kansas City Royals, 38–40, 178
Kay, Dan, 119
Keillor, Garrison, 53, 124
Kemp, Jack, 88
Kennedy, John F., 17, 202
Kennedy, John Forbes, 159
Kennedy, Robert, 24–25
Kennedy, Teddy
 and Bork nomination, 74
 on immigration reform, 105
 Limbaugh on, 47, 101
Kerry, John, 108
Keyes, Alan, 88
Keynes, John Maynard, 7
KFBK, 41–44
KFIX, 39
KGMO-AM, 23, 25
Kinder, Frank, 14, 16–17, 20
King, Larry, 124, 144–45
King, Martin Luther, Jr., 9, 25,
 172–73, 183
King, Rodney, 75
Kissinger, Henry, 57
Kondracke, Mort, 152
Koppel, Ted, 49, 53, 66–67
KQV-AM, 35–36
Krauthammer, Charles, 102, 104, 135
Krischer, Barry, 97
Kristol, William, 104
Krugman, Paul, 186, 202
KUDL-FM, 37, 39
Kudlow, Larry, 4
Kurtz, Howard, 148

Labor unions, Limbaugh on, 65
Lacey, Sam, 39
Landon, Alf, 13
Lanier, Bob, 82
Latzman, Phil, 68
Lauer, Matt, 90
Leadership, Limbaugh on, 71
Lehrman, Lewis, 56
Leibovich, Mark, 164
Leno, Jay, 59

Letterman, David, 53, 59, 148,
 150, 164
Levin, Mark, 5, 27, 123, 144
Lewinsky, Monica, 90–91
Liberals
 Bush (George W.), view of, 102
 on conservative thinking, 54–55,
 136–37, 140
 Limbaugh's view of, 44, 65. See also
 Democratic Party
 and media. See Media
 Reagan on, 70
 view of Limbaugh, 44, 49–52,
 137–40
Liberty University, 111
Lichter, Linda S., 212
Lichter, S. Robert, 212
Limbaugh, David (brother)
 background information, 12,
 26–29, 51
 collaboration with Rush, 62
 and Hannity, 5
 on Obama, 28
 on R. H. Limbaugh, Sr., 16–17
Limbaugh, Johannes Michael (first
 Limbaugh in America), 12
Limbaugh, Julie (cousin), 133
Limbaugh, Marta (wife), 94, 130–31
Limbaugh, Michelle (wife), 41,
 42–43, 46
Limbaugh, Millie (mother), 14–15, 36
Limbaugh, Rush Hudson, III
 on abortion, 50, 58, 68
 on Abu Ghraib, 102–3
 on affirmative action, 58
 on Afghanistan surge, 199–200
 on AIDS, 58, 68–69
 anti-corruption campaign, 77–79
 anti-Semitism accusation, 51–53
 apolitical period for, 24–25,
 48–49, 173
 audience, growth of, 42, 53, 57, 59,
 122–23, 151
 awards to, 125, 144–45, 203
 on big government, 65, 101, 144

Limbaugh, Rush Hudson, III (*cont.*)
  and Bill Clinton, 85–87, 89,
    106–7, 119
  and Bo Snerdley (James Golden), 68,
    84, 113, 127–28, 157–59, 190
  and Clinton/Bush election (1992),
    81–85
  on communism, 48, 65, 66, 101
  and congressional elections (2009),
    192–96
  conservatism in writings of, 62–66
  at Conservative Political Action
    Conference of the American
    Conservative Union Foundation,
    141–52
  conservative thinking, influence on,
    136–37, 143–44, 186, 196–201
  conservative views on air, early years,
    41, 42, 44, 49
  on crime, 64, 72
  cutaways, 126–27
  deafness, 92–94, 115, 130
  on Democratic Party/liberals, 6–7,
    9–10, 44, 65, 70–71, 73–74
  Dittoheads, profile of, 128–29,
    136–37, 211–12
  on Drive-By Media, 5, 107, 119,
    162, 177
  drug use, 9, 94–98, 182
  earnings, 42, 57, 64, 122–23
  on economy, 7–8, 56, 70
  on education, 72
  as El Rushbo, 1, 43–44, 60
  on environmental movement, 44,
    65–67, 71
  Excellence in Broadcasting (EIB)
    Network, 1, 44, 57, 64
  Excellence in Broadcasting tour, 69
  family/background information,
    12–31, 48–49
  on feminism, 44, 50, 73
  on gay marriage, 98
  gender gap and listeners, 128–29
  and George H. W. Bush, 81–85
  and George W. Bush, 100–106

  girlfriend (Kathryn Rogers), 12,
    129–30, 190–91, 204
  as GOP de facto head, 6–10,
    149–50, 153, 197
  -Gore debate, 66–67
  Harry Reid letter auction, 108–10
  on health care reform, 86–87,
    187–90, 203–4
  on Henry Gates incident,
    171–72, 191
  hospitalization (2009), 203–4
  on immigration reform, 104–6,
    170–71
  on Iraq war, 101–2, 107–8
  and John McCain, 100, 111–16
  on judicial activism, 74
  Kansas City Royals job, 39–41, 178
  on labor unions, 65
  on leadership, 71
  liberal media opinion of, 53, 97,
    115, 136–37, 139, 148–53, 157,
    165–66, 183
  liberal view of, 44, 49–52,
    137–40
  Limbaugh Letter, The, 64
  Magic Negro (Obama as)
    controversy, 154–58, 177
  marriages, 38–39, 41, 130–31
  Michael J. Fox parody, 103
  misfired humor, examples of, 51–53,
    59–60, 68–69, 103
  on moderate Republicans, 194–96
  on multiculturalism, 44, 70
  on NAACP, 177
  national show, 44–57
  New York establishment, reaction to,
    49–54, 56–57
  and Obama. *See* Obama, Barack
  Operation Chaos, 116–19
  Palm Beach, move to, 92–93
  Palm Beach residence, 120–22,
    131–34
  Palm Beach studio secrecy, 112–13
  personality traits, 7–8, 40, 53–54,
    56, 60, 72, 204–5

political figures, comments on. *See individuals by name*

and presidential primary (2000), 111–19

racial bias, 85, 168–77, 179–85

radio as preferred media of, 60–61

radio broadcasting, early interest, 21–23, 26

radio jobs, early, 21–22, 25, 32–44

as radio pioneer, 125–29, 137–40

Reagan as hero, 55, 57, 60, 65, 71, 75, 144–45, 204

religiosity of, 28–29, 73

and Republican congressional election (1994), 76–80

Republican roots of, 13–14, 16–18, 24, 28, 47–49, 204

Rush to Excellence tours, 144

St. Louis Rams bid controversy, 182–85

satire, examples, 47, 59–60, 68–69, 77–79, 84–85, 90–91, 102–3, 154–58, 188–90

satire/comic spots, development of, 33–34, 37, 43–44, 126–29

See, I Told You So, 64, 65–66

on sexual behavior, 71

social and family life, 131–34

on Sotomayor nomination, 167–71

Sunday NFL Countdown issue, 179–82

targets/themes of, 6–7, 44, 65, 70–75

on taxes, 70, 101

and Tea Party movement, 186–87

on televangelism, 33, 63

35 Undeniable Truths column, 47–48

35 Undeniable Truths of Life, 68, 70–71, 104–5, 198–99

TV show, 57–60

and Vietnam war draft, 82–83

Wanda Sykes on, 165–66

Way Things Ought to Be, The, 62–65

and William F. Buckley, 54–57, 135

See also specific topics and persons

Limbaugh, Rush Hudson, Jr. (father), 5, 14–18, 36, 48, 58, 60, 65, 122, 204

Limbaugh, Rush Hudson, Sr. (grandfather), 12–14, 64, 205

Limbaugh, Steven N., Jr. (cousin), 12, 27

Limbaugh, Steven N., Sr. (uncle), 27

Limbaugh Institute for Advanced Conservative Studies, 136–37

Limbaugh Letter, The, 64, 119

Liston, Sonny, 7–8

Little, Rich, 165

Live with Regis and Kathie Lee (TV program), 57–58

Louis, Joe, 8

Lowry, Rich, 150

Lugar, Richard, 88

Lujack, Larry "Superjock," 23, 36, 41

Luntz, Frank, 80

Lupica, Mike, 181–82

MacBeth, Jesse, 107–8

McCain, John
campaign, failure of, 5
as GOP spokesperson, 153
on immigration reform, 105–6, 114, 170
Limbaugh's view of, 100, 111–16, 195
view of Limbaugh, 112

McClatchy, C. K., 41

McConnell, Mitch, 5–6, 197

McDonnell, Bob, 192

McHugh, John, 193

McLaughlin, Ed, 44, 51

McNabb, Donovan, 179–82, 184

McNair, Steve, 180

McNeely, Roxy Maxine, 38–39

McVeigh, Timothy, 89

Maddow, Rachel, 161

Magno, Joana, 203

Maimone, Mike, 126

Malcolm X, 172–73

Marconi Radio Awards, 125
Marine Corps–Law Enforcement
 Foundation, 109–10
Marr, Bruce, 44
Martin, Chuck, 24
Martin, Joseph, 80
Matalin, Mary, 121, 134, 148
Matthews, Chris, 161
Mays, Mark, 109
Meadows psychiatric hospital, 96
Media
 Drive-By Media, 5, 107, 119,
  162, 177
 elite, political affiliations of, 212–13
 liberal compared to conservative
  (1988), 137–38
 liberal media on Limbaugh, 53, 97,
  115, 136–37, 139, 148–53, 157,
  165–66, 183
 liberal talk radio attempts, 124–25n
Media consumers, informational/
 educational level of, 211–12
Media Matters, 108
Mencken, H. L., 62–63n, 86, 136
Michaels, Al, 134
Michel, Bob, 84
Miers, Harriet, 103–4
Mondale, Walter, 57
Morris, Dick, 88
Morrison, Toni, 154
Mosbacher, Robert and Georgette, 54
Mull, Johannes, 12
Multiculturalism
 Limbaugh on, 44, 70
 Limbaugh racial bias, 85, 168–77,
  179–85
Musial, Stan "the Man," 26

Nathan, Bob, 43
National Association for the
 Advancement of Colored People
 (NAACP), 177
National Association of Broadcasters
 Hall of Fame, 125
National Review, 54–57, 135–36

Nevitte, Neil, 212
Nichols, Terry, 89
Nickell, Frank, 14, 19
Nightline (TV program), 66
Nixon, Richard, 17, 36, 49, 57, 81,
 137, 173, 178
No Child Left Behind, 101
Nordlinger, Jay, 135–36

Obama, Barack
 black dialect/gestures by, 159–60
 failure, Limbaugh's hope for,
  3–6, 147
 FOX News assaults on, 61
 health care reform, 187–90
 and Henry Gates incident,
  171–72, 191
 Limbaugh's view of, 3–5, 65,
  144, 199
 Magic Negro satire, 154–58, 177
 as "Messiah," 8, 163
 Official Obama Criticizer, 157–58,
  162–63
 and Operation Chaos, 116–19
 outreach to Republicans, 3–4, 6
 presidency, assessment of, 196–200
 remarks about Limbaugh by, 6–7,
  9–10
 and Sykes at WHCA dinner,
  165–66
 teleprompter use, 163–64
Obama, Michelle
 DNC speech, mockery of, 161–62,
  175–76
 slave blood, 158
O'Brien, Larry, 202
O'Donnell, Brett, 111
O'Donnell, Norah, 161
Ohlmeyer, Don, 134
Oklahoma City bombing, 89
Oliver, Marie Watkins, 26
O'Neill, Rose, 26
Operation Chaos, 116–19
O'Reilly, Bill, 124, 144
Owens, Bill, 193–94, 196

Palin, Sarah, 187, 193, 194, 200,
201–2
Parker Meridien Hotel, 46, 51, 52
Pataki, George, 141
Paterson, David, 127
Pat Sajak Show, The (TV program), 58
Paul, Ron, 143
Pawlenty, Tim, 201
Pelosi, Nancy, 6, 187, 193, 196
Pence, Mike, 142
Perkins, Marlin, 26
Perot, Ross, 81, 88
Plouffe, David, 118, 148
Podhoretz, Norman, 57
Povich, Elaine, 213
Powell, Colin
  endorsement of Obama, 152, 195
  on Republican Party, 152
  view of Limbaugh, 152–53
Project Dignity, 59
Project Vote, 117

Radio Equalizer, 152
Radio Hall of Fame, 125
Ray, James Earl, 183
Reagan, Ronald
  Fairness Doctrine, repeal of, 85
  as George Gipp, 178
  immigration policy of, 104
  letter to Limbaugh, 60
  Limbaugh's view of, 55, 57, 65,
    71, 75
  Reaganism, Limbaugh on return to,
    144–45, 204
Reid, Harry, 6, 105, 197
  Limbaugh auctions letter from,
    108–10
Religion, Limbaugh on, 28–29, 73
Reno, Janet, 85
Republican Party
  approval of Limbaugh, 60, 80, 84
  election of 1994 victory, 76–80, 87
  GOP spokespersons, 153
  and Limbaugh family, 13–14, 16–18,
    24, 28, 47–49, 204

Limbaugh as GOP de facto head,
  6–10, 146–47, 149–50,
  153, 197
moderates, Limbaugh on, 194–96
portrayal by liberal media, 137–38
Powell on, 152
Reynolds, Joey, 36
Rhodes, Randi, 124
Rice, Constance, 136
Rich, Frank, 187, 195, 202
Richards, Ann, 100
Richardson, Marvin, 127–28
Robertson, Pat, compared to
  Limbaugh, 63
Robinson, Eugene, 161
Rogers, Kathryn, 12, 129–30,
  190–91, 204
Romney, Mitt, 111, 141, 142, 201
Rook, John, 36
Roosevelt, Franklin D., 13
Rose, Charlie, 114
Rosow, David, 132, 134
Rostenkowski, Dan, 78–79
Rothman, Stanley, 212
Rove, Karl, 77, 116
Rueseler, John, 39
Rush to Excellence tours, 144
Russert, Tim, 49
Rusty Sharpe Show, The, 25

Safire, William, 89
Sahl, Mort, 173
St. Louis Rams, Limbaugh rejected
  from purchase bid, 182–85
Sajak, Pat, 58
Sanchez, Rick, 183
Sanders, Bernie, 109
Scalia, Antonin, 135
Scarborough, Joe, 151
Schlafly, Phyllis, 142
Schakowsky, Jan, 108
Schneider, Bill, 146
Schroeder, Pat, 59
Schultz, Ed, 150
Schwarzenegger, Arnold, 141, 195

Scott, Dred, 26
Scozzafava, Dede, 193
Scully, Dr. Mark, 24
Secure Borders, Economic Opportunity and Immigration Reform Act (2007), 105
See, I Told You So (Limbaugh), 64, 65–66
Seebaugh, Jan, 21–22
Segal, Nathan, 52, 59
September 11 attacks, 61, 101, 160
Shanklin, Paul, 126
Shapiro, Mark, 181
Sharpe, Rusty, Limbaugh as, 21–22, 25, 45
Sharpton, Al
 dialect of, 159
 Limbaugh's racial bias, reaction to, 181–84
 Limbaugh's view of, 177
 view of Limbaugh, 155–56
Shock radio, 41
Shuster, David, 187
Shuster, Stan, 134
Silver, Ron, 52, 84–85
Sixta, Michelle. *See* Limbaugh, Michelle (wife)
Slater, Michael, 117
Smith, DeMaurice, 183–84
Snerdley, Bo. *See* Golden, James "Bo Snerdley"
Solid Rockin' Gold Show, 32
Sotomayor, Sonia, Limbaugh attacks on, 167–71
Sowell, Thomas, 135, 140
Specter, Arlen, 88, 197
Spitzer, Eliot, 127
Spring Fling, 134
Steele, Charles, 158
Steele, Michael, 9, 147–48, 195, 197
Stem cell research, 103
Stern, Howard, 41, 51, 125, 175
Stewart, Jon, 164
Stumwasser, Steven, 96–97
Sullivan, Jeremy, 134

Sullivan, Tom, 44
Sunday, Billy, 17–18
Sunday NFL Countdown, 179–82
Surnow, Joel, 134
Sykes, Wanda, 165–66

Taft, Robert, 54
Tapper, Jake, 170
Taxes, Limbaugh on, 70, 101
Tea Party movement, 186–87
Televangelism, Limbaugh on, 33
Television
 FOX News, 61
 Limbaugh on, 57–60
35 Undeniable Truths column, 47–48
35 Undeniable Truths of Life, 68, 70–71, 104–5, 198–99
Thomas, Clarence, 74, 131
Thomas, Evan, 97
Thompson, Fred, 111, 141
Thurmond, Strom, 54
Trilling, Lionel, 54
Truman, Harry, 18–19, 26
Twain, Mark, 11, 26, 203

Van Susteren, Greta, 172
Varsity Barber Shop, 20, 30–31
Veblen, Thorstein, 14
Villaraigosa, Antonio, 106–7

WABC, Limbaugh at, 44–47
Waco, Texas, massacre, 85, 89
Wallace, Chris, 195
Wallace, George, 24
Wallace, Mike, 51
Warner, Mark, 192
Warwick, Dionne, 69
Washington, George, 59
Washington, Martha, 59
Waters, Maxine, 196
Way Things Ought to Be, The (Limbaugh), 62–65
Webber, Vin, 80
Welfare, Limbaugh on, 74
Welfare reform, 87

White House Correspondents'
    Association dinner, Sykes on
    Limbaugh, 164–65
Whitman, Slim, 43
Wilbon, Michael, 183
Will, George, 3, 104
Williams, Dave, 43
Wills, Maury, 22
Wilson, John K., 117
Winfrey, Oprah, 129
WIXZ-AM, 32–35

Wolff, Michael, 4, 122–23, 151
Women, gender gap and listeners,
    128–29
Woodruff, Norm, 41–42, 69
Wright, Jeremiah, 61, 142,
    160–61

Young, Steve, 179–80

Zakaria, Fareed, 152
Zerin, Dave, 183